Mission-Critical Lotus Notes

David S. Marshak

Prentice Hall P T R, Upper Saddle River, New Jersey 07458

Library of Congress Cataloging-in-Publication Data

Marshak, David S.
    Mission-critical Lotus Notes / by David S. Marshak.
        p.   cm.
        Includes index.
        ISBN 0-13-472671-5
        1. Lotus Notes for Windows.   2. Groupware (Computer
            software)
        3. World Wide Web (Information retrieval system)   I. Title.
        HF5548.4.L692M37   1996
        650'.0285'46—dc20   96-7974
                                                                                          CIP

Editorial Production: *bookworks*
Acquisitions Editor: *Mark Taub*
Manufacturing Manager: *Alexis R. Heydt*
Cover Design Director: *Jerry Votta*
Cover Designer: *Mary Jo DeFranco*

 © 1996 by Prentice Hall P T R
Prentice-Hall, Inc.
A Simon & Schuster Company
Upper Saddle River, NJ 07458

The publisher offers discounts on this book when ordered
in bulk quantities. For more information, contact:

> Corporate Sales Department
> Prentice Hall P T R
> 1 Lake Street
> Upper Saddle River, NJ 07458
> Phone: 800-382-3419
> FAX: 201-236-7141
> E-mail: corpsales@prenhall.com

Printed in the United States of America

10 9 8 7 6 5 4 3 2 1

ISBN 0-13-472671-5

Prentice-Hall International (UK) Limited, *London*
Prentice-Hall of Australia Pty. Limited, *Sydney*
Prentice-Hall Canada, Inc., *Toronto*
Prentice-Hall Hispanoamericana S.A., *Mexico*
Prentice-Hall of India Private Limited, *New Delhi*
Prentice-Hall of Japan, Inc., *Tokyo*
Simon & Schuster Asia Pte. Ltd., *Singapore*
Editora Prentice-Hall do Brasil, Ltda., *Rio de Janeiro*

For Nancy, Lindsay, and Nathan.
You are the best.

Contents

Contents vii

CHAPTER 7   NOTES DEVELOPMENT ENVIRONMENT   73

CHAPTER 8   NOTES IS WORKFLOW   85

**CHAPTER 9   NOTES WORKFLOW ARCHITECTURE
                AND FUNCTIONALITY   93**

Foreword

I can't imagine a better title than *Mission-Critical Lotus Notes*. The "killer application" of this decade will clearly be centered around the convergence of Messaging, Groupware, and the World Wide Web, and Notes is the fundamental platform supporting such a convergence. Neither can I imagine a more appropriate or capable author than David Marshak, as he has chronicled and indeed influenced the evolution of Notes since its commercial beginnings six years, and millions of users, ago.

While a large amount of information systems value will continue to be garnered by our traditional transaction-centric systems and applications, experience shows that the R.O.I.'s being derived from Lotus Notes far surpass returns typical of our data-centric systems. The richness of the information-sharing experiences grows exponentially each year with continually expanding ubiquity. Notes deployments range from small workgroups and departments to a majority of Fortune 500 enterprises, and, most critically, beyond our historic definitions of the enterprise to partners, suppliers, and ultimately all of our customers. And, Lotus Notes at this point in time represents better than ten calendar years, and a half billion dollars, in research and development.

As David discusses in this text, Notes Release 4 has also become a critical element of something much larger: the Internet and World Wide Web, which now offer us even richer collaboration opportunities we could only dream of a few years back. Clearly the widespread emergence of Internet/Intranet phenomenon is the single most important paradigm shift any of us will experience in our working careers. In order to fully realize the incredible potential this network of networks offers us we must however view the critical infrastructure we employ to support it as a single, integrated continuum. This single continuum must embody the unstructured application development we typically refer to today as groupware, with world-class messaging and ubiquitous support for publishing and accessing highly distributed Web-based content. We must do so in an agnostic hardware and Operating System fashion from UNIX to NT to Windows and the Macintosh. The future holds much to be excited about with yet increasing rates of advancement central to this area of technology.

I'd like to give David great credit for taking on all of the beforementioned facets of this compelling but complex technical maze in this book. Additionally, as has typically been the case with David's past works, he adeptly weaves in a significant number of user experiences in an enlightening and highly readable way. User experiences with Notes are vast and run the gamut from simple messaging and discussions to full-blown "killer applications." David's choices of the cases studied here offer important insights and a look at the many sides of the Notes experience.

Let me conclude with a few not so objective predictions. I predict the prowess of Notes will make it the central applications platform for this increasingly network-centric world. I predict this world will be expanded beyond today's ambitions with the commercialization of Notes-based objects or OCX/ActiveX-based applets that will form the basis for even more powerful application building blocks. While this new era will begin with the arrival of Lotus' own component library in mid-1996, those efforts will be greatly eclipsed in scale by the enormity of the third-party industry that has been the central success behind the proliferation of Lotus Notes from the beginning. I predict, and fully expect, David and the Patricia Seybold Group to continue to play a central and leading role in that industry, now more than 15,000 organizations strong.

I'll end with a simple thank you to David for all the good work past, present, and future; and a final prediction that you the reader will find this text a very worthwhile investment of your time.

Jeff Papows
Executive Vice-President & Chief Operating Officer
Lotus Development

Preface

I am an industry analyst, a consultant, an "expert." In my job, I constantly answer questions about the best use of leading-edge technologies such as electronic mail, the Internet, groupware, and Lotus Notes. These questions range from the seemingly simple "What is groupware?" to "Can Lotus Notes scale to enterprise applications?" These questions also range from the highly technical, "How does Notes Release 4 improve replication performance?", to a high business orientation, "How do I use technology to get closer to my customers?"

The common thread running through these questions is a decision that has to be made. This decision, though often couched in technical or product terms ("Should I use Notes to . . . ?"), is really a decision designed to impact strategic parts of the business directly by making it more flexible, competitive, and responsive to customer needs. In fact, many of these decisions consciously or unconsciously result in completely transforming existing business and customer relationships or in creating new business opportunities and brand new businesses.

Mission-Critical Lotus Notes addresses the key questions surrounding the Notes decision, including:

- What is Notes?
- Which applications is Notes best used for?
- Is Notes a workflow platform?

- How do I build interenterprise applications on Notes?
- How does Microsoft Exchange stack up against Notes?
- Will the World Wide Web make Notes obsolete?
- What is the significance of Notes Release 4?

The last question, on Notes Release 4, is dealt with in two ways. Chapters 12 and 13 describe the Notes R.4 enhancements and their significance in the business and technical arenas. At the same time, the technical sections, particularly those on the Notes user environment and on the Notes development environment, are based on the functions and features of Notes Release 4.0.

A critical decision such as investing in Lotus Notes needs to be taken from two perspectives: the technical ("Is Notes the correct platform?") and, more important, the business ("Will this affect my business?"). This book is designed to help in both decision processes. Each of the in-depth chapters has a business orientation or a technical focus. The business chapters focus on the business reasons for using Notes and on how specific companies have used Notes effectively to transform their businesses. The technical chapters focus on Notes as a product, including its architecture, development environment, and specific features that enable advanced applications such as workflow or interenterprise electronic commerce.

Some of you may want to look only at the business-oriented chapter, whereas others may read the technical chapters exclusively. Some may look at both aspects of a given issue (e.g., interenterprise applications or Notes Release 4), and others may want to take in the whole picture. And some teams of business and technical people may want to divide the reading according to their areas of expertise. None of these approaches is incorrect, and it is hoped that any of them will lead you closer to making your own business-transforming decisions.

Please let me know how you do, in hopes that we can help others to follow in your path.

David S. Marshak
dmarshak@psgroup.com

Acknowledgments

This book is the culmination, but not the end, of work that has gone on for over eight years. There are more people who have directly or indirectly influenced this work than I could ever list. I would like to emphasize the contributions of at least some of them, knowing that I will suffer the embarrassment of leaving out at least one very important person. So my first thanks goes to that very important person who is not on my list below, but should be—you know who you are.

My first real set of acknowledgments go to the staff at Prentice-Hall and Bookworks, particularly Mark Taub, Beth Sturla, and Lisa Garboski, who made the publication of this book possible.

Next, I would like to site the work of Iris Associates, the division of Lotus Development which conceived, created, delivered, and is constantly improving Lotus Notes—the product which has transformed many businesses and changed many lives. My interactions with people such as Ray Ozzie, Tim Halvorsen, Steve Beckhardt, Len Kawell, Mussie Shore, Rob Slapikoff, and many others at Iris have always been warm and stimulating.

I also wish to recognize the efforts of many at Lotus who, over the years, have helped me understand (and let me in my own small way influence) this thing we call Notes. These "Loti" past and present include: Jim Manzi, Mike Zisman, Jeff Papows, Larry Moore, Eric Sall, Brownell Chalstrom, Frank Ingari, John Landry, June Rokoff,

Bruce Hitchcock, Eileen Rudden, Terry Rogers, Jane Eisenberg, Don Bulens, Steve Sayre, Cheryl McPherson, Elena Fernandez, Mike Laginski, Scott Durgin, Ian Richmond, Joe Forgione, Jeff Brown, John Blanchet-Ruth, Tony Walsh, Nancy Lipstein, Arlene Greene, Cindy Null, Bill Flanagan, Mary Murphy, Alan Rogers, Jay Fiore, Sharon Ricci, Schott Eliot, Scott Prather, Judy Jalbert, and, especially, Peter O'Kelly.

This book would not have been possible if not for the Notes users, from Sheldon Laube to Bob Kantor to David Daniels to Jim Wilcoxon and the hundreds more, who have graciously given of their time to help me understand what Notes really means. These people continually demonstrate that while a piece of software may be marginally interesting, what is remarkable is the way people take that software and push the envelope of their businesses, their organizations, and their cultures.

A special thanks to a select group that I am lucky to call friends: George John, A. J. Dennis, Peter Rothstein, Robb Kushner, and Warren Sirota. I have never officially worked with any of these great people. Yet I have worked with each of them for over half a decade to understand how people can best use technology, and, on the way, solve the problems of the world many times over.

Finally, I want to thank Patty, my sister Ronni, and the whole crew at the Patricia Seybold Group. Each is a uniquely talented individual and a pleasure and an honor with whom to work. And as a group they prove daily that the whole is greater than the sum of its parts. I have been given many titles and worn many badges, and the one I am most proud of is that at Patricia Seybold Group forum I can wear the white ribbon marked "Staff."

And to all of the above I can only add, "What a long, strange trip it's been."

David Marshak

About the Author

DAVID S. MARSHAK is vice president and senior consultant with the Patricia Seybold Group. He specializes in Lotus Notes, groupware, electronic mail, multimedia, electronic commerce, and new technologies. He provides consulting services to systems and software vendors and large end-user companies, particularly in the areas of developing, selecting, and implementing distributed information solutions such as LAN-based electronic mail, workflow, calendar/scheduling, and Lotus Notes.

Marshak directs the Patricia Seybold Group's innovative interactive electronic information services program which includes *Notes on Information Technology*, the industry's first publication delivered exclusively via Lotus Notes and now available on the World Wide Web. He is also the author of *Understanding and Leveraging Lotus Notes* and the *Notes Strategist Series*.

Marshak has appeared as an expert commentator on PBS and the CNBC television network. His analyses are frequently quoted in publications such as *The Wall Street Journal, Forbes, The New York Times, Business Week, Investors Business Daily, Datamation, PC Week, InfoWorld, Infoweek, PC World, Computer World,* and *Network World,* as well as on National Public Radio. He is currently serving on the board of directors of the Society for Management of Professional Computing (SMPC).

Marshak has spoken at U.S. and international industry events such as Comdex, Groupware, NetWorld, InterOp, LotusSphere,

International Multimedia and CD-ROM Conference, Lotus World, UniForum, Executive UniForum Symposium, the Danish Unix Users Group, and the Canadian Information Processing Association He has also lectured on new technologies at academic institutions including Massachusetts Institute of Technology and Babson College.

Marshak's articles have appeared in the *Workgroup Computing Report, Open Information Systems, Distributed Computing Monitor, Byte, Connect, Network World, Optical Insights, Communixcations,* and *Computer World.*

Marshak holds a B.A. in history from Rutgers University and an M.A. in history from Concordia University in Montreal.

Introduction

Jim Wilcoxon Transforms His Business with Lotus Notes

Jim Wilcoxon installs swimming pools. Actually, his company, Wilcoxon Construction (Rockville, Maryland), subcontracts four of the nine steps involved in installing residential swimming pools: installing the gunnite (concrete shell), coping stones and tile work, decks, and plaster. Wilcoxon does not handle the excavation, plumbing, reinforcing steel, electrical work, or fencing. His customers are large and small pool companies in the Maryland–Washington–Virginia area. These companies sell the pools and manage their installation, but they subcontract out the actual construction.

In 1993, Wilcoxon put in a 10-pack of Lotus Notes to track internal jobs. In a very short time, Notes greatly improved his company's internal processes, keeping everyone aware of the status of all jobs. He saw quickly that these benefits could be extended, as much of his information flow is with other companies, including both the pool companies and the other subcontractors on a particular job.

Wilcoxon began a plan to convince his customers and compatriots to use a computer-based system to manage the installation process. "The pool companies had very little computer use. I thought if I introduced the same software that I was using, they'd appreciate the training, and it would ensure standardization between companies." Wilcoxon offered the pool companies free introduction to and training on a number of software packages, including Windows, Lotus SmartSuite, and Lotus Notes. When the pool builders came over because of their curiosity about PCs and took the classes and tutorials, Wilcoxon approached the owners of the pool companies and told them he was starting a network called "PoolNet," which he developed with the help of consulting services provided by Mike Mazan of Chesapeake Technology Group and Kit Davis of Solutions By Design. He offered to help set up the pool companies, train them free for the first location, and charge them $300 per month or by the hour to participate in Pool-Net. He would provide full support.

This would be an interesting story if Wilcoxon had stopped right there. But he took it a step further. He recognized that pool builders are not really interested in *installing* pools. Their interest lies in *selling* pools. With the two largest pool companies, Wilcoxon built a lead-tracking database to automate and manage their sales process. When the lead turns into a sale, a Notes form that matches the pool company's sales contract (a slightly different one was developed for each of the companies) and all of the information needed to install the pool goes into the Notes construction database, which tracks the construction steps. Wilcoxon's name appears automatically under the four steps that the company handles. A set of affiliated subcontractors' names appears automatically under the other steps. The pool company's job scheduler can change these assignments but, in practice, tends not to. The scheduler adds due dates and financial information. As the installation of the pool continues, the scheduler updates each step and follows the progress in the construction database. From the pool builder, the construction database is replicated to Wilcoxon and then replicated to the other subcontractors. Each pool builder has its own construction database. Each subcontractor has a single database that shows the status of all jobs from all pool builders in which the subcontractor participates.

Wilcoxon is currently updating the application to add mail-based workflow notification and updating, and he is continuing to bring new pool companies onto the network.

The results: According to Wilcoxon, "We already had a good percentage of the market, and we have increased that percentage. We have increased contact with our customers, and we have given them added value. It is really very low cost for a whole lot of benefit to us and our customers. I've been in business for 30 years, and it really makes a big difference. It makes stuff work better."

Asked about continuing extending his Notes applications, Wilcoxon responds, "I talked to my banker today, and she's going to ask her boss if she can get hooked up on our Notes network."

Wilcoxon's may be one of the smallest companies redefining its business and relationships using Lotus Notes, but it is certainly not alone. The promise of business transformation is there for big and small alike. According to Jim Wilcoxon, "We're just a small organization, but the business principles are the same. We've got people who work out of their basement or their home. Information-wise, they are now not at any disadvantage from the person in the corner office of a high-rise."

1

What Is Lotus Notes?

Lotus Notes can be looked at in a number of ways. For example, it can be looked at architecturally, as a set of services (such as document management, security, messaging, etc.), a set of clients to access those services, and a development environment to build applications on top of those services; this is precisely what we do in the technical chapters of this book. Notes can also be looked at as an advanced, client/server electronic mail system or as a sharable document database. Or Notes can be looked at as the leading groupware application that provides support for groups and teams by enabling information sharing and business-oriented discussions.

These views are all correct, yet they all fail to capture the essence of Notes, which is much more than any one, or all, of these views.

Notes is not just a set of technologies, services, or applications. Rather, *Notes is a platform for developing and deploying business process applications*. Each word of this definition is important:

Platform: Notes is an infrastructure that must be exploited to gain benefit. It is the basis on which other things of value can stand.

Developing: Notes is valuable only when it is customized to meet a particular need. This requires developers (in some cases, these can be business users) and planned development. Notes encourages rapid, iterative, and cooperative development that enables meeting users' needs and establishing user buy-in.

Deploying: Notes provides its own method for getting users into applications and for updating both the data within the applications and the applications themselves. Notes is particularly beneficial in deploying applications across locations and to remote and mobile users.

Business process: The key to the value of Notes is enabling and supporting business processes, ranging from product development to prospect tracking to customer service to sales force automation. Notes can provide value at several levels—E-mail, groupware (discussions and information sharing), workflow, and interenterprise applications. In particular, the workflow and interenterprise applications make the greatest use of Notes capabilities and provide the highest benefit.

Applications: The model for using Notes is the application, be it the customer application, the product development application, the contract approval application, or any other business process. In its best use, the user interacts with the application by taking actions that affect the business. This is very much like transaction-based applications or, to use an old term, line-of-business applications. Notes thus differs in this respect from enhanced messaging systems (for which the model is putting mail in folders) or the World Wide Web (for which the predominant model is searching for information).

THE ARCHETYPAL NOTES APPLICATION

One way to understand Notes (in fact, the *only* way) is to look at how Notes is used. Throughout this book, we look at representatives of some of the best applications built on Notes. Before we begin, however, it is probably best to look at a specific Notes application and see why Notes is so appropriate and the value that Notes adds.

An archetypal Notes application is customer support. Let us look at a typical scenario, in which the same information needs to be viewed and acted upon by different people in the organization.

A customer calls into Acme Widget Company and says, "My widget is broken—I need someone to fix it." The representative on the telephone fills out a Notes form, putting in the customer's name, address, or any information unique to that customer. The Notes form automatically goes out to a relational database and brings into the form all the other information about the customer, such as the widget model, when it was purchased, and if it is under warranty. The representative on the phone confirms this information and tells the customer that someone will be there within 24 hours.

When the form is saved into Notes, a number of things happen: The service manager is notified that a new outstanding widget call has been added and assigns it to the best widget repair person. The widget repair person, who is at a remote service office, looks at a local copy of the application (which has since "replicated" with the home office) and sees her assignments for the day, presented under her name. She goes to the customer's home, fixes the widget, and updates the status of the service call in Notes. She also learns that the customer was visited last week by a salesperson from Omega Widgets—Acme's chief rival—and was offered a 10 percent discount to switch to Omega. This information is also entered into Notes.

While this is going on, the Acme customer service manager is monitoring the status of outstanding service calls by call and date and is very happy that they are being satisfied in less than 18 hours. At the same time, the product manager for the widget that failed is looking in Notes and sees that the failure rate of this model is getting worse. He calls in his product design team to find out why this is happening. The quality assurance manager is also aware of the problem, having looked at Notes by product, as has the purchasing manager, who is checking to see whether the bad parts are coming from one or more sources, by looking at part numbers.

At the same time, the salesperson who sold the widget to the customer has become aware of the service call by looking in Notes by customer account. He decides to call on the customer the next morning. That night, from a nearby hotel room, he learns of the visit from Omega Widget. He puts in an urgent request to his manager to allow a 15 percent discount on new widget purchases to this customer. The next morning, he looks in Notes and sees that his request has been approved. He sets off to visit the satisfied customer, whom he is about to make happier.

NOTES APPLICATION TYPES

In a business sense, Notes is a *tabula rasa,* a clean slate on which strategic applications can be built and deployed. Note the term *applications.* Many people sec Notes as a product to enable discussions and other group activities. Although Notes can certainly be used to enable groups and teams, this is a limiting view, which does not take into account the areas in which Notes is used for mission-critical applications. These areas include:

- Customized applications
- Workflow and business process management
- Interenterprise applications

We will look specifically at each of these Notes application areas in Chapters 6–11.

CATEGORIES OF NOTES APPLICATIONS

Crossing these application areas are the specific categories for which Notes is used most often. The "big three" of Notes applications are:

- Sales force automation
- Customer service/support
- Product development

Sales Force Automation

Sales force automation has become the classic Notes application and the entry point for Notes in many organizations. Sales force automation takes advantage of many of the unique strengths of Notes, particularly support for mobile users. Notes applications are used to deliver product and price information to the field, roll sales transactions back to corporate headquarters, track prospects, and manage the whole sales cycle from lead to fulfillment. Notes also enables sales people on the road to feed qualitative information about customers and competitors to their colleagues and management, as well as have access to competitive intelligence generated by others. Managers can instantly view the current status of the business: Information can be presented categorized and filtered by prospects, customers, order status, territory, sales person, or any other way the user thinks about the information.

Customer Service/Support

Customer service and support constitutes the second major entry point for Notes in many organizations. This ranges from using Notes as a "Help Desk" repository, to tracking open service requests, to delivering collateral information and updates directly to the customer. The service request application discussed above is very useful in illustrating the power of Notes. Using Notes for this application provides the following advantages: All of the participants in the process can see the critical information from their own point of view, and wherever they may be located. The process can be tracked, and the time taken to provide service to this customer can be decreased. And the overall information about the business can be captured and used to improve the process.

Product Development

Product development is a third major category of Notes applications. Many product development applications begin as Notes discussions and brainstorming. For many companies this has evolved into managing the whole development process, from product conception to build milestones to completion. This evolution clearly demonstrates Notes as a conferencing platform and Notes as an application platform. When engineers and designers discuss the types of products they would like to build, and marketing people add their view of the customer response to such products, we have an interactive discussion. When other constructs are added—such as responsibility (who will be the product manager, who will research trademark, who constitutes the product team, etc.), milestones (what are the key steps in the process), due dates, and current status—the discussion becomes a business process management application.

And Many, Many More

While these major categories describe a large set of Notes applications, examples of other strategic uses of Notes range from Chase Manhattan Bank's approval process for multimillion-dollar loans to a Dell Computer application that assigns new part numbers to computer parts. In this book, you will see many more examples of strategic Notes applications. You should also be able to envision new ways that Notes can be applied to your business. After all, in many ways, the only thing that limits your use of Notes is your imagination.

NOTES TRANSFORMS BUSINESSES

Ultimately, the technical definition and the capabilities of Notes do not really make much of a difference. The reason that companies bring in Notes and continue building and deploying applications on it is that Notes has the potential to transform a company's business. This transformation can come internally, from better communication, better decision making, and better managed processes. More often, however, this transformation has an external face, one that affects customer relationships directly. Here the transformation ranges from exquisite customer service to the ability to better anticipate and meet customer needs and desires, to actually including the customer in the process, creating the stronger bond of partnership out of the supplier/customer relationship.

Throughout this book, we will look at many examples of how businesses large and small have transformed themselves using Lotus Notes.

CASE STUDY

BOSTON MARKET: A BUSINESS TRANSFORMED

BOSTON MARKET EXPERIENCES UNPRECEDENTED GROWTH

Boston Market Incorporated (née Boston Chicken) had a problem. Its problem was that it was becoming too successful, too fast. The company, with its emphasis on providing consumers with fresh, convenient, home-style meals, was able to create a unique niche for itself between fast food and formal dining and had rapidly become one of the nation's best known food retailers. With its initial public offering in 1993—considered the most successful IPO in that year— the company established its presence in the financial consciousness as well as the culinary mind.

Boston Market's growing reputation was matched by explosive expansion in the number of stores: the company successfully opened more than 300 restaurants in 1994 and planned to open an additional 325 outlets in 1995. This expansion rate of close to a new store opening each day is virtually unprecedented in the retail food arena.

FAST EXPANSION DRIVES NEED FOR BUSINESS REORGANIZATION

The pace of its success, while certainly welcome, created significant challenges for Boston Market. By far the greatest challenge for Boston Market has been to make its organization evolve to keep up with its explosive expansion. It is these organizational needs that drove Boston Market to use Lotus Notes to redesign its business operations.

BOSTON MARKET STRATEGY: CONSCIOUS DECISION TO CHANGE THE ORGANIZATION

According to Stephen Elop, Boston Market vice president of Systems, the rapid expansion of the business has forced the organization of Boston Market's Support Center (i.e., corporate headquarters) to evolve from a traditional stable of hierarchical departments to a process-oriented collection of teams. These teams have been organized to take end-to-end responsibility for the business processes that are critical to Boston Market's high-growth environment, and they comprise a mix of support center, market partner (i.e., franchisee), and vendor staff.

In order to keep up with the pace of its business, Boston Market made two conscious organizational decisions:

1. Form process teams
2. Re-form the departments around the processes

These events happened sequentially rather than simultaneously. In fact, the second decision was enabled by the success of the first.

DECISION 1: FORM PROCESS TEAMS

Prior to the reorganization, Boston Market was organized into standard departments: systems, marketing, and so on. In 1994, when it was opening almost one store per day, it became clear that no organization had complete "ownership" of any of the key processes. The response was a conscious decision to provide an overlay organizational structure, with each of the key business processes getting its own focus. For each business process, a process team was formed. The process team took ownership and accountability for each of the processes. In order to be successful, the process team had to include people from multiple departments, market partners, suppliers—all of the stakeholders in the process.

As people became members of process teams, they also maintained their identities within their original departments. Individuals thus had dual and multiple roles.

Ultimately, 18 process teams were formed, including:

1. *Concept Evolution,* for long-term profitability
2. *Marketing,* to build store sales by increasing customer base, frequency, and usage
3. *Product Development,* to ensure that Boston Market has great tasting, safe, and cost-effective food and appropriate packaging
4. *Procurement,* to ensure that all stores have the quality and quantity of food and paper items necessary to meet demand at the lowest total cost
5. *Field Employee Experience,* to identify constraints of the HR systems and tools in order to enhance the effectiveness of the field employees and the partner(s) HR organizations
6. *Facilities Design,* to design store prototypes, select vendors, and develop programs that maximize revenue and return on investment
7. *Store Performance,* to design and develop the systems and tools for store performance improvement and new store openings, and to ensure adherence to quality, service, and cleanliness standards
8. *Development,* to create the tools and technology to enable the identification, selection, and acquisition—through lease or purchase—of excellent real estate, and to determine the best construction methods and continual reduction of store investment cost
9. *Partner Development,* to acquire, develop, and maintain the legal and financial relationship with partners and provide the company legal support
10. *Systems,* to ensure that the Boston Market enterprise utilizes information technology to its competitive advantage). [Note: This process is focused on building systems-related infrastructure (networks, selection of tools, etc.), not on the development of systems, per se, to support the store performance process.]

11. *Financing,* to ensure timely access to capital to fund enterprise growth consistent with balance sheet strategy and at the lowest cost

12. *Investor and Public Relations,* to ensure successful positioning with key constituencies through timely, accurate, and consistent delivery of information

13. *Support Center Administration,* to develop and maintain the SC environment, facilities, human resources, and administrative activities to facilitate customer, partner, and employee focus

14. *Entity Direction,* to provide vision, leadership, and resource allocation

15. *Measurement and Learning,* to ensure that the enterprise has the information necessary to measure process performance in a timely and accurate manner and thereby make fact-based decisions

16. *High-Performance Management,* to facilitate successful projects with broad participation and reduced cycle time

17. *Deployment,* to change/improve employee behaviors within stores, partner offices, and Support Center consistent with project teams' expectations

18. *Enabling the Execution,* to enable the improvement of repetitive out-of-store processes, thereby maximizing enterprise-wide efficiency—i.e., lowest cost with acceptable error

LOTUS NOTES-BASED PROJECT MANAGEMENT

This organizational evolution has been made possible in large part by a suite of workflow-oriented, Lotus Notes-based tools known collectively as "Project Office." Every current or planned project being managed by every process team is chartered and tracked using the Project Office databases. These tools facilitate the widespread dissemination of information as well as the participation by process stakeholders regardless of their physical location or corporate affiliation. As well, interested parties not involved directly with a particular process can observe activities elsewhere in the organization, allowing groups to anticipate better the needs of others.

At Boston Market, a process team's basic job is to collect ideas for projects. The team then assesses and prioritizes the ideas. The ones to be implemented are turned into "Chartered Projects." These are then organized, executed, tracked by status report, and completed. This whole process, which includes individuals in different departments and locations and may include market partners, is managed via a set of Notes applications.

The processes of the project teams are managed by two Notes applications which constitute Project Office:

Project Idea. Project Idea is designed to enable the preapproval process for new projects. Here process team members' ideas are collected, discussed, chartered, prioritized, and approved for funding (see Figure 1.1).

Process and Project Information. The Process and Project Information application maintains a record of active projects. This includes weekly status reports and completion reports.

DECISION 2: RE-FORM THE DEPARTMENTS AROUND THE PROCESSES

The success of the process teams led to the next logical step in the evolution of the Boston Market organization. Old departments were abolished and new ones that more closely matched the key process were formed. The new organization is structured as follows. The departments are:

- Marketing
- Research and Development (R&D)

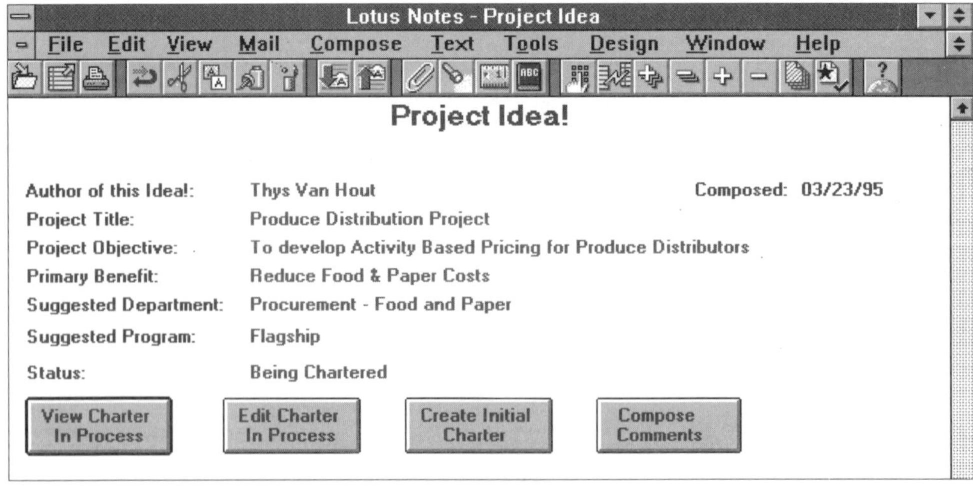

FIGURE 1.1   The Project Idea form is used by the Boston Market process teams to introduce, discuss, and approve projects.

- Procurement—Food and Paper
- Procurement—FF&E and Construction Materials
- Operations Services—Human Resources
- Operations Services—Training
- Operations Services—Store Performance
- Operations Services—Deployment
- Design (i.e., of facilities)
- Real Estate and Construction
- Franchise Development
- Legal
- Systems
- Financing
- Communications
- Support Center Administration

The cross-departmental process teams that live on are:

- Measurement and Learning
- Enabling the Execution
- Concept Evolution
- High-Performance Management
- Entity Direction
- Boston Market's New Notes-Based Processes
- Project Office Facilitates and Manages the Process Teams

NOTES WITHIN SPECIFIC BOSTON MARKET PROCESSES

Although the support of the process teams is Boston Market's most strategic application, the company has many other Notes-based business process.

OPENING RESTAURANTS

A series of Notes databases and Sybase database components is used to manage the process of opening new restaurants. Notes applications track the steps of site location, negotiations for buying or leasing land or mall sites, restaurant construction, obtaining permits, and so on. InfoPump (from Trinzic) is used to integrate Notes database and Sybase tables. For example, a construction manager at each location continually updates the project status in a local copy of a Notes database. This replicates back to a central Notes real estate database. InfoPump is then used to update the Sybase database. Reports are then produced from Sybase.

In addition to construction, every time a new restaurant is bought, there is a series of systems steps. These involve both the point-of-sale computers (NCR 7450s) and the Intel-based back-store computers. Steps to be tracked and managed include coordinating the wiring and configuring the computers (including menus, recipes, and prices). This type of information is downloaded on an ongoing basis to the point of sale via XcelleNet (which is also used to bring financial data up).

All of these processes are managed via a Notes database, which is tracked locally and replicated centrally and to the partner locations. This database also shows all the current configurations of all the stores (see "In-Store Information" below). Workflows are enabled by providing mail message notification to the next person who has to do something. Boston Market is considering integrating and managing these workflows in Notes or via an external product that integrates with Notes.

IN-STORE INFORMATION

As noted above, Boston Market's Support Center maintains Notes databases that contain all in-store information (see Figure 1.2). Specifically, the Store Systems Department uses Notes to maintain store information (address, phone, hardware/software configuration), data update request tracking (e.g., a store manager calls asking for a menu price change), vendor issues tracking, roles and responsibilities (organization chart-like views, job descriptions in documents), and a point-of-sale document library (maintains history of changes to POS database files).

SOFTWARE DISTRIBUTION

The Support Center also distributes software via Notes. For this application, Boston Market uses the Notes C API to further automate some functions. For example, files are attached to documents in the software distribution database. The "change manager" section has a button to execute an API program that will detach the attached files to appropriate directories on the XcelleNet Electronic Software Distribution server (the directories correspond to a specified list of store numbers in a text list field).

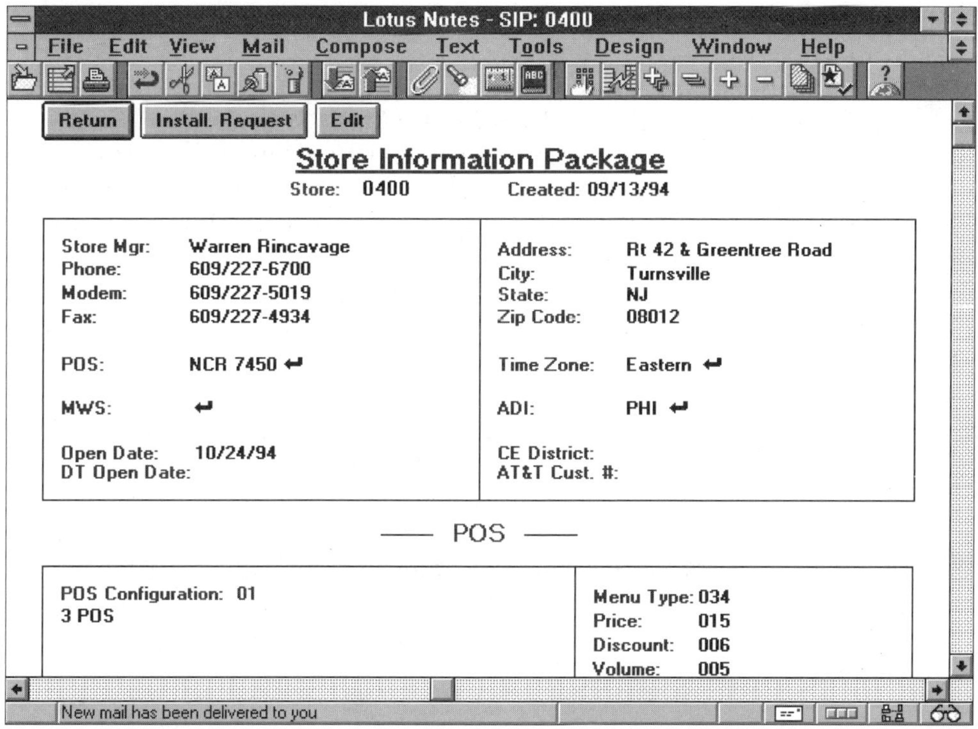

FIGURE 1.2 Most information about each Boston Market location is stored in the In-Store Information Database.

HELP DESK

A Store Systems Help Desk is maintained in Colorado. This provides support to any restaurant location or market partner office.

CONCLUSION: THE IMPACT AT BOSTON MARKET

This approach to the management of a multiunit retail concept is now permitting Boston Market to leverage its processes across multiple concepts. For example, Boston Market managed its bold move of renaming itself from Boston Chicken in order to expand its market by adding new main dishes to its menu. These new main dishes (ham, turkey, and meatloaf) will continue to appeal to the same customers while offering them more variety—they can now eat at Boston Market more than once a week.

In addition, the company recently announced a significant investment in Progressive Bagel Concepts Incorporated (PBCI; an amalgamation of three regional bagel chains). Boston Market is providing support services to this organization, including the immediate establishment of processes that parallel those at Boston Market, the introduction of Project Office concepts, and the application of many of the process-enabling applications that were originally developed for Boston Market.

RESULTS: KEEPING UP WITH THE PACE OF THE BUSINESS

For Boston Market the key result of using Lotus Notes has been the ability to transform its organization to manage the pace of the business. This transformation ranges from supporting the core business processes of opening almost one new store per day and of maintaining immediate update of material (menus, recipes, training materials, prices) to hundreds of sites, to the general effort to reorganize the whole organization.

According to Stephen Elop, "Without the conscious decision to reorient its business around its key processes, and without the formation of process teams comprising representatives of the support center, the market partners, and suppliers, Boston Market would not have been able to achieve and maintain the pace of growth for which it is so well known. Given the diversity of geography, time zones, and work patterns, the process teams could not function without the use of the Lotus Notes-based tools."

2

Notes as a Business Decision

Notes is a business decision. It is best undertaken with a specific business goal in mind. One of the most frequent mistakes is to say, "We need groupware" or "We need more communication." Most companies that have implemented Notes successfully and virtually all companies that are transforming their businesses with Notes are doing so with specific goals in mind.

These goals are frequently promoted by those with specific business, rather than technical, responsibilities. It is very common for a marketing vice president or customer service director to be the key sponsor of a Notes application.

The goals may be expressed in a variety of terms, but they usually include addressing one or more of the following critical business issues:

Improving customer relationships. This includes more responsiveness, better service, higher-quality products, and to be the leader in and meeting customer needs and desires.

Decreasing cycle time. This includes order processing, product delivery, and product development and improvement.

Sharing strategic information. Most common is providing information about customers, competitive intelligence, product information (specifications, prices, current promotions), and future plans to all who need it (particularly mobile users).

Managing business processes. This goal, which frequently includes the others, is aimed at automating and managing business processes, while empowering the individual, the team, and the whole organization.

It is important to note that all of these goals have a direct impact on a company's customers—in fact, it is arguable that the definition of "strategic" is *having an effect on your customers.* Many companies are taking this a step further by including the goal of involving the customer directly in the process—via direct interaction, information dissemination, and electronic commerce.

Thus the primary decision surrounding Notes is: Can it be used to further these customer-oriented goals? The results should be best measured in increased orders and customer satisfaction.

NOTES RETURN-ON-INVESTMENT STUDIES

Most companies embark on a Notes implementation without explicit return-on-investment (ROI) goals. Their stated goals fall into the categories described above: improving customer relationships, decreasing cycle time, sharing strategic information, and managing business processes. There have been, however, two studies of ROI in companies deploying Notes, and both have returned encouraging, if not astonishing, results.

The first study, *The Impact of Lotus Notes on Organizational Productivity*[1] by Telesis, surveyed 39 companies in 1992. The study reported results that accrued to these companies averaged:

- 3-month payback of actual investment
- 400 percent 3-year return on investment

This was followed in 1994 by a more in-depth study by International Data Corporation (IDC) of 65 Notes customers, *Lotus Notes: Agent of Change.*[2] The IDC study was designed to be more "conservative," and used additional financial factors (such as taxes,

---

[1] *The Impact of Lotus Notes on Organizational Productivity, Evidence of Customers,* Telesis, Providence, RI, 1992.

[2] *Lotus Notes: Agent of Change, The Financial Impact of Lotus Notes on Business,* International Data Corporation, Framingham, MA, 1994.

depreciation, and less than 100 percent productivity) that lowered the ROI numbers. The results were still very impressive:

- 2.0-year median payback; 2.4-year average payback period
- 117 percent median 3-year return on investment; 179 percent average 3-year return on investment

---

CASE STUDY

MILLIPORE MAKES A NOTES BUSINESS DECISION

Millipore Corporation (Bedford, Massachusetts) is the leading manufacturer of filtration systems used in medical, scientific, and industrial companies throughout the world. Millipore provides expertise in applications ranging from bacteria testing of water, to sterilization of biopharmaceutical proteins, to eliminating contamination from gases used in manufacturing semiconductors.

The Millipore Laboratory Water Division provides products and services that purify water for a variety of applications requiring the highest standards of purity. These applications include microelectronic production, medical research and treatment (such as *in vitro* fertilization), and various analytical chemistry protocols requiring high-purity water. The Laboratory Water Division derives revenue from both capital equipment and expendables—i.e., the consumables, such as filters, used in the purification process. The expendables business is driven by equipment sales, which themselves have a long sales cycle ranging from 3 to 9 months.

The North American Laboratory Water Division consists of approximately 50 sales, service, and administration personnel. The sales force is driven by leads, which are generated from multiple sources, including trade shows, advertising, and direct mail. Additional leads are generated through phone calls to the Millipore Technical Services and Customer Service organizations.

STREAMLINING THE PROCESS

Millipore was faced with a major business problem: how to streamline the process used by the sales force to respond to leads. The existing process had two major drawbacks.

First, leads were collected and entered into an Oracle database. They were then printed and, on a weekly basis, mailed to the sales people at their homes (see Figure 2.1). According to Bruce Dawson, director of North American Operations, this process produced two inevitable results: The sales people were working with "cold" leads, and the company's management had no way of following up on the leads to determine their quality and how well a particular marketing campaign has faired. In addition, 50 percent of the leads, those that came through Technical Services and Customer Service, were not even captured in the leads database. There was no record of them at all.

The second drawback forced the sales people to go through a difficult, time-consuming process to respond to the leads. Once the sales people received the lead, they had to do three things in order to follow up:

1. **Create the quote.** This was done by hand, writing on a quotation form, putting in the items to be ordered, part numbers, quantities, prices, and any custom information. This then had to be faxed to the Millipore internal quote-generation group, where it would be typed up and mailed to the customer.

2. **Request collateral literature.** The sales people also had to create a request for collateral material (product description, specification sheets, etc.) by hand. This request was then faxed or E-mailed to Bedford. The material was gathered and then mailed to the sales person's home. The sales person would then mail it to the customer, in hopes that it would arrive at the same time as the quote.

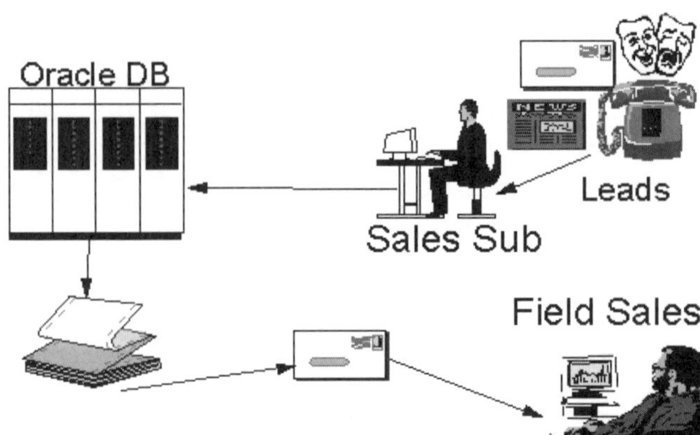

FIGURE 2.1 **Millipore lead flow diagram (pre-1994).** The Millipore Laboratory Water Division Lead Flow process before 1994 was designed to mail leads to sales people on a weekly basis.

3. Customize the cover letter. Each quotation required a cover letter that described the quote. The cover letter might be customized for the specific prospect industry or application. The sales person had to create the letter, print it at home, and then mail it together with the collateral material.

This process made responding to leads very difficult. Millipore has a highly mobile sales force, but because of the requirement to deliver collateral material and cover letters directly through the sales people, they could only respond to a request for a quote from their own homes. This meant that the quotes would get even more stale, waiting until the sales person returned home. It also meant that, because of the amount of time the sales people needed to process the responses and material, and their need to return home frequently, they produced fewer quotes and spent less time following up on them.

MAKING THE BUSINESS CASE

Bruce Dawson saw the problem clearly, and recognized that improving the system would provide tremendous revenue opportunities for the Millipore Laboratory Water Division. First, he articulated his vision:

> Each morning a sales person replicates and receives the 10 hottest leads. A few clicks by the sales person creates the quote. Automatically the lead status is entered, a quote is created with a professional-looking cover letter, and the appropriate collateral material is sent. This all arrives to the customer in a single, professional-looking package within days, if not hours, after the customer made the request.

He then reasoned as follows:

> The process described above previously took 60 minutes on average and can be reduced to 10 to 15 minutes. If the system enabled the average sales person to make two additional quotes per day, assuming a 10 percent closure rate and average pricing, during a 12-month period a conservative estimate of $3.1 to $5.2 million in incremental revenue would be realized.

Although he was well aware that these were estimates, it was clear that they could just as easily be on the low side as on the high side—for example, these numbers do not take into account a likely higher closing rate because customers receive more professional quotes, receive them complete with the collateral material, and receive them more quickly. It also does not take into account sales people's improved ability to follow up on quotes because of time savings and the ability to travel without constantly having to return to their homes.

REACHING THE SUMMIT

Under the direction of Kevin Danehy, Millipore Manager of Workgroup Application Development, and with sales/marketing input provided by Glen Gagnon, Manager of North American Field Marketing, the company began to design a new system called SUMMIT (Sales Ultimate Market Management Information Tool). The project involved redesigning the lead flow process (see Figure 2.2) and creating a Notes-based application for use by all sales people on their laptops. SUMMIT rollout began in April 1995; by mid-August complete rollout had been achieved, with 100 percent sales force participation.

The new process takes the leads from the existing lead tracking database, adds the leads from Technical Services and Customer Service, and delivers them via Notes to the appropriate sales person. The sales person—who can be at home, in an office, in a hotel, or at a customer site—has full access to all of the leads and the information required to create a quote.

The quote is created via a Notes form that is simply filled in, mostly by picking from lists of items (see Figure 2.3). The form automatically sets up the products, product number, description, price,

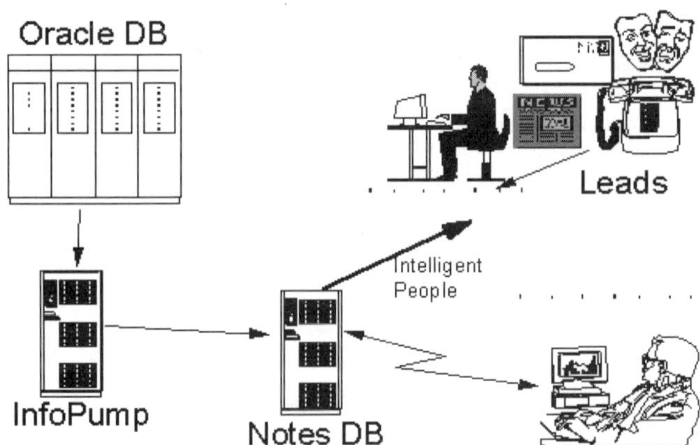

FIGURE 2.2 **Millipore lead flow diagram (today).** The new lead flow process eliminates paper and speeds up delivery of leads to the sales force.

and so on. The sales person can choose from predefined product packages—product packages are convenient and they assure that the customer is quoted on all the needed equipment to get up and running (see Figure 2.4). Choosing a package automatically fills in the appropriate areas of the quote (see Figure 2.5). The sales person can modify a package (e.g., discount an item—Millipore sales people have some latitude in discounting prices) and save the modified package as a personal package for later requoting to the same customer.

The sales person can then fill out a form to select appropriate collateral material (see Figure 2.6), and automatically create a standard format or customized cover letter to accompany the quote and the collateral. When the sales person next connects to the office, the process is updated: The lead status is automatically entered, and new leads are downloaded to the sales person.

At Millipore headquarters, the Notes application assures that the quote is automatically created with a professional-looking cover

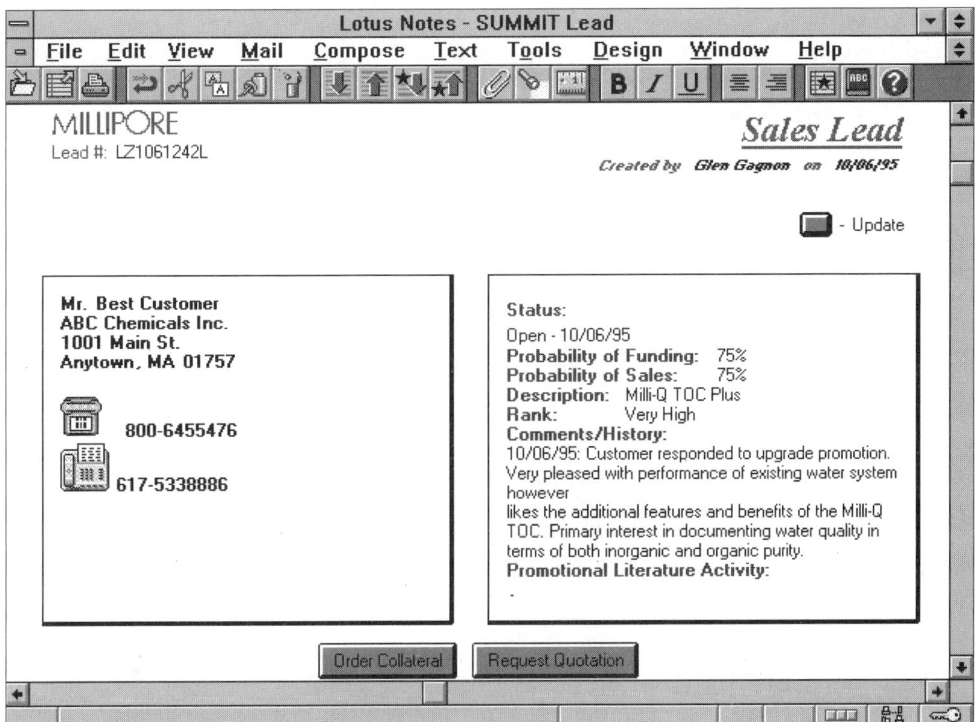

FIGURE 2.3 Processing a lead. Screen shot from SUMMIT application showing a customer lead.

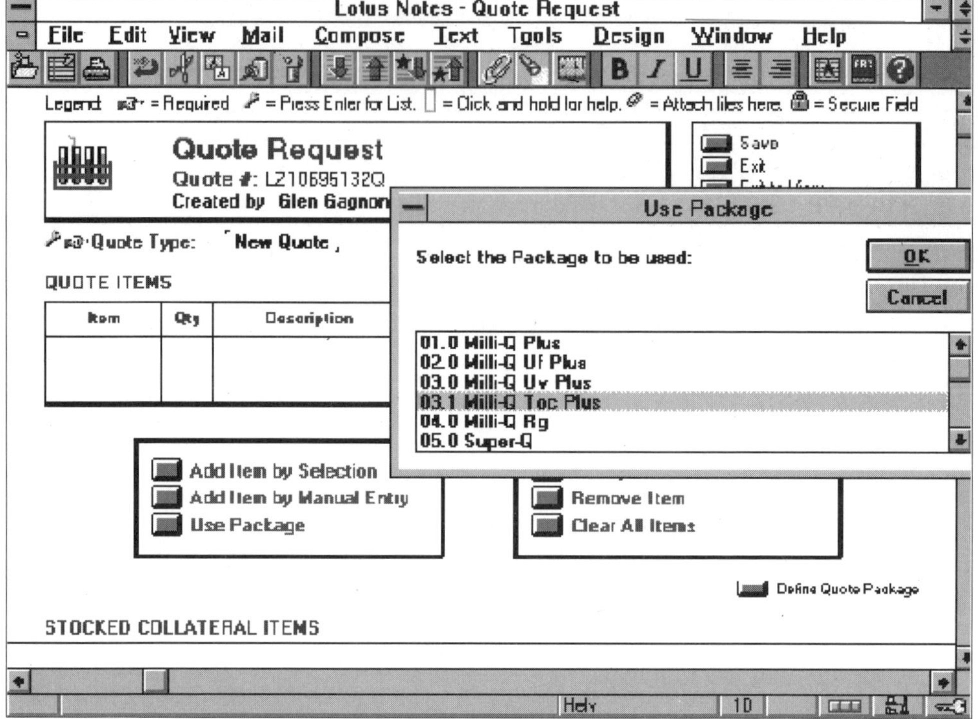

FIGURE 2.4 **Selecting a package.** The sales person can select a predefined package to create a quote.

letter, and the appropriate collateral material is gathered. All pieces are then sent together to the prospect.

At all points, sales people and managers can track the fulfillment of the quote, sending collateral material, and the cover letter process. Managers can also track quotes and orders against marketing efforts or specific promotions. They now have access to won–lost statistics, as well as qualitative information on customer satisfaction. And they can now make strategic judgments about deploying their resources with much more confidence.

SUCCESS FACTORS

Glen Gagnon attributes the success of SUMMIT to two major factors. First, the case made was a business case, not a technology case. And with the prospect of a multimillion-dollar return, the business case was easily made.

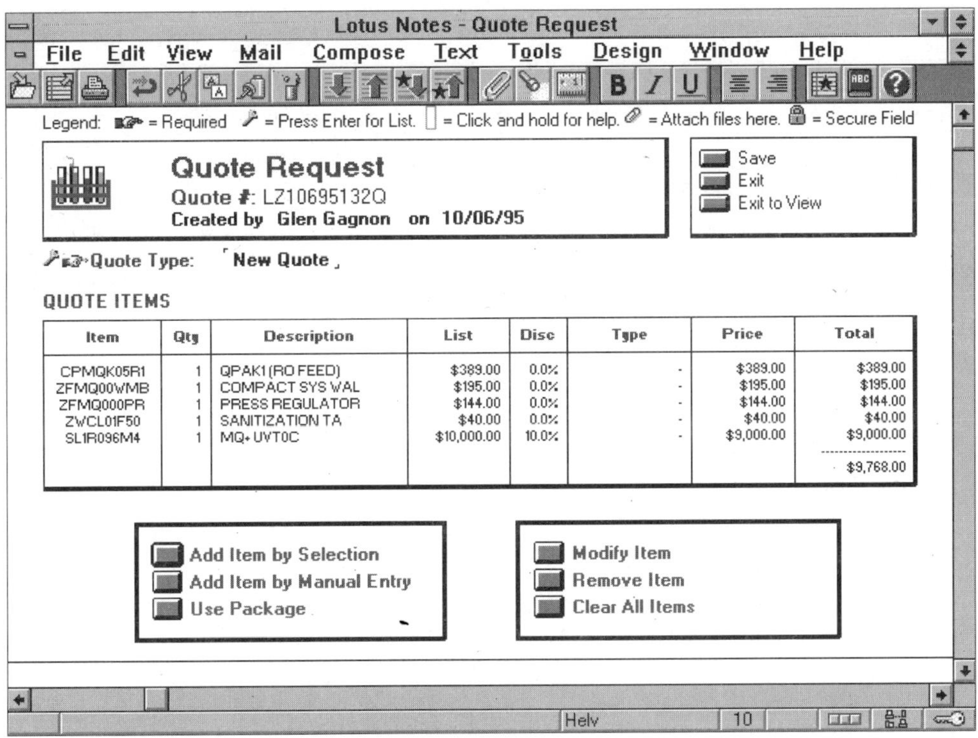

FIGURE 2.5 **Generating the quote.** The package automatically fills in the appropriate information, including items, description, list price, and discount.

Second, the application was built with two design goals: creating a better and more manageable process, and making the sale peoples' job more convenient. Whereas the former was required for the business case, the latter was required to make it work. Millipore understood that it is essential to obtain user buy-in and that users need to perceive that the management aspects are not threatening and do not require additional work on their part. Millipore sees this as emphasizing the *carrot* over the *stick*. Millipore also obtained significant input from the field, and is engaged in ongoing update and extension of the application. According to Gagnon, the sales organization is vigorously encouraged to provide feedback related to how SUMMIT can enhance sales productivity and provide more professional and informative customer presentations.

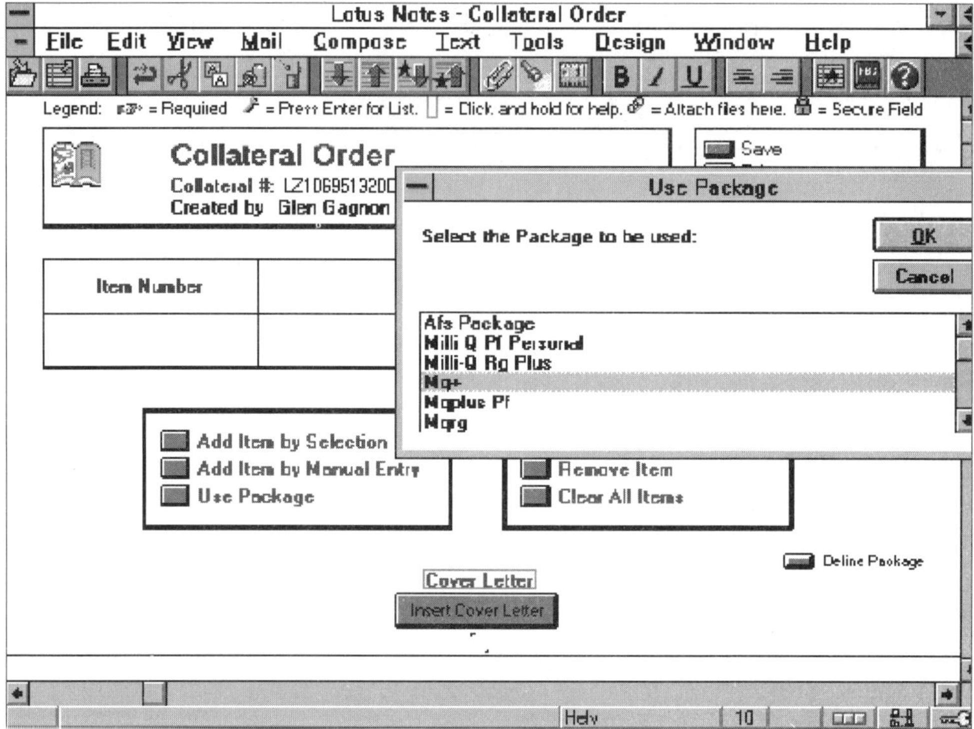

FIGURE 2.6 **Selecting collateral material.** The sales person can then select a package of collateral material to accompany the quote and cover letter, which can also be generated from this form.

RESULTS

SUMMIT has been fully deployed for only a few months, and actual return figures are not yet available. According to Bruce Dawson, however, there is no question that it will "quickly return our under-$100,000 investment many, many times over."

FUTURE DIRECTIONS

Millipore is implementing a number of additional Notes applications that will affect its business directly. One of these will automatically deliver a customer request for price and availability directly to a sales person's pager. This will enable very fast response to this type of request. Bruce Dawson notes that speed in responding to this type of request is critical: "When we get these calls, we know that the customer is shopping around. If we don't respond quickly, the opportunity will likely be lost to one of our competitors."

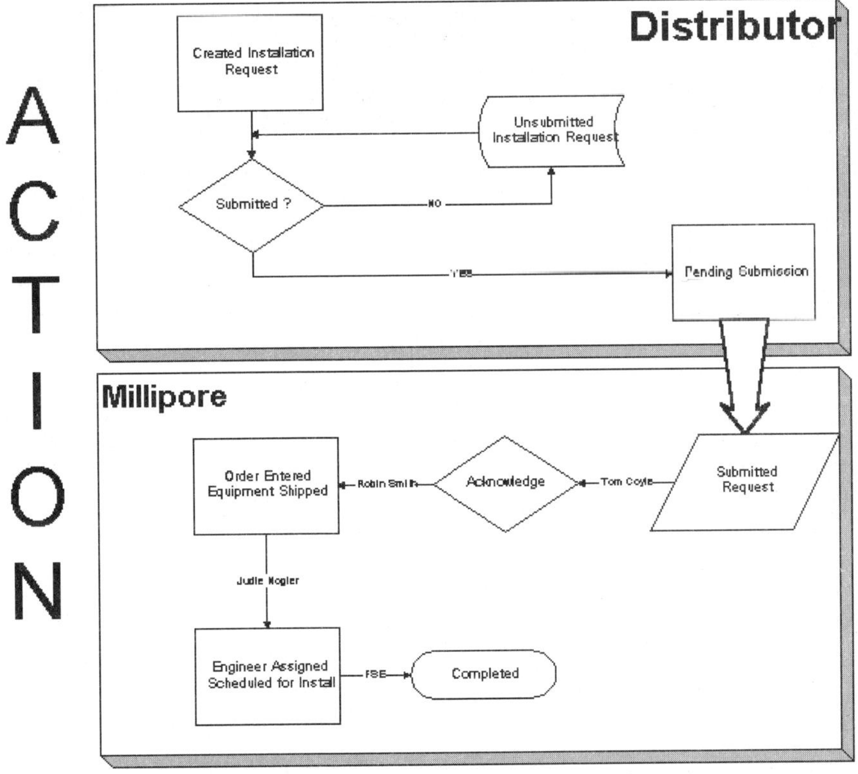

FIGURE 2.7   Millipore ACTION. The ACTION system coordinates delivery and installation of sales via the Millipore distributor.

A second new application at Millipore connects the company directly to its major distributors, and is a very good example of interenterprise workflow (we will see more examples in Chapter 10). The application—called ACTION (Automated Customer Transfer of Installation Order Needs)—allows both Millipore and the distributor to schedule and track product delivery and installation steps. The process is as follows: The distributor sells a Millipore product to one of its customers. The product must be drop-shipped at the customer site, and a Millipore engineer is scheduled to arrive soon after to install the unit (see Figure 2.7).

The benefits of this application, according to Millipore National Accounts Manager Tom Coyle, and Workgroup Application Specialist Jeff O'Halloran, include:

- Accuracy
- Efficiency

- Common implementation
- Tracking ability
- Remote access
- Easy understanding

Moreover, as Bruce Dawson emphasizes, this application ties Millipore "much closer to our distributors and creates more of a partnership relationship."

3

Notes as a Technical Decision

Notes is a technical decision. It is essential that Notes functions and features be appropriate for the application and implementation under consideration. One of the greatest mistakes is to be seduced by Notes as "neat technology," and assume that it is good for everything. Another great error is to assume that because "Notes is not _________" (the reader should substitute his or her favorite technology such as relational database management systems or the World Wide Web), it "really isn't good for anything except simple discussions."

Notes needs to be evaluated as a solution for a specific set of technical issues—such as multiuser access to information, rich document storage and management, support for remote and mobile users, and so on. This, of course, merges the Notes technical decision with the Notes business decision, as different business processes require different technical implementations.

IDENTIFYING APPROPRIATE APPLICATIONS FOR NOTES

OPERATIONAL APPLICATIONS VERSUS BUSINESS PROCESS APPLICATIONS

One way to distinguish the class of applications for which Notes is the best platform is to distinguish between two categories:

transaction-oriented applications and communication/coordination-oriented applications.

Transaction-oriented applications tend to center on an organization's operational applications. Typically, these applications are designed to capture and analyze business transactions such as order entry, inventory control, and payroll processing. They are usually part of back-office operations. Their focus is on the data they capture and on maintaining the integrity of the data's relationships as well as a consistent real-time transaction state. These applications have traditionally been built on host-based transaction processing systems and, for the past few years, have been migrating to client/server-based relational database management systems (RDBMSs). Characteristics of platforms that support these applications include being transaction-oriented, providing continuous access, implementing pessimistic locking, and supporting two-phase commit.

Communication/coordination-oriented applications center on business process management applications. They are designed to define and coordinate the activities of people working collaboratively to perform the tasks that make up a business process. These processes may involve small workgroups, or they may encompass an extended organization, including customers and suppliers. Their requirements are different from those of operational applications. They need to share, track, and route many types of information. Business process management applications focus on maintaining the integrity of the work process as well as managing the information needed to support the business function. Characteristics of these applications include being optimized for management of unstructured information (including text, image, voice, and video), supporting communication and collaboration among users, assuring security to enable interorganizational applications, enabling remote and mobile users to participate in the business process, and providing mechanisms to track and manage the task and workflow.

PROFILE OF APPLICATION REQUIREMENTS THAT CAN MAKE BEST USE OF NOTES SERVICES

A second way to look at an application to determine if Notes is the appropriate platform is to map each application requirement to the services required to deploy it. The following application requirements are particularly well supported by the Notes environment (see Table 3.1). Although few applications have all these require-

TABLE 3.1   Notes Application Requirements Checklist

Application Requirement	Notes Service	✔
Document orientation	Notes object store, document management	
User notification of events	Notes client, messaging	
User browsing of documents	Notes client, Notes object store	
Rich content	Notes object store, companion products	
Integrated mail and messaging	Messaging, directory, security, gateways	
Support for multiple users	Document management, directory, security, replication	
Support for multiple locations (remote sites, remote users)	Replication, messaging	
Support for mobile users	Replication, messaging, gateways (pager, wireless, phone)	
Security	Authentication: RSA public/private keys, password, digital signatures Encryption: RSA Authorization: granular access lists by server, by database, by document, by document section	
Application integration	OLE (and Notes/FX), DDE, Apple Publish and Subscribe, LEL	
Access to external data	DataLens, NotesSQL	
Workflow management	Server-based macros, structured fields (status, due date, etc.), routing, digital signatures	
Application deployment and management	Replication, application templates, data dictionary	
Platform independence	Multiplatform clients, servers, networks	
Support for standards	OLE, DDE, ODBC, TCP/IP, SPX/IPX, NetBIOS, VIM, MAPI, X.400, X.500, SMTP/MIME, HTML, HTTP, SMNP	

TABLE 3.1   (continued)

Interenterprise capabilities	Security, replication, Internet, WWW, Notes Public Networks	
Rich, scalable development environment	Notes development tools, LotusScript, C-API, forms and workflow builders, data access and reporting tools, client/server GUI builders	

ments, any that meet more than a few of them should be considered good Notes candidates. In some cases a single requirement—e.g., support for mobile users or interenterprise needs—could make Notes the most, if not the only, appropriate platform upon which to build the application. The requirements list, which is not all-encompassing and could include many more items, is as follows.

Document orientation, a requirement for dealing with documents or documents as containers for other objects. The Notes object store and document management features allow users to interact easily with documents. Notes's support for Object Linking and Embedding (OLE 2.0) allows the Notes compound document to be a container for other objects and applications.

User notification of events, a requirement to notify users that a task must be done or that a condition of the application has changed. Notes integrated messaging can be accessed by users or agents to send notifications to other users.

User browsing of documents, a requirement to allow users to access documents when they do not have precise and unique data for locating them. The Notes user interface and object store enable applications where users can browse through data without formulating precise queries. Users can traverse a Notes document hierarchy in an outlinelike manner by expanding and collapsing document categories. Users can also access documents via graphical Navigators or via full-text query.

Rich content, a requirement for information that is not just numerical and unformatted text. The Notes object store supports rich text, images, audio, and video.

Integrated mail and messaging, a requirement for messaging and electronic mail from within the application. The Notes integrated messaging, directory, security, and gateways provide a complete platform on which to build mail-enabled applications.

Support for multiple users, a requirement to support access to data and documents by multiple users. Notes provides a full set of services to support concurrent and asynchronous access to information by multiple users. These services include document management (including versioning), directory and security for access control, and replication.

Support for multiple locations, a requirement to deploy the application across multiple locations. The Notes replication, messaging, and security support the participation of users in multiple sites in Notes applications.

Support for mobile users, a requirement to provide access to the application for mobile users. The Notes replication, messaging, and gateways (pager, wireless, phone access) all provide the premier platform for mobile users.

Security, a requirement for security in any or all aspects of the application. Notes provides full authentication (including digital signatures), authorization, and encryption services that can be applied to virtually any Notes object.

Application integration, a requirement to integrate the application with other applications such as word processors, spreadsheets, graphics programs, and forms packages. Notes provides tight integration on multiple platforms through DDE, OLE 2.0, Apple Publish and Subscribe, and the Unix LEL. Notes/FX provides field-level data interchange between Notes and embedded OLE applications, and enables workflow capabilities across OLE-compliant applications.

Access to external data, a requirement to import or access external data into the application. The Notes import/export, ODBC drivers, NotesPump, and the NotesSQL facilities enable data to be integrated between Notes and most popular applications and databases.

Workflow management, a requirement to track and manage tasks that make up a business process. Notes supports both the message-based and database-centric models of workflow. The Notes server-based agents, structured fields (e.g., Status, Due Date, Person Assigned), intelligent routing, access to external data, and digital signatures all enable advanced workflow applications.

Application deployment and management, a requirement to easily deploy and update applications and to maintain corporate application standards. The Notes replication, Design Templates, and data dictionary enable effortless distribution and maintenance of applications.

Platform independence, a requirement not to limit an application to a single client/server/network platform. Notes supports a wide variety of client, server, and network platforms.

Support for standards, a requirement to protect current and future investments by supporting established *de jure* and *de facto* standards. Notes supports OLE, DDE, ODBC, TCP/IP, SPX/IPX, NetBIOS, X.509, VIM, MAPI, X.400, X.500, SMTP/MIME, HTML, HTTP, and SNMP.

Interenterprise capability, a requirement to implement the application across enterprise boundaries. Notes replication and security provide a unique platform for building secure interenterprise applications. With Internet integration and access to the Notes Public Networks for commercial-grade hosting services, Notes is a compelling option for interenterprise applications.

Rich, scalable development environment, a requirement for a rich set of development tools that can scale from end user to professional developer. The Notes development environment is easy enough for the power user and powerful enough for the professional developer. The environment is enhanced by access to the Notes API Library and by LotusScript, a full Visual Basic-like scripting language with integrated script editor and debugger. Notes developers also have access to a variety of additional development tools, including forms designers, data query and reporting tools, and workflow builders, as well as alternative development environments such as PowerBuilder, SQLWindows, and Visual Basic.

APPLICATIONS REQUIREMENTS BEST SUPPORTED BY OTHER PLATFORMS

Some applications have requirements that are not supported by Notes services and therefore should be built on different platforms. These applications tend to be transaction processing in nature or to involve a high degree of calculation (see Table 3.2). They also fre-

TABLE 3.2 Application Checklist for Non-Notes Applications

Application Requirement	Platform	✔
Simultaneous and frequent updates	RDBMS, host-based OLTP	
Continual access to latest data	RDBMS	
Two-phase commit	RDBMS	
Large databases (over 4 GB)	RDBMS, host-based	
Query-based access and reporting	RDBMS with SQL, data access, 4GLs, and reporting tools	
Complex calculations	Spreadsheet	
Mass publishing to unknown individuals	World Wide Web (Notes will include a Web server in mid 1996.)	

quently involve direct and complex queries, or data manipulation by users.

Some of the requirements that are not well supported by Notes include the following.

Simultaneous and frequent updates. Notes best supports an additive model of data, rather than constant updating of the same data. Notes has an optimistic locking scheme; frequent updates may require pessimistic locking. This requirement is best handled by an RDBMS or a host-based online transaction processing (OLTP) system, and it may require a separate transaction monitor.

Continual access to latest data. Notes is designed to operate in an occasionally connected system, making for lower expectations of complete accuracy of data at all sites. Although real-time access to the latest data can be maintained on a fully connected local or wide area network, applications with this requirement are generally better built on a continually accessible RDBMS-class system.

Two-phase commit. Notes supports document versioning and notifies the user of replication conflicts but does not support roll-back, roll-forward, or two-phase commit. These features can be found in advanced RDBMS products.

Very large databases. Notes databases are limited to 4 GB in size. Notes supports the external storage of large objects, such as images and other objects, but does not support multimillion-record databases. Databases this size should be built on RDBMS or host-based systems.

Query-based or report-based access. Notes access is via views or advanced full-text search. It does not support SQL query techniques such as joins or manipulation of cursors (data sets), nor does it include a report writer. These requirements are best handled by front-end tools for RDBMSs such as 4GLs, query builders, or report writers.

Complex calculations. Notes supports a number of mathematical functions but is not designed for complex, processing-intensive calculations. These functions are probably best provided by spreadsheet products.

Mass publishing to unknown individuals. Notes is a very powerful platform for business-to-business information delivery or electronic commerce. However, it cannot compete with the World Wide Web as a platform to deliver information to a mass of individual consumers. Notes, itself, will include a Web server in mid-1996.

COMBINING NOTES CAPABILITIES WITH OTHER PLATFORMS

The selection of Notes versus an RDBMS or versus the World Wide Web as an application platform need not be an "either/or" proposition. In fact, many applications can make use of a combination of platform services (see Table 3.3). In brief, platforms can be combined as follows.

Notes and RDBMSs. Notes and RDBMSs (as well as other non-Notes data) can be integrated via DataLens, which brings relational data into Notes databases; NotesSQL, which allows Open Database Connectivity (ODBC) calls to access data within Notes; NotesPump, or third-party integration products, which have processes that translate and move data between relational and Notes database servers.

Notes and data access and reporting tools. Data access and reporting tools can be used to display, manipulate, and create reports on Notes. This can be done via OLE, DDE, and Notes/FX.

TABLE 3.3   Integrating Notes and Other Application Platforms

Application Platform	Interfaces
Notes and RDBMS	DataLens, NotesSQL, NotesPump, third-party products
Notes and data access tools	OLE, DDE, Notes/FX, NotesSQL
Notes and spreadsheets	OLE, DDE, Notes/FX
Notes and World Wide Web	InterNotes Web Publisher, InterNotes Web Navigator, Notes Web server

Notes and spreadsheets. Integration with spreadsheets can also be accomplished via OLE, DDE, and Notes/FX.

Notes and the World Wide Web. Notes can be integrated with the WWW via the Lotus InterNotes Web Publisher (which allows Web users to access Notes data) and the Lotus InterNotes Web Navigator (which allows Notes users to access Web servers). With Notes Web server, due in mid-1996, the Notes server will provide native support for HTTP, HTML, Java, and JavaScript, thus providing direct support for Web browsers as Notes clients.

4

Notes for the User

A TECHNICAL DESCRIPTION OF NOTES (FOR NONTECHIES)

The technical chapters of this book provide an in-depth look at the Notes architecture, development environment, workflow capabilities, and so on, that are required to make a technical decision about Notes. It is also beneficial for the business person to have at least some idea of what Notes is and what functions it performs. It is also useful for business people to be able to speak "Notes"—that is, to be able at least to identify terms such as databases, views, and replication.

Notes is a document *database* with integrated *messaging* that allows documents to be accessed and shared among connected and remote users. Users access Notes applications (which is generally synonymous with Notes databases) via the Notes Desktop (see Figure 4.1).

When users open a Notes database, they are presented with a three-pane window that provides access to the contents of the database (see Figure 4.2), specifically via Notes *Folders* and *Views*.

Folders and Views allow different people to see information in different ways. Items are not actually stored in Folders or Views; rather they are *virtual* collections of documents. Folders and Views present the user with a certain set of information, sorted and

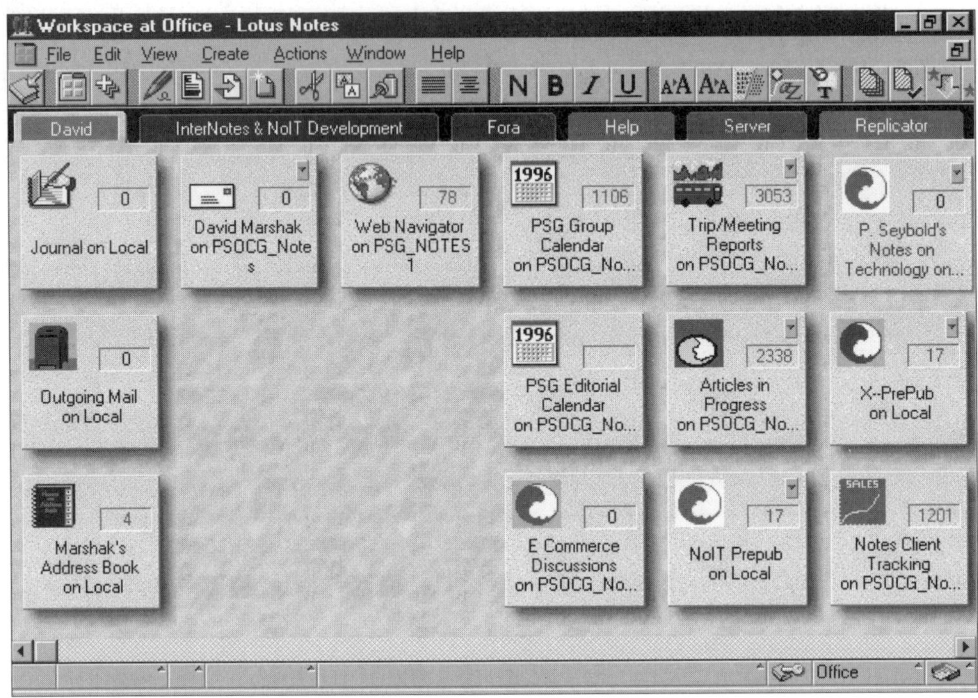

FIGURE 4.1 **The Notes desktop.** Users access Notes applications via the Notes desktop. Users can organize their work by using the tabbed pages.

categorized in a customized manner. This helps support business processes in which people have different roles in dealing with the same information. The key distinction between Folders and Views is as follows. Documents appear in Views because they match a specific formula—e.g., all documents pertaining to open sales quotations (sorted by customer), all documents pertaining to open sales quotations (sorted by account manager), all documents pertaining to open sales quotations (sorted by dollar amount). Documents appear in Folders because a user (or an Agent) has consciously dragged-and-dropped them into the Folder. Examples of Folders could include: My Hot Items, My Customers, Do Today, Look at When I Have Time, and so on.

Notes allows threaded discussions, enabling users to respond to one another and allowing other users to easily navigate through the conversation.

Notes includes a development environment that enables customization of the user interface, including providing graphical ac-

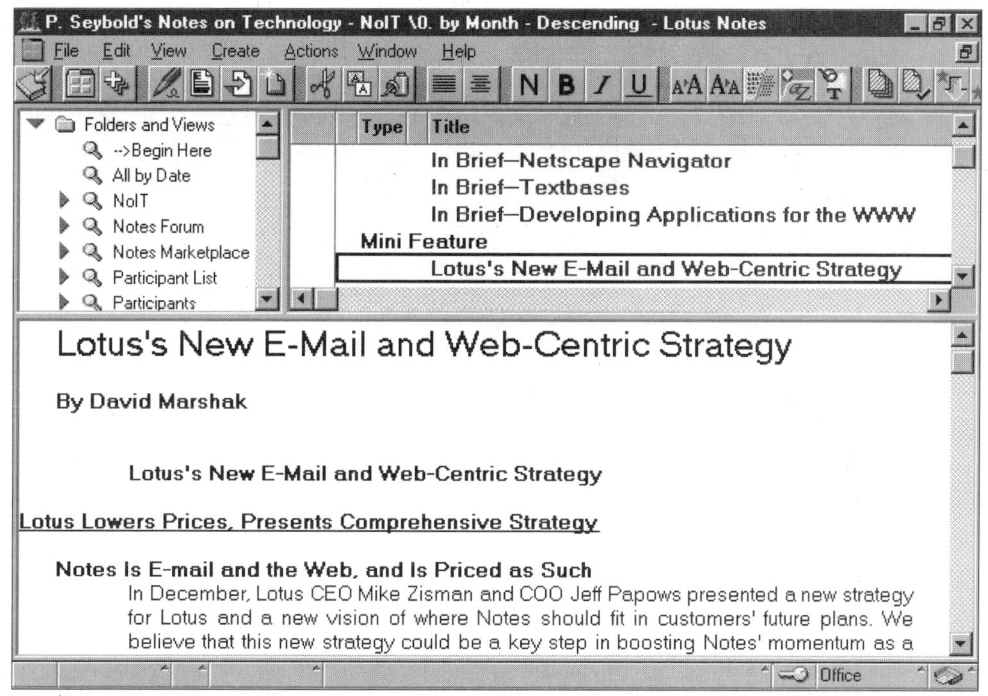

FIGURE 4.2 **Notes Views.** The Notes three-pane window presents a hierarchical picture of the Notes documents. The Navigation pane on the left shows the Folder/View hierarchy. The Browser pane on the right shows the documents within the Folder/View hierarchy. The Document pane across the bottom shows the contents of the selected document. User can also open a document in its own window by double-clicking on it.

cess (e.g., via pictures or maps) to information via *Navigators* (see Figure 4.3). It also enables sophisticated programming to build in application logic. Notes provides server-based *Agents* that can be used to drive applications, such as workflow. Notes enables users to customize their environment by creating their own Folders and Views or building their own Agents.

Notes provides a full set of electronic mail capabilities, including rich person-to-person mail and support for mail-enabled applications. Notes provides advanced security, including authentication, authorization, and encryption. Notes also supports *digital signatures,* which are particularly useful in workflow applications.

Perhaps Notes's most unique characteristic is its support for distributed environments, which can consist of servers in multiple locations and/or remote and mobile users. Notes *replication*

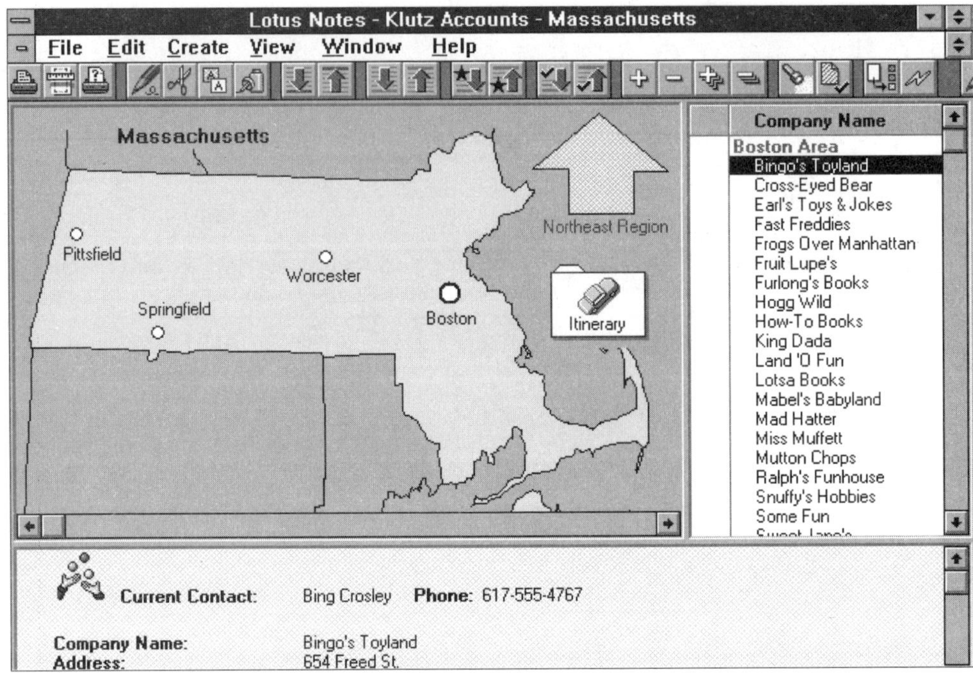

FIGURE 4.3 **Notes Navigators.** Notes Navigators provide graphical access to Notes applications.

provides synchronization between "copies" of a Notes database. This enables users at multiple sites, including mobile users who are only occasionally connected to the network, to work as if they were connected to a single site with all of their information available.

NOTES USER ENVIRONMENT

Lotus Notes offers three distinct user environment products:

- Full Notes
- Notes Desktop
- Notes Mail

These products differ in whether the user has access to design capabilities (Full Notes), access to all Notes applications (Full Notes and Notes Desktop), or access to electronic mail and a limited number of Notes application types (Notes Mail). The key elements of all of them are:

- Notes Workspace
- Views, Folders, and Navigators
- Documents and Forms
- Full-Text Search
- Agents
- Mobile Use
- Access to the World Wide Web

NOTES WORKSPACE

Users interact with Notes through the Notes *Desktop,* or Workspace. Each Notes database (best seen by the user as an *application*) appears as an icon on the Workspace. Users can organize their databases by grouping them on different pages, each with its own tab and user-selectable name. Customizable SmartIcons—shortcuts to highly used functions—are available from the Workspace and from any Notes screen. System information is provided by the Smart Status Bar at the bottom of the screen. This information includes direct access to and manipulation of mail and user location (connected to the network, connected via phone line, disconnected, etc.).

A typical Workspace has the user's mail database, personal Name & Address Book, and one or more Notes databases. (See Figure 4.1.) These databases can reside on the user's own hard drive (generally used only for private databases or databases under development by that user) or on any Notes server on the network. Databases on remote servers can also reside on the desktop—and with Release 4, replica databases can be grouped together for clarity. From the Workspace, users can see how many unread documents there are in each database.

Users can receive new-mail notices at the Workspace or within any Notes application. If new-mail notification is selected, an audio tone sounds, and an envelope icon appears in the Smart Status Bar.

The Notes Workspace is only a click away (via either the Window menu or a SmartIcon) from any Notes application. This allows users to easily open multiple Notes databases and navigate among them using the Window menu.

Users open a Notes database by double-clicking on the database icon. Alternatively, databases can be opened by name from the File menu. The first time a user opens a database, a policy document that provides information about the application and its proper use is automatically displayed. Each database can also have its own Help document.

The designer of the database can designate that an action other than simply opening the database take place upon double-clicking. Other actions that can be taken include:

- Opening a designated View or Navigator
- Launching a DocLink
- Launching an attachment

These capabilities, combined with Notes support for OLE 2.0, allow external applications to be seamlessly launched upon "entering" a Notes database. This effectively means that the Notes Workspace can be used as a desktop to give the user access to Notes and non-Notes applications.

VIEWS, FOLDERS, AND NAVIGATORS

When a database is opened, the user is presented with a navigation window. This window contains three panes:

- Navigation
- Browsing
- Document

The Navigation pane presents the user with a list of elements, such as Views, Folders, Agents, and Design Options. This pane can also contain a Navigator—a way to provide graphical access to Notes data or actions. The Browsing pane shows the items found within the element selected in the Navigation pane, such as the documents contained within a Folder or View. The Document pane, which can be optionally closed on open, allows the user to preview the contents of the item selected in the Browsing pane.

Views

Users gain access to information in Notes via Views. A View is a listing of all or a subset of documents within a given Notes database, arranged in an outline fashion. Notes Views are virtual—they do not represent actual storage of documents, and any document can appear in more than one View.

Each View lists a certain set of documents in the database, providing a specific selection and presentation of the information.

The selection is made by a formula that can involve one or more fields of the database—e.g., all documents created after 1/1/95, all sales leads from the northeast region, or all outstanding customer complaints. The presentation is determined by the columns of the View, allowing the user to see a specifically categorized set of information about selected documents (see Figure 4.2.)

Typically, a View is named for its selection or categorization criteria. For example, a client-tracking database may have Views that display documents "By Client," where the items are grouped by client and client names, which appear in the first column; "By Region," where the items are grouped by region, which appears in the first column; or "By Sales Person," which is grouped by the sales person's name in the first column. The information that appears in other columns is defined by the database designer. Generally, its purpose is to help identify the documents for the user, but it can also be used to give specific information, such as the total of other columns.

One of the most significant Notes capabilities is that users can create Private Views for their own use. Private Views, which are available only to the user who created them, allow listings with sorting or selection criteria not anticipated by the designer in one of the publicly available Views. For the most part, any user can learn to create Private Views in minutes.

Notes Views act like outlines: They can be expanded or collapsed as needed by the user to navigate through the documents. From within the View, users can select one or more documents to print, delete, or forward to someone via E-mail.

Folders

Folders, a new Release 4 feature, behave exactly like Views. The difference is how documents "get into" Views and Folders. Documents appear in Views by formula—that is, because they match a View's selection criteria. Documents appear in Folders because they have been specifically dragged-and-dropped by a user into a Folder (Agents can also place documents in Folders). Folders, like Views, are virtual—the document never really moves. Documents can appear in multiple Folders and in any combination of Folders and Views.

Navigators

Perhaps the most exciting user interface enhancement to R.4, is the ability to manipulate the Notes environment directly via graphical Navigators. Navigators can be used as Views to provide access to a selection of documents. They can also be used to provide access to a specific Notes document or to launch a Notes action. They can even be used to launch external applications.

Navigators are best used as graphical representations of what the user is trying to do. Good examples of Navigators include maps (e.g., to allow access to territory or state information) and process diagrams (to enable participation in a workflow).

DOCUMENTS AND FORMS

Notes information is stored as documents. Notes documents can contain a rich variety of information—text, formatted text, numbers, tables, sounds, graphics, images, video, attached files, and embedded applications. Notes documents also support DocLinks, hypertext links between documents in the same or another Notes database.

When a Notes document is opened, it appears in the Notes editor, which lets the user read, edit, print, mail, delete, copy, and so on. These abilities are dependent on the permissions that the user has for the database, the document, and even the specific field.

Notes documents can be made to open automatically into an alternative application (or editor), such as a full word processor.

Notes data are stored in documents as a set of fields. In order to create, display, or print a document, Notes requires a Form. The Form defines the fields, as well as how they are laid out. A document can be created in one form (such as a data entry form) and displayed or printed in another. This provides great flexibility in building customized applications.

FULL-TEXT SEARCH

Another way to navigate through Notes information is by using the Notes full-text search facility developed by Verity Incorporated (Mountain View, California). Notes supports text search within databases and across several databases, Boolean operators, and relevancy ranking. Relevancy ranking, a hallmark of Verity's "concept-based retrieval" capability, returns documents that meet the search criteria in a ranked order according to how relevant they are to the search criteria.

AGENTS

Notes Release 4 provides an enhanced end-user Agent facility that includes an Agent Builder and schedule- and event-based, server-based Agents. Users have easy access to very powerful Agents that can be used to manage their personal information and work. These facilities can also be used to create workflows that manage specific business processes. (For a fuller discussion of Agents, see Chapter 13.)

MOBILE USE

Notes's most distinguishing feature is its support for mobile users' almost full participation in their business environments. Notes does not limit remote users to receiving and replying to new messages. Rather, through its replication capabilities, it provides a full work environment to users on their laptops or remote desktop machines.

Notes supports remote users with two modes of operation. First, the user can dial into the network (or directly into the server) and work on a database on that server. This is useful for occasional access to a specific database. Second, a replica copy can exist both on one or more servers and on users' remote machines. The users can then work on the database locally—at home, in a hotel room, at a client site, on an airplane—and, upon reconnecting to the network (either directly via a docking station or PC card or by dialing into the network or Notes server), replicate with the server database. All additions that the user made between replications are now reflected on the server database, and all additions that anyone else made are added to the user's local database.

The advantages of operating in this mode are significant: Users can create a virtual office and have access to all of their critical information. Sales people on the road can see all of the interaction between their company and their clients. Managers can run their businesses from the road. And business processes can be carried out wherever an individual happens to be.

There are some drawbacks to operating in a replicated environment. First, the information cannot be guaranteed to be accurate past the last time of replication; thus, most inventory applications should not be run that way. However, because most Notes applications deal in qualitative and historical information, a latency of 24 hours is generally not much of a problem, particularly when compared with not having access to the information at all.

The second limitation is that the responsibility to replicate is on the users. They must remember to replicate in a timely fashion to receive up-to-date information and to make sure that the information they have added can be seen by others.

Since Notes introduced the possibility of true mobile work, many improvements have been made to ease the burden on the user (and to distance Notes further from competitive products). These enhancements include:

- Background replication, which enables the user to keep working in Notes or other applications while replicating
- Selective replication, which allows the user to choose which documents to download—e.g., only those added in the last 10 days or only those under 100 KB
- A set of enhancements—including field-level replication, server pass-through, replication management, location management, and stacked replica interface—which are part of Notes Release 4. (For a fuller discussion of these enhancements, see Chapter 13.)

ACCESS TO THE WORLD WIDE WEB

With Release 4, Notes provides direct access to the World Wide Web for all Notes users, including those with Notes Mail and Notes Desktop. This functionality, called the InterNotes Web Navigator, uses the Notes server to provide access to HTML pages on the World Wide Web. The pages look and behave exactly as they do when viewed by any Web browser—for example, all links between documents are live, and the user can follow them across the Internet or within Intranets.

Notes users not only have the same access to the Web as those who use other browsers, they have this access with all of the capabilities of Notes, including using different Views, putting items in Folders, running Agents, and replicating Web documents to their laptops for use when they are not connected to the network. In addition, the InterNotes Web Navigator provides companies with a wide set of security and access management tools that enhance those found in current Web-oriented technology. (For a fuller discussion of the InterNotes Web Navigator, including its architecture and a set of screen shots, see Chapter 14.)

NOTES CLIENT OPTIONS

All of these features can be found in each of the Notes client options—Full Notes, Notes Desktop, and Notes Mail. The differences between these options are as follows.

NOTES CLIENT

Also known as Full Notes, the Notes Client allows users to access any Notes application for which they have appropriate rights. In addition, the Notes Client comes with an integrated application development environment, which allows users to design applications for personal, workgroup, or corporate use.

NOTES DESKTOP

Notes Desktop is a less expensive, runtime version of Lotus Notes. Notes Desktop is exactly the same as the full Notes Client, with a single exception: The Notes Desktop user does not have access to Notes design capabilities. Notes Desktop users can participate fully in all Notes applications, including creating Agents for their own use.

NOTES MAIL

Notes Mail actually has two meanings: the mail facilities within Notes and the mail-only version of Lotus Notes.

Notes mail is a full client/server mail user agent that uses the Notes document database as its message store. Notes Mail supports all of the Notes facilities and paradigms (many of which actually come from the E-mail world), including rich, compound documents, hierarchical Folders and Views, server-based agents, replication to remote machines, serial routing, task management in the To Do Folder, encryption, digital signatures, and so on. Notes mail is included with all Notes clients.

The Notes Mail *product* contains all the mail features of Notes. It is Notes! However, the Notes Mail user is limited to using mail and to participating in a set of defined application types. These applications include the following.

InterNotes Web Navigator. Notes Mail users have full access to the R.4 InterNotes Web Navigator. They can use the InterNotes Navigator to browse the World Wide Web. In addition, if someone E-mails a universal resource locator (URL) to them, they can click on it to launch the Web document.

Discussions. Notes Mail users have access to discussion applications that use a discussion template with limited, minor modifications. They can participate in discussions with other Notes Mail users and full Notes and Notes Desktop users.

Journal. Notes Mail provides users with a template to create and maintain a personal diary.

Document Library. Notes Mail users have access to the Notes Document Library application that supports document management of Notes, Lotes SmartSuite, Microsoft Office, and other documents. The Document Library includes canned workflow (serial review, select reviewers from Name & Address Book, collect responses and edits, define allotted time for review, timed reminders to reviewers, notification by each reviewer or after all reviews) within which Notes Mail users can participate.

Room Reservations. Notes Mail users can participate in resource reservation applications. This is a precursor to participation in an eventual Notes-based calendar/scheduling system.

5

The Notes Architecture

Notes provides a full client/server architecture that enables companies to develop and deploy workgroup, enterprise, and interenterprise applications. Notes uses remote procedure calls (RPCs) between clients and servers and between servers and servers. The Notes architecture is inherently multiplatform, with virtually equal functionality available on each. Clients run on Windows95, Windows NT, Windows 3.x, OS/2, Macintosh, and Unix. Servers run on Windows NT, OS/2, NetWare, Unix, and Windows. Notes supports most networking protocols, including NetWare IPX/SPX, NetBIOS, TCP/IP, X.25, SNA, and Asynch dial-up.

Notes provides the following set of services on which developers can build applications (see Figure 5.1):

- Document management
- Messaging
- Replication
- Security
- Server-based Macros/Agents
- Full-text search

FIGURE 5.1 Notes services architecture. Notes services (document management, messaging, directory, replication, security, server agents, data access, full text retrieval, etc.) are supplemented by Notes Companion Services (imaging, OCR, phone, video, fax, etc.). They are accessible via the Notes Client, Notes API, ODBC, Notes F/X, and, in mid-1996, HTTP.

DOCUMENT MANAGEMENT

Notes provides a range of services that make it the most powerful distributed document management system available today. These services include:

- Notes Object Store
- Document hierarchy
- Versioning
- DocLinks
- Full-text search

In addition, Notes document management is enhanced by other Notes services such as replication and highly granular security, which are described below.

NOTES OBJECT STORE

At the heart of Notes is the Object Store, which is a database of all *notes*—the technical term for all Notes objects. The Object Store contains all of a Notes database's design elements (Forms, Views, Agents, etc.), the Access Control List (ACL), and all other information relating to the database. Most important, the Object Store contains documents. In Notes, the document is the container for virtually all information in the database. Documents in Notes act very much as records in relational databases; that is, they contain the specific information about each item in the database.

The Notes document can contain a variety of data types: numeric, text, rich text, compound-document objects, multimedia, images, links to other documents, and embedded applications. It also contains information such as what database it is in, whether it is a response (or a parent) to another document, when it was created and last modified, who can read or modify it (or individual sections of it), and who created it. This information allows Notes to manage the documents to enable multiple users to read and interact with the information.

A Notes document can store a wide variety of objects, including text, formatted text, graphics, images, voice, video, and other applications.

DOCUMENT HIERARCHY

Notes is perhaps best known for its built-in document threading, a facility that lets users create documents that are then bound to the original document (i.e., responses). The Notes Object Store preserves this parent–child relationship even when the documents are copied to another database, and this relationship is maintained across different Notes views.

VERSIONING

Document versioning is a key feature of Notes. Notes can handle versions in two ways: Edited documents can become responses to the original document, or the last updated version can become the main document with all previous versions displayed as responses. The choice of method and whether to invoke versioning at all are controlled by the database developer. The developer also controls the order of display in the same way that he or she specifies the order in which a view's documents are sorted.

The greatest advantage of versioning is not in the traditional document management function of allowing access to multiple versions of documents, though this capability may be useful in certain Notes applications. Rather, the importance is that the use of versioning minimizes possible inconvenience when multiple people edit the same document simultaneously. In addition, it can be used to eliminate replication conflicts that occur when the same document is edited at two different sites between replications.

DOCLINKS

Notes enables links between documents in the same or in different Notes databases. These links are maintained when the document with the link in it is mailed to another user or copied to another database. The target document can be in any replica copy of the target database (see "Replication," below). This allows DocLinks to be maintained and managed in a distributed, occasionally connected network.

FULL-TEXT SEARCH

Notes provides sophisticated text search and retrieval capabilities using a search engine licensed from Verity. Notes supports text searches across multiple Notes databases, Boolean operators, and relevancy ranking. Relevancy ranking, a hallmark of the Verity "concept-based retrieval" capability, returns documents that meet the search criteria in a ranked order according to how relevant they are to the search criteria (see Table 5.1).

Notes full-text queries can be run on either the server or a client machine. The search is generally run where the database is stored: on the server for server databases, on the client for local databases. This architecture lets connected users have the indexing process and their searches run on the server and not tie up their machines, while at the same time giving disconnected users full access to the Notes search capabilities.

A key strength of the Notes full-text facility is the ability to launch actions (send documents, enter or change data in specific fields of documents matching the search criteria, etc.) based on the results of a query. These actions can use Notes Formulae, with access to Fields, Forms, and @Functions. This capability, coupled with

TABLE 5.1 Notes Full-Text Query Features

Search across multiple databases	Searches across multiple databases are supported. The target databases must be specified.
Boolean search operators	ACCRUE, AND, OR, and NOT are supported. ACCRUE is an operator used by the Verity engine to provide relevancy ranking.
Proximity operator	The ability to search for multiple, discrete text strings in relative proximity to each other (i.e., within the same sentence or same paragraph) is supported.
Wild-card operator	Wild-card operators (*, ?) are supported.
Phrase searching	The ability to search for multiword phrases is supported.
Incremental indexing	Incremental indexing occurs on the server automatically. For each database on the server, an index priority determines how frequently (hourly, daily, specific schedules) an index is updated. The default is "immediate," which causes databases to be incrementally indexed whenever a user closes the database. Local databases on workstations are incrementally indexed upon user request.
Field-based retrieval	Text searches limited to a specific field are supported.
Date-based retrieval	Searches can be constrained based on the creation date of the document.
Numeric value searching	Numeric value-based searches are supported, including both integer and floating-point values. Operators for numeric and date fields include $<, >, <=, >=, <>$.
Word positions returned for highlighting purposes	Words are returned from a query and displayed in context. Values that match search criteria are highlighted.
Relevancy ranking	Documents may be returned in ranked order of relevancy. ACCRUE and weighting operators are supported.

the ability to run queries automatically on a timed basis, provides the support for building applications based on text-based agents—a unique facility within Notes.

The Notes full-text capabilities can be accessed from the Notes client or from other applications via the published full-text API.

MESSAGING

Lotus has developed its next-generation mail services as an integral part of Notes Release 4. Notes Release 4 messaging is standards-based, with native support for X.400 and SMTP/MIME transports and X.500 directory shadowing. Notes also supports all the popular mail APIs, including XAPI, VIM, CMC, and MAPI. This allows developers to build mail-enabled applications to their interface of choice and run them on a Notes infrastructure.

Notes messaging provides all the components of a mail system: transport, message store, and directory, as well as a highly functional mail client. Developers can easily build mail-enabled applications on the Notes platform without having to know a lot about mail and messaging. Notes messaging functionality is also continually available to the user.

TRANSPORT: THE NOTES ROUTER

The Notes Router is the store-and-forward communications process supported by Notes. The other major Notes communication process is replication, which is simultaneous synchronization of different copies of a Notes database. The Notes Router uses two databases to forward mail: MAIL.BOX, where the Notes workstation client (User Agent or the Notes Mailer) deposits mail; and NAMES.NSF, the public Name & Address Book, which includes the directory of users (and their local mailboxes, other Notes mailbox locations, foreign mail addresses, and connections between servers that allow the routing of mail within and between Notes domains).

The Router is a continuous process that runs on the Notes server. It is one of several Notes server processes (including database server, replicator, login server, name server) that run simultaneously on the Notes server.

Notes Mail is a cooperative client/server process. Some of the work is done in the client (the Mailer), and some is done by the server (the Router). Sometimes, the mail process appears as a single event, and, at other times, such as with delayed sending of remote mail, a significant amount of time can elapse within the process (e.g., the user may wait until the next day to connect to the server and actually send the mail).

MESSAGE STORE: THE NOTES DATABASE

The Notes Message Store is simply a Notes database. Thus it has all the features of Notes databases, including customizability, support of compound documents, rich text, graphics, images, sounds, video, executables, OLE objects, and links to other documents. Notes maintains a separate store for each user. The user may keep a replica copy on a laptop for full access to Notes Mail functionality and to his or her mail messages when disconnected.

DIRECTORY: THE NOTES NAME & ADDRESS BOOK

The Notes Name & Address Book is the directory service for Notes. It provides for registration of users and servers, mail addressing, and security information for encryption and digital signatures. The Notes Name & Address Book is synchronized and propagated via the Notes replication service.

The Notes Name & Address Book is also just another Notes database. Thus, it is customizable and extensible for an organization's specific needs. For example, a Signing Limit Field could be put in each Person Record in the Name & Address Book. This field could then be used by a workflow application to determine routing of request-for-approval forms.

Hierarchical Naming

Notes is designed to support X.509 hierarchical naming (part of the X.500 definition). Each Name & Address Book entry contains the following naming parts:

- Country
- Organization
- Organizational unit (up to four levels are supported)
- Common name (such as user name or server name)

Entries logically form a tree representing the distinguished name hierarchy. Each entry in the name hierarchy is responsible for managing the name space below it. As a result, each entity with descendants becomes the naming authority for its descendants. Lotus recommends associating each naming authority with a certifier of the same name, creating a one-to-one correspondence between certifier and naming authority. This is consistent with what is becoming the *de facto* industry standard for X.500 space management.

The naming convention applies in a number of contexts, including:

- Name & Address Book (mail addressing)
- Database access control lists (ACLs)

- User ID certificates
- Author fields in Notes documents

NOTES MAIL CLIENT

One of the standard Notes databases is a full-function rich mail client that is available from anywhere within Notes. The Notes mail client provides users with all the common mail functions—send, reply, forward, etc.—as well as advanced features, such as full compound-document support. The Notes Release 4 mail client is based on the cc:Mail for Windows client.

REPLICATION

Replication is the process of keeping multiple copies of a database in synchronization. It allows a database to be distributed (i.e., reside in multiple locations). Users in remote locations or in separate companies can work on the same process, and the system automatically updates their respective copies of the database. Replication is particularly powerful in its ability to allow users to work on documents and tasks when they are disconnected from the LAN. As soon as they connect (either directly to the LAN or via dial-up modem), the databases copies can be synchronized, with both copies reflecting all changes made in either database while they were disconnected.

Thus, after a replication cycle, all documents added or deleted in either copy will be added or deleted in the other. For documents that are changed in one copy, the modified version replaces the older version in the other copy. If a document is modified in both copies between replications, Notes keeps both copies (since it cannot know whether each user was aware of the other's changes) and flags the conflict. This may then be resolved by a user or administrator.

Notes Release 4 introduces the concept of field-level replication, where only the altered field is sent from one copy of the database to other copies. When compared with sending the whole changed document (which could itself be multiple megabytes in size), this can provide significant savings in communications time and cost.

In the Notes model, replication is essentially peer to peer, with changes being sent in both directions between two servers or between a user and a server. The model supports both complete replication, which produces identical copies, and selective replication, where only a subset appears in one of the locations. Selective replication is particularly useful for laptop users, for whom disk space can be an important issue. The criteria for selective replication is controlled by user- or administrator-defined parameters. Replication is subject to all of the Notes security facilities. (See "Security," below.)

Since replication is a Notes system service, developers do not have to build anything special into their applications to make use of the facility. In a sense, all Notes applications are "occasionally connected-aware" and are ready to be distributed. This brings two key benefits to developers: First, the developer can build applications that are not constrained by connectivity limitations. Unlike most applications built on other database architectures, which depend on continuous user access, Notes allows the developer to conceive and implement connection-independent applications.

Second, replication eases software distribution, making it a virtual nonissue in a Notes environment. New applications can be distributed to users whenever they are connected to a server. Connected users can instantly use a new application on the server; they can be instantly notified of the application via an E-mail message or database posting with a link to the new application. For disconnected users, distribution can be as simple as electronically mailing a replica copy of the database, which will then synchronize with the server copy upon next connection.

Maintaining and updating existing Notes applications is even easier. Any change made to the application design is instantly available to all connected users and is incorporated into remote users' applications as soon as they next replicate. All of this occurs without any overt action on the part of the developer or users.

SECURITY

Notes provides advanced security services that are readily available to developers and, at times, to end users. Notes supports all three classes of security—authentication, authorization, and encryption—each of which can be applied at various levels of granularity within an application.

AUTHENTICATION

Authentication securely identifies users using the X.509 hierarchical naming syntax. In Notes, authentication is built on a system of certifiers and certificates. The system ensures that both the user and server are who they "say" they are and are certified to communicate with each other. The certification system allows secure control of interaction between organizations, as well as within domains.

Authentication is also used to support *digital signatures*, a significant security feature and an important foundation for authorizations within a workflow. Digital signatures ensure that a given message is from whom it says it is from and verifies that it has not been modified in transit. Digital signatures can be user-initiated, and they do not require any design on the part of the developer.

AUTHORIZATION

Authorization allows the authenticated user or server to access objects or services. This is done via access control lists (ACLs), which can be placed on servers, databases, documents, views, forms, sections, and fields. Access rights in Notes are hierarchical (i.e., every one at a certain access level has all the permissions of the levels below them). Notes access rights levels (from highest to lowest) are as follows:

Manager	Has control over the ACL.
Designer	Can modify the structure of the database.
Editor	Can modify all documents.
Author	Can create documents. Can modify or delete only those documents that he or she created.
Reader	Can only read documents.
Depositor	Can create documents but cannot read them.
No Access	Cannot access the database.

These access rights apply to each database. Individual forms, documents, sections, and fields can also have read or read/write access for individuals. These are defined by role lists for each application.

ENCRYPTION

Notes encryption ciphers information using the RSA Public Key Cryptosystem. Encryption is available at three levels within the system: Users can encrypt individual messages (or parts of them); the Notes administrator can force encryption on anything stored or moving on the network; developers can build encryption directly into the databases so that only specific users can read them.

SERVER-BASED AGENTS

Notes lets applications be launched by the Notes server and Agent processes (macros) to run directly on the server. Agents can be run on a periodic basis (every hour, day, week, etc.), or they can be launched by specific events (e.g., a new document being pasted or mailed into a database).

Notes Agents can perform most actions a user can and can invoke Formulae and @Functions, including launching external processes and applications. Notes Agents are a key component of workflow tracking and management applications.

EXTENDED NOTES SERVICES

Lotus has extended the Notes service environment by offering a set of companion products. The extended services available to developers include:

- **Imaging.** Lotus Notes: Document Imaging both enables desktop imaging within Notes and supports a mass storage subsystem for image-intense Notes applications.
- **OCR.** Lotus offers server-based optical character recognition as part of its companion product line.
- **Phone.** PhoneNotes lets developers build Notes-based Interactive Voice Response (IVR) applications, which allow users to access and manipulate Notes information via the telephone.
- **Video.** VideoNotes provides viewing capabilities and a large object store for video objects within the Notes environment.

6

Notes Custom Applications

From its earliest days, Notes has been used to create custom applications to match specific business activities of companies. Even classic Notes discussion databases in many cases become business-oriented applications. For example, a "brainstorming" discussion about new products will frequently evolve to encompass the business processes of getting the products built and to market. Thus what began as topics and responses takes on new characteristics (Notes fields), such as Status, Due Date, Next Action, Next Actor, etc.

The range of custom Notes applications is nicely illustrated by two of the earliest Notes applications that I encountered as a judge for *Computerworld's 1992 Lotus Notes Application Awards:* On the macro level is an application that Chase Manhattan Bank uses to evaluate its risk with multimillion-dollar loan prospects, and on the micro level is an application that Dell Computer uses to save 4 minutes when assigning part numbers to computer parts.

CASE STUDY

CHASE MANHATTAN CREDIT RATING COMPARISON SYSTEM

The Case Manhattan Credit Rating Comparison System (CRCS) is a Notes application developed for Chase's North American Sector

Credit Policy Group, which is the bank's business unit. This unit serves large U.S. and multinational corporations with loan products, structured finance products, "big ticket" leasing, merchant banking, and other related services. CRCS was written by IS specialist Joan McAuliffe and Vice President Susan Garaviglia to provide the senior credit executive, his direct reports, and the credit-support managers with timely and easy-to-access information about key credit-related facts they need to know about each customer.

CRCS is a complex Notes application that combines information from two internal Chase databases and two external databases for display on a single screen. These inputs include internal credit ratings and credit ratings from two major independent agencies (Standard & Poor's, and Moody's), which show the user key facts about credit rating, financial exposure, industry classification, names of the client executive and credit officers, and dates of last

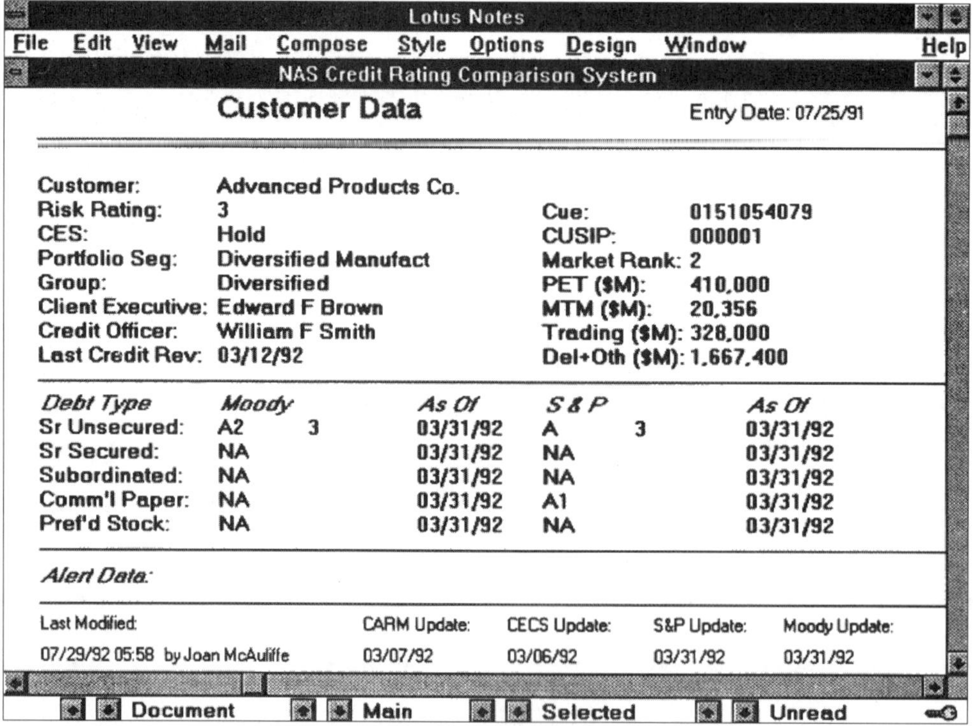

FIGURE 6.1   **Chase Manhattan CRCS Customer Data form.** In a single document, Chase executives can see all of the credit-related information about any customer.

update for each data source. This information creates a Customer Data document for each Chase customer (see Figure 6.1).

A "response document" is created by a continuous process that updates the application every 30 minutes with current bond-rating information extracted from news wire services. The application uses the Desktop Data real-time feeds and E-mail capability to extract news messages and create ASCII files based on predefined keyword profiles. An artificial intelligence-based text understanding program (Arity Corporation's Prolog) reads each extracted message and summarizes it as well as tripping the header and control information from the text.

CRCS has 13 Views (see Figure 6.2 for the Main View). One of the most important of these shows credit officers the customers for which Chase's risk rating is better than the rating of at least one of the external rating sources. This View thus displays the companies

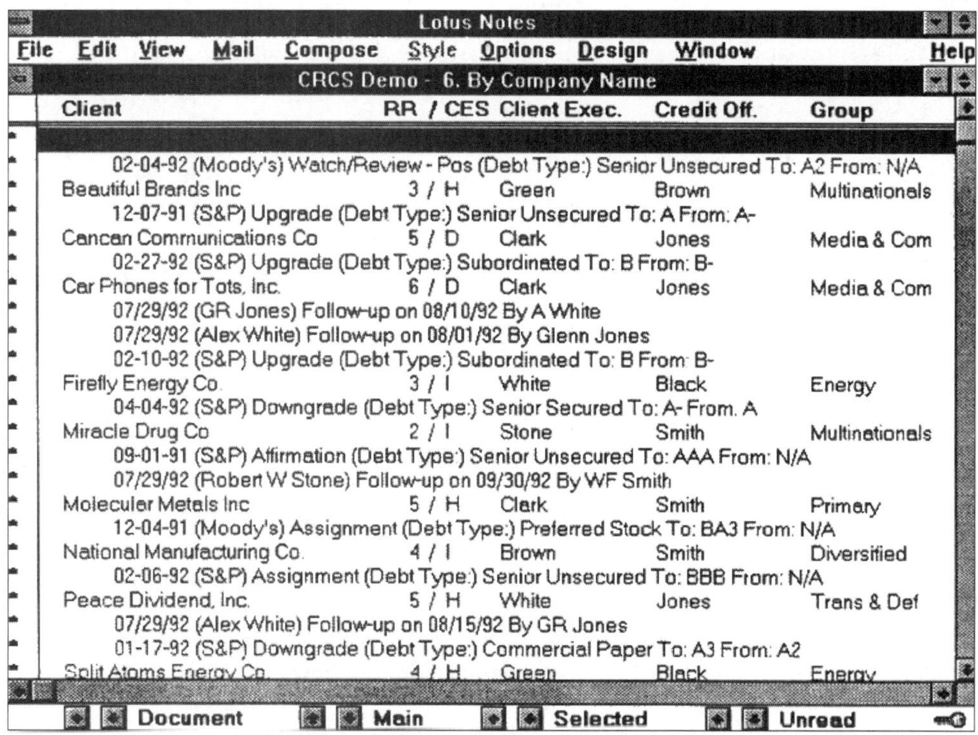

FIGURE 6.2 **Chase Manhattan CRCS View by Company Name,** one of the CRCS Notes Views.

on which Chase has taken a less conservative position than S&P or Moody, and is used as an indicator of where Chase may be at greater risk. A similar View shows companies where Chase's rating is lower than the rating agencies, indicating where Chase has taken a more conservative position.

Two of the other Views facilitate analysis by industry grouping and total principal exposure. Other administrative Views show customers by credit officer assigned, follow-up dates, and last review date. And another View shows current related news release by bond-rating action (e.g., upgrade, downgrade, credit watch). Thus credit professionals can, without waiting for the next day's newspaper or actively monitoring the news wires, get an answer to the question, "What companies were upgraded today?"

In addition to the automatically compiled information in CRCS, the senior credit executive and his direct reports may create additional documents that contain free-form comments about a customer. These responses act as "ticklers" through a follow-up system that tracks who must follow up and by which date the follow-up must be done.

Chase has seen high user satisfaction with the application, noting its users say the application saves them time by putting key information from various internal and external sources on a single screen. In addition, the continuous updating with news wire stories helps them obtain critical information much more quickly. Users can also print Views and use them for various analysis tasks. And the application has been described as a great time saver by the credit policy group, who point to the fact that the "intuitive and attractive Notes interface puts information right in the credit officers' hands." Users report that they can use the application without extensive training or intervention by others.

Chase describes the benefits of the CRS application as follows:

The information that senior credit management uses to make credit decisions is contained in a number of internal and external data sources. Gathering the key data elements from both internal and external databases was very time consuming, and one had to do this company by company. The CRCS helps credit people get control over both information and the actual financial risk involved.

Although the benefit of this type of on-demand availability should be obvious, the importance of this cannot be overstated in the current economic climate. With major household names suffering bankruptcies and other economic crises, credit professionals have to be ready with the facts when the chairman calls them into his office. Using CRCS, a credit professional can get financial exposure information on a single company or industry group and compare Chase's risk rating of any company to that of external agencies. It now takes seconds to determine an absolute financial exposure and Chase's position relative to "the market."

In general, CRCS helps Chase credit management respond to unexpected inquiry or event as well as plan ahead to avert future difficulties. It gives any credit executive unprecedented control over the risk portfolio and increases the bank's profitability by making credit management more effective in preventing losses.

CASE STUDY

DELL DESCRIPTION GENERATOR

Dell Computer's Description Generator is a good example of the use of Notes to achieve significant benefits in a small part of the large process of designing and manufacturing computers.

The Description Generator addresses the process of assigning part numbers to computer parts. To obtain a part number under the former process, an engineer first had to consult Dell's *Naming Standards Dictionary,* a detailed 50-page hard-copy document, which explains how to describe everything "from a screw to a hard drive." (This document had to be reprinted and mailed to all users whenever a change was made.) The person requesting a part would fill out a cc:Mail form, referring to the *Naming Standards Dictionary* to describe the part, and mail it to the group responsible for receiving and processing such requests. This group would check that all the correct information was entered, sending the form back to the originator if any of the information was incorrect. This tended to be quite time consuming; describing the parts was very tedious, and the part descriptions themselves were constantly changing. A significant number of parts would slip through the process and be approved without matching the *Naming Standards Dictionary.*

Dell decided to build a new program to manage the process. The program would not let people request incorrect parts and, at the same time, would reduce the time required to check part information manually. The objective was to build a system that would:

- Bring more control to the part-number process
- Provide an easy-to-use user interface
- Be data driven
- Allow more accessible information to the originator
- Be flexible for future change

The resulting application, built by Ralph Arvesen, systems engineer, combines a number of Notes databases, dBase files, Clipper indexes, and locally developed applications (using Microsoft C, Windows SDK, Codebase, and the Notes API). The system works as follows (see Figure 6.3).

APPLICATION COMPONENTS

User ini file. An initialization file that contains information about the user and the user's environment, this enables the application to be brought back up in the state the user left the application.

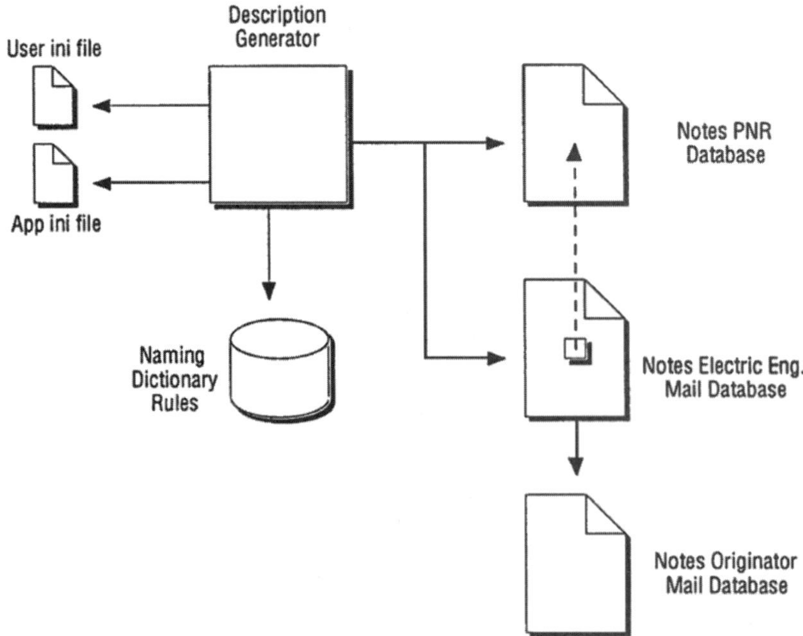

FIGURE 6.3 **Dell Description Generator architecture.**

App ini file. An initialization file that contains information about the Notes environment, this includes server names for the part-number requests (PNRs) and Name & Address Book databases, directory names, and database names. This adds flexibility to the deployment of the application.

Naming Dictionary Rules. This is a set of dBase files and Clipper indexes that contain the former hard copy of the *Naming Standards Dictionary* rules, available vendors, and abbreviation cross-references. The rules database makes this process data driven. A group at Dell maintains the rules files. All changes to the rules files are instantly available to all users, compared to several weeks under the old process. The database also includes information that previously was not available to all users at Dell.

Description Generator. The Description Generator provides an artificial intelligence interface to the rules database and eliminates the need for users to research this information manually. It supports a number of concurrent users by maintaining record-level locking of the rules database. It uses the Notes API to open and close Notes databases, search for specific documents, create documents, and create documents that have a DocLink to other Notes documents. This application is about 10,000 lines of C code.

Notes PNR Database. This Notes database holds the documents created by the Generator. The Generator can create a number of different documents, depending on the user's request. These include: Initial Part Request, Delete Part Request, Change Part Request, Change Part Description, Change Part Bill of Materials, Change Part Approved Supplier List, and Change Part Systems Affected. A group at Dell monitors this database for new requests and acts appropriately. This combination of the Generator and this database eliminates the human resource of tediously checking the requests. It also provides previously unavailable information to all Dell employees. And users can now get immediate feedback on the status of their requests.

Notes Electrical Engineering Mail Database. Any electrical part request requires specific approval from electrical engineering. With this type of request, the Generator creates a document in the Notes PNR database and then creates a Memo document in the Electrical Engineering mail database. The document includes information on the requester and what is being requested. The Generator also creates a DocLink to the appropriate document in the PNR database.

Notes Originator Mail Database. A receipt document is automatically created in the user's mail database. This informs the originator that the electrical engineer has received, read, and/or acted upon the request.

APPLICATION FLOW

- The user launches the program. The user than selects the type of request from the Generator menu bar. The user then answers a series of questions and selects from a series of options presented by the Generator. The questions and options are generated by accessing the rules database. Thus any changes in the rules are immediately reflected. The Generator also checks the validity of the user's answers (see Figure 6.4).

- The Generator creates a document in the Notes PNR database. If the requested part is an electrical part, the Generator also creates a memo document in the Electrical Engineering mailbox (or mail database) with a DocLink to the appropriate document in the Notes PNR database. A receipt is sent back to the user when the engineer reads the request. The user can continually monitor the status of the request in the PNR database (see Figure 6.5).

BENEFITS OF THE APPLICATION

Dell has documented the following benefits from the Description Generator:

Benefits to the Originator. The process of requesting a part is a lot easier. Time and money are saved on each part number request. Productivity is improved because the originator no longer has to search through a hard copy *Naming Standards Dictionary.* The originator feels insured that the information is correct and will not be getting a disapproved request due to incorrect information. This saves the originator time and saves Dell money because the originator does not have to resubmit the same request.

It would take the average user about five minutes to request a part under the old process. It would take the same user about one minute to request a part number with the new process. The time savings is significant if you consider that some users might

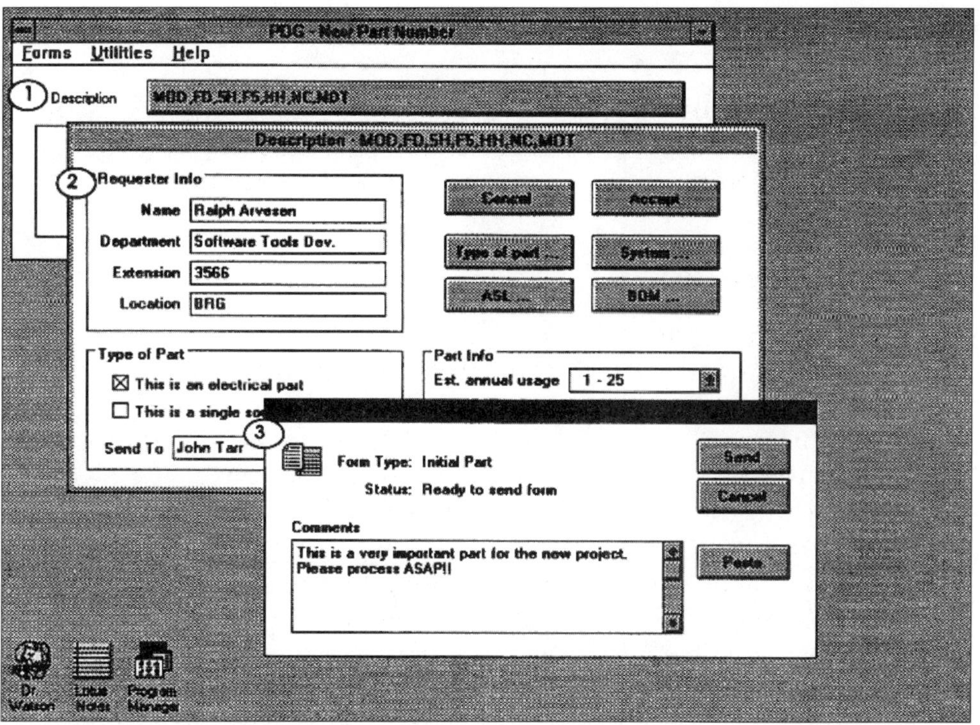

FIGURE 6.4 **Dell Description Generator screens.** (1) The main window of the Generator. This is where the user is prompted to select from items that are retrieved from the naming rules database. (2) A dialog box appears after the user has successfully selected all items. This dialog box retrieves more information about the user and the part. (3) A dialog box appears before every Notes transaction. This allows the user to enter comments. It informs the user what type of form will be created in the Notes PNR database. In this case it is an Initial Part. It also displays the status of the Notes transaction. The transaction status will start as "Ready to send form," change to "Creating form," and then to "Success" or "Failure." If a failure occurs, an error message will be displayed.

request up to 100 parts in one day. The productivity increase of a user can be seen with the following example: In eight hours, the user could make approximately 96 requests with the old process. The same user could make approximately 480 requests with the new process. The new process is also a magnitude of time simpler for new employees to learn. This saves time and money for Dell and enables the new employee to be more productive more quickly.

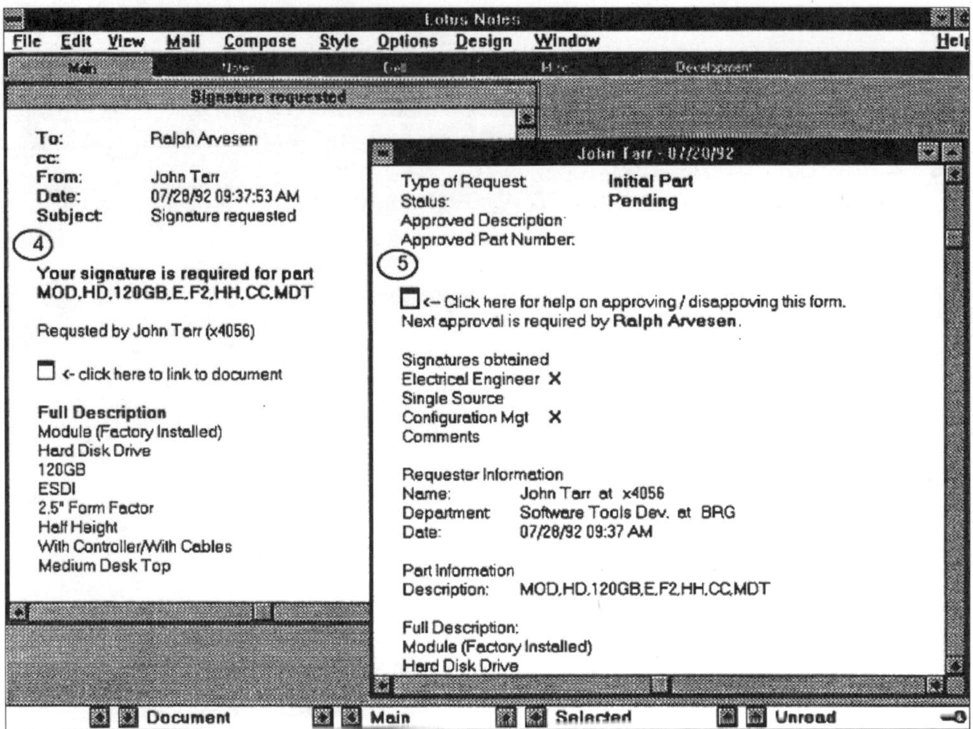

FIGURE 6.5 **Dell Notes screens.** (4) This is the Memo document that the Generator creates in the Electrical Engineering mailbox. The document includes who is requesting the part, information about the part, and a DocLink to the appropriate document in the Notes PNR database. (5) This is the document that the Generator creates in the Notes PNR database. The document contains detailed information about the requester and the part.

Benefits to the Electrical Engineer. The electrical engineers' productivity increases. When a request needs their signature, they receive a memo in their Notes mailbox with a DocLink to the appropriate document. This decreases the time required for the engineers to review and sign the request.

Benefits to Dell. The benefits are overwhelming. People no longer have to have personnel that do the tedious work of checking part number request information. People know it's correct; otherwise the program would have rejected the request. Money and time are saved because the information is substantially more organized and people do not have to spend time answering calls from originators on where in the process their request is. It improves Dell's service to employees.

All users of the program instantly see whatever changes are made so there is no need to print and ship hard copies of the *Naming Standards Dictionary.* This results in a substantial savings and reduces paper shuffling and waste involved when hard copies are used.

7

Notes Development Environment

Notes applications are generally built with a set of tools delivered with every Notes Client. Accessed via the Notes Design menu, these tools allow anyone from professional developer to end user to build or modify Notes applications.

NOTES DEVELOPMENT TOOLS

Each full Notes Client includes a full development environment for building Notes applications. This allows knowledgeable users to prototype their own applications or (given proper permissions) modify existing applications. At the same time, the Notes development environment gives the professional developer direct access to Notes services and enables rapid application prototyping and development. In fact, with Notes, there is little difference between prototyping and actual development, because Notes applications are ready to be deployed as they are being built. In a production environment, an application generally moves from prototyping to deployment after rigorous testing and the requisite data population.

The rapid development and instant feedback it provides makes Notes ideal for interactive development processes where both the developer and user take part. Examples of this interactive process are found in many, if not most, successful Notes implementations, and it is a key element in the high level of user acceptance of Notes applications.

NOTES DESIGN ELEMENTS

The basic Notes design elements include Databases, Forms, Fields, and Views, which allow the creation of and multiuser access to the distributed document database. Advanced elements include a rich set of Formulae and Functions, as well as an Agent facility that can be used to automate processes on the server or the client.

DATABASE

All Notes documents are stored in a Notes database. A Notes server houses many Notes databases, including the server's Name & Address Book, the server's log, users' mailboxes, and any number of application-specific databases. The database stores all documents, as well as design elements such as Forms, Fields, Views, Formulae, and Agents. Each database has its own access list and replica ID. The former maintains security, while the latter allows the database to be distributed across multiple servers and client machines.

User access to Notes applications is generally through the Database in which the appropriate documents are stored (access is through the Database icon on the Notes desktop or via a DocLink from another database).

FORMS

The fundamental design element of Notes applications is the Form. This is the medium by which information is entered and displayed. Often, the form is a container for a compound document created with the user's desktop applications. Once the user (or an external process) has completed data entry, the information is then stored as a document in the Notes Database.

Subforms are shared objects that can be used within forms or as forms themselves. They can be as simple as a background with a company logo, or they can be highly complex, containing Agents, LotusScripts, and Action Bars.

FIELDS

A Form is made up of Fields, such as author, date, summary, and document body. Each Field is assigned a specific data type. Notes data types include text, number, time, keywords, author names,

names, sections, and rich text. Rich text can contain formatted text (including fonts, color, and tabular data), images, audio and video objects, embedded OLE objects, attachments, and links to other Notes documents. Some Fields, such as time and date, can be filled in automatically, using the systems clock or using the user ID. Other Fields may require the user to choose from a list of keywords, which can be displayed in a separate window or as a check box or radio box. Formulae can be used to populate fields with calculated or default data and to validate user input. Fields can inherit values or lookup values from other Fields or from other documents or records from both Notes or external databases. Fields can be defined with a number of attributes and properties (lists of readers and authors, encryption, whether hidden or on display, editing, etc.).

Notes supports both unique Fields, which have value only in the specific form or database, and Shared Fields, whose definitions and value can span Forms and Databases.

Developers add and modify the attributes and properties of Fields in a Notes Form via a set of dialog boxes. Developers can also use the Notes SmartIcons to access all design commands directly.

VIEWS

Views allow users access to Notes documents. Notes Views present to the user a list of documents; Field data associated with each document are presented in columnar form. The document list is selected, sorted, and categorized according to the developer's design. Document selection is handled via Formulae, which can look at any Field (other than rich text) and make calculations on it. Sorting can be ascending or descending and can take place on any column. Categorization allows the documents below a field and a column to be expanded and collapsed by the user.

Views can display calculations, such as the sum of a specific column. Views can also be used to inform users which documents they have read and which they have not, and which have been modified since they were last read. This information is stored separately for each user.

Views can be public (created by the database designer) or Private (created by any user for his or her own use).

FORMULAE

Notes Formulae are similar to mathematical formulae, consisting of variables, constants, and arithmetic functions (e.g., +, −, *, /), which can be used against integers and scientific notation. Equally important, if not more so, Notes also provides a full set of string-handling features, including string concatenation. Notes Formulae can use operators such as =, not =, >, <, and, or, and if . . . then constructs.

Formulae can be used to perform a variety of functions, including the following:

- Calculate values for display in documents and Views
- Validate and translate new values entered into documents
- Select documents to include in a View
- Change, add, or delete values in a document based on functions of values in another Field or Database
- Determine which Form to use for displaying data in different situations

@FUNCTIONS

Notes is shipped with more than 100 predefined @Functions, which perform a variety of calculations with different data types. Most @Functions return a value of text, number, time-date, or a Boolean value. @Functions fall into six categories:

1. String @Functions, which recognize and manipulate strings
2. Mathematical @Functions, which compute calculations using numeric values
3. Time-Date @Functions, which are used for time-date generation and manipulation
4. Logical @Functions, which produce values based on the result of conditional statements
5. View Statistics @Functions, which are used to view column formulae to maintain view statistics and hierarchy
6. Database and Document Statistics @Functions, which calculate and display database and document information

AGENTS

Agents are macros or rules that automate routine tasks. They can force specific action based on given values, thus providing a key mechanism to monitor and track the status of Notes applications.

Technically, Agents are a special set of @Function macros that, in addition to performing some type of calculation, perform some

DESIGN ELEMENTS SHARED ACROSS DATABASES

Shared design elements provide a more granular level of inheritance. Developers can copy Fields from Design Templates (remember, any database can be designated as such) into another database. Notes prompts the developer if an inheritance link is desired. If the developer chooses, this Field will now inherit any changes to the Field in the Design Template, including formats, formulae, and keyword definitions. The developer can now place this Field in the new database in any Form.

Subforms can also be used to share design elements across databases. Subforms create a new level of reusability in Notes applications. Certain features, such as input forms, routing rules, Actions, or graphics, can be managed centrally and accessed as needed. An organization can designate a set of Subforms to be used in creating new forms. This provides both management and efficient use of compound design elements; it obviates the task of recreating each combination of elements every time it is needed.

DATA LINKED ACROSS DATABASES

The corollary of being able to link database design elements—such as the design of a Field—across individual databases is the ability actually to link data elements—such as the value in a Field—across databases. This capability has three major benefits:

1. Eliminating multiple entry of identical information
2. Controlling redundancy and maintaining consistency
3. Moving information from one database to another to create workflows or multidatabase Notes applications

Notes provides two mechanisms for moving information from one Notes database into another: @DbLookup and @DbColumn. Both of these operate on a pull model; that is, data values may be retrieved from another database but data may not be moved to another database (only full documents can be sent to another database).

Each of these functions can be used in the following ways:

- A Field in one database can contain a formula that sets its value as being equal to the value of a Field in another database.

- An Agent can be written to look at the value of a Field in a database and take a specific action based on that value.

- A Keyword List Field can be defined to match the values found in a specific column in a View in another database.

MANAGING SHARED DESIGN ELEMENTS

The Notes application model is designed to encourage distributed development because any authorized developer has access to all corporate designs. Notes allows the enforcement of application standards in three ways:

1. Developers can protect the design of an application. Once an application is developed and saved as a template, the designer can elect to close the design from further modification using the Notes Application Design Protection. Users who try to modify the design will see the Design Menu item disabled (grayed out).

2. Developers can be allowed to modify standard templates. If the developer allows a template to remain open, departmental developers can make whatever modifications they wish. The purpose is to enable these developers to add new Fields and Formulae while maintaining standard Fields that preserve consistency across applications.

3. Applications can inherit changes. When a standard template is borrowed for use as the basis for a customized application, all its attributes are inherited in the copied template. If the original template is modified later, all changes are propagated to any application that inherits from that template, ensuring consistency across applications.

Notes also assists application management by being self-documenting. Every application contains an About Document, which explains to the user (and to developers who may need to modify the design during maintenance) the overall purpose of the database and how it should be used.

In addition, Notes provides a Design Menu option that displays all the attributes of the application design in a single location. This feature displays all the information about the Database's Forms, Views, Fields, Macros, Access List, and any other attributes that can be specified with the Notes user interface.

THE EXTENDED NOTES APPLICATION DEVELOPMENT ENVIRONMENT

Key attributes of the Notes environment are the extensions to its application development environment, which are enabled by the set of available interfaces, including the Notes API, OLE and Notes/FX, NotesSQL, and, with Notes Release 4, LotusScript. These interfaces are currently being taken advantage of by Lotus and many third parties to integrate a wide variety of development tools for use with Notes.

The extended Notes application development environment consists of Lotus tools and third-party tools. It allows developers to do the following:

- Build alternative clients for Notes applications. This capability includes using graphical development tools, such as ViP (now owned by Revelation Technologies), Powersoft's Power-Builder, Gupta SQLWindows, and Visual Basic to integrate Notes data with relational data.
- Run desktop productivity applications on top of and within Notes.
- Provide end-user data access, manipulation, and reporting.
- Graphically create workflow applications.
- Maintain data integration and synchronization.

There are two major reasons for selecting a third-party tool to develop Notes applications. The first is that the developer is looking for a particular functionality that is not currently available with the Notes toolset. The justifications in this area tend to change with time. For example, with Notes Release 3, developers had to go to an external tool in order to build graphical user interfaces or to make use of a powerful scripting language. Developers no longer have to exit Notes for these functions, because Notes Release 4 Navigators and LotusScript provide them.

The second reason for selecting a specific development tool is the developer's familiarity with it or corporate standardization on a particular tool.

A number of tools providers have adapted their products to work directly with the Notes API. These include the most popular client/server tools (such as Powersoft's PowerBuilder and Gupta's SQLWindows), as well as Visual Basic, which, through third-party additions from companies such as Brainstorm Technologies and Lotus itself, can be used to develop applications that access Notes databases.

In addition to integration with specific products, developers can choose any tool that supports Open Database Connectivity (ODBC) to develop Notes applications via the NotesSQL function. This has the advantage of making Notes instantly available as a quasi-relational data source without any changes being made by the tool vendor. The disadvantage of this approach is that ODBC does not provide interfaces into all of the Notes API functionalities, such as accessing the Notes View mechanism directly.

There are two approaches to using alternative Notes development tools. One is to build alternative clients that provide a non-Notes environment and experience for the user. Tools such as Notes ViP, Visual Basic, PowerBuilder, or SQLWindows can be used to develop applications that execute from the Windows Program Manager and have little to do with Notes. This is certainly appropriate if the purpose of using the alternative tool is to build an application that matches a non-Notes corporate application standard.

However, if the company has already invested in Notes training, and particularly if the company has made a large commitment to Notes as the home for its users, then providing the user with both Notes applications that access Notes data and non-Notes applications that access Notes data makes little sense. In this case, the same tools can be used to create applications and screens that can be called from within a Notes application. Although the Notes users see another window opening with, for example, more information, they feel as though they are still living in Notes.

This "enhancing" of Notes applications can be accomplished via a button and an @Command or, using Notes object activation, by embedding the application developed by ViP, Visual Basic, or other tools in the form. In the last case, the external application or screen is launched instantly when the document is opened. Embedding the application has the advantage that changes in the application can be propagated easily, because the form can be updated everywhere whenever the database is replicated. This allows a degree of version management that is not normally found outside of Notes.

8

Notes Is Workflow

One of the great (and pointless) debates is whether Notes is a workflow platform. Those opposing this view point to the lack of a workflow mapping tool in the Notes development environment and the fact that Notes lacks a real-time "state" engine found in *pure* workflow products. Those supporting this view point to Notes features such as intelligent routing, server-based agents, and digital signatures—all of which are certainly important to workflow.

The reason that this debate is pointless has little to do with the validity of these two positions—technically they are both correct. The fact is that whether or not Notes meets someone's personal definition of workflow, it has been used from its beginnings by Notes customers to automate, track, and manage business processes (see the Value Behavioral Health case study below)—in my mind this is the best definition of workflow to date.

Invariably, these process tracking/management applications involve individuals in specific roles. Participants use Notes to find their work (or they are notified by Notes of what they have to do on a specific project or account), and they update the status of the workflow as they complete the steps. Individuals can easily see what their own workloads are and what role they play in the whole process. Managers can see the status of a process and the tasks that specific individuals have on their plates. Notes also lets managers look at aggregated information, such as how many processes are at a given step or how long specific steps take, on average.

A second element of Notes as a workflow platform is the fact that virtually all workflow products integrate with Notes (a number, in fact, are built exclusively on Notes), using the Notes infrastructure and Notes client as key elements of the process. The Notes infrastructure can serve as a data store, messaging system, security system, directory, and so on, while the Notes client enables users to receive or access tasks via mail or in Notes databases.

The third element is the actual Notes architecture and functions that support multiple workflow models, which have been enhanced in Notes Releases 3 and 4 to support business processes even better. Chapter 9 focuses on these Notes technical features.

CASE STUDY

VALUE BEHAVIORAL HEALTH MANAGES THE HEALTH-CARE PROCESS IN NOTES

Value Behavioral Health (Troy, New York) contracts with some of the nation's largest medical insurance companies to oversee the approval and monitoring of health-care cases, specifically in the area of mental health and substance abuse. The company employs experts who review treatment plans submitted by health-care providers. Virtually all treatment, care authorization, and medical claims must be approved by Value Behavioral Health before the insurance company will authorize treatment or pay a claim.

The company's goal is to assure the highest-quality care for patients while saving money for the program by lowering the overhead of providing, monitoring, and managing patient care.

The job involves monitoring each patient's case. The company has to approve or deny each request for treatment authorization, and it has to provide an appeals process to review denied requests. It must be able to provide reports on individual cases and statistics about such areas as the accumulated claim amounts approved, denied, or pending. In addition, the company must be able to quickly provide information about case status and eligibility requirements to all participants in the process: patients, employers, care providers, and the insurance company.

MOVING FROM PAPER TO ELECTRONIC WORKFLOW

In 1993, the unit that handles the authorizations for its Empire Plan, which provides services to more than 90,000 employees, began to examine its options for automating its paper processes. The existing processes created and dealt with a great amount of paper, forcing the same information to be entered, filed, and retrieved multiple times in multiple places. According to Jim McNierney, director of information services, "the whole system was becoming overloaded with disconnected paper and databases." The company found that, in order to meet its goal, its employees had to work harder. It wanted to try to let them work "smarter" by applying technology to the business process.

DESIGNING THE NEW APPLICATION

Mapping the Interrelationships

The first step was to map the existent paper flow and the interrelationships among databases to represent the ideal workflow. After a couple of days of intensive meetings, this map materialized on a whiteboard. In the middle was a "Magic Gray Box," which would make it all work.

Requirements of the Application

The application had two distinct requirement areas: security and performance. A high level of security was required because of the sensitivity of the information being handled—information about individuals' mental health and substance abuse. A high level of performance was required because of the company's contract with the insurance company. This contract includes certain metrics that produce "severe financial repercussions if not met." Some of these metrics include:

- Turnaround time from the receipt of a request payment authorization to the notification of the provider of the approval
- Abandonment rate of calls (the number of calls that go unanswered)
- The time it takes to answer a call (this must be within 20 seconds or the call is considered abandoned)

In addition to meeting these requirements and managing the workflow, the application was expected to integrate with various other data sources. These included the insurance company's host-based payment system and the paper-based records of the existing process.

FINDING NOTES

The department first looked at internal sources to automate the process, but quickly found that a case management software product that had been developed for other areas of the company did not meet its needs. The software did not scale to the required volume, its modules were not fully integrated, and it was not at all flexible.

After months of looking for appropriate products, one member of the automation team heard about Lotus Notes and began to wonder whether it would be appropriate for the department's business process. With help from ComputerWorks (Albany, New York), a Notes consultant specializing in workflow and the health-care market, the company determined that Notes indeed could handle its workflow.

MAPPING THE BUSINESS PROCESS

The team started by going over foot-high stacks of papers consisting of descriptions and diagrams of the current processes, paper stores, and databases. They quickly determined that this approach was not getting them anywhere, so they basically started from scratch, taking each paper form and tracking its movement through the system.

The team found that the company has two basic processes: information dissemination and case management.

There are two types of information dissemination. The first is done by the company's Resource Information Center, which refers patients, employers, or health-care providers to health-care resources; the Resource Information Center is a gateway from patients to an extensive network of quality health-care providers, including 16,000 in-patient and out-patient facilities and 30,000 practitioners. The second point of information dissemination is handled by Customer Service, which takes all calls from patients, employers, or providers concerning eligibility, benefits, and the status of a case or claim. Customer Service also is where providers call to request authorization for treatment.

Case management is the process that tracks the case from the request for certification to approval for payment of benefits. It includes monitoring and evaluating the ongoing treatment plan for each patient. Value Behavioral Health handles a tremendous volume of cases. The process accommodates two distinct types of clients: out-patients and in-patients. The company decided to work on the out-patient process first.

USING LOTUS NOTES

The first step was to build several Notes databases to anchor the workflow. Initially, the Customer Service database, which recorded and tracked all inquiries, was built. Next was a set of reference databases to be used to find relatively fixed information, such as providers and facilities. These databases would be used to fill in information automatically, such as the provider's address, in a case-tracking form. Another database, built in dBASE, was created to hold the information about enrollees in the insurance plan. This database is an extract from the insurance company's host-based system, and is updated once a month.

Two case management databases were then built. The first is the Out-Patient Case Management database, which tracks the cases in progress. The second is the Appeals Management database, which tracks all cases that have been appealed.

THE RESULTING WORKFLOW

The Out-Patient Approval Process

The steps in the Out-Patient Approval Process workflow, shown in diagram form in Figure 8.1, are as follows.

- A Provider (1) requests a form for authorization of treatment from Customer Service (2). (The company eventually plans to have the workflow begin when the call is first made to the Resource Information Center, but this is not yet implemented.) Customer Service (2) sends the approval form to the Provider (3), who fills out the information about the case and requests approval for a specific treatment.
- The request for treatment is sent to the unit that prepares the case (4). Preparing the case consists of creating a case document in the Out-Patient Case Management database and scanning in the treatment approval request. When the Preparer is finished, a button is pressed on the form, and the case goes into the case assignment queue for a Case Manager (5).
- The next available Case Manager (5) reviews the case based on the information in the Notes document, the information in the treatment request and any updates, and historical information about the patient.

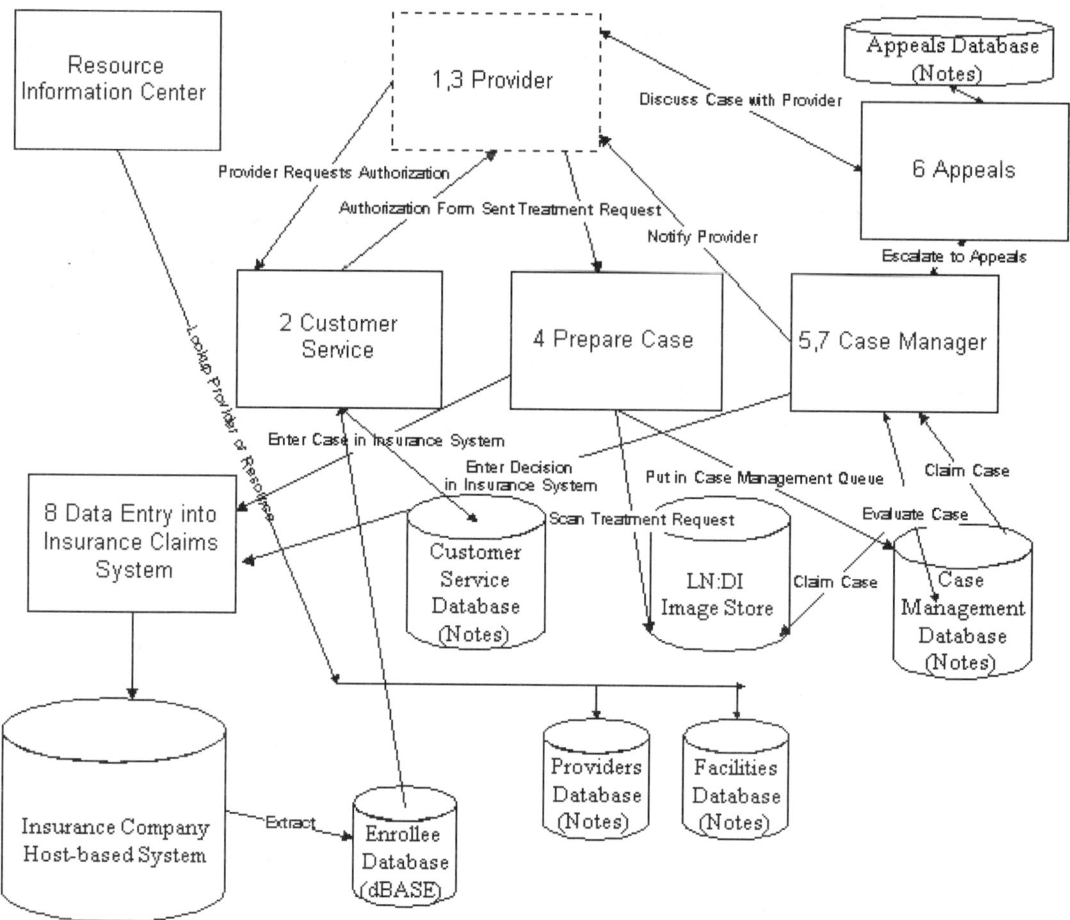

FIGURE 8-1 VBH Out-Patient Approval Process. The numbers in the boxes represent steps in the workflow.

■ If the Case Manager does not approve the treatment, it is escalated to an appeals process (6), where an Appeals Manager (a medically trained person) contacts the Provider (3) and discusses the best treatment. When the original request or new treatment is agreed upon, it is sent back to the Case Manager (7), who approves it. Letters detailing this information are then automatically generated to the Provider and the Patient. The information is then sent into a queue for entry into the insurance company's claims system (8). The company would like to automate this entry process in the future.

Throughout the workflow, all the documents (both Notes and scanned) are available to the Case Manager, Appeals Manager, and Customer Service.

IMMEDIATE SUCCESS

In a very short time, the project proved to be a remarkable success. First, the speed of implementation has been nothing short of amazing. The actual development process started in January 1994; within 5 weeks, the first part of the application, the Customer Service tracking piece, was done and rolled out.

The benefits from this were immediate and striking. Client inquiries that might have taken days to answer before were now taking hours or even minutes, with the average having dropped from 3 days to under 1 hour. In many cases, calls are being answered right on the phone, without a return call (or Callback). Callbacks have been reduced from 1,000 to 48 per month!

The second part of the application, the Out-Patient Case Management Workflow, was rolled out 4 weeks later. Again, the company experienced immediate and significant benefits in its ability to process and manage new cases.

In addition, Value Behavioral Health has benefited from the elimination of over 250,000 documents—with significant savings being accrued in saved filing time and office records space.

Users of the system have been very pleased with their ability to access information quickly (currently there are over 1.2 million documents in the system), be it in a Notes document or an image, and many have commented on the benefit of more than one person being able to deal with the same case document at the same time. Chris Baker, Director of Quality Improvement for Value Behavioral Health, explains: "With Notes, our managers have access to much more information than they ever had before. We're not looking at the business retrospectively anymore. Now we can manage the day-to-day operation with the most up-to-date information possible."

And, John Hill, Executive Vice President of Value Behavioral Health, concludes: "With its communications and workflow capabilities Lotus Notes and ComputerWorks allows us to improve our administration and to be more efficient as an organization. It's been a godsend to us. In the first year alone, I can say we have saved several hundreds of thousands of dollars—and that's a conservative estimate."

9

Notes Workflow Architecture and Functionality

In the previous chapter, I argued that Notes's specific workflow capabilities are immaterial to the definition of Notes as a workflow platform. This argument is based on the fact that most strategic applications that are currently being built by Notes customers are easily seen as workflow applications or, at the very least, have some elements of tracking and process management within them.

Once this argument is made, it is important to note that with two key exceptions (the lack of a workflow mapping design or participation interface, and the lack of a real-time state engine), Notes provides a complete and highly functional environment for building and deploying workflow applications. This is true for two reasons:

1. The Notes architecture supports workflow and a variety of workflow models.
2. Notes provides a rich set of workflow-oriented functions for the developer and user.

MODELS OF WORKFLOW

In order to understand Notes's architectural advantages as a workflow platform, it is important to be aware of the two major models for building workflow applications:

1. Routing-based workflow (also known as mail-based workflow) model

2. Shared database model

ROUTING-BASED WORKFLOW MODEL

When most people think of workflow, they think of the automatic routing of documents, such as expense reports. Routing-based workflow generally uses the underlying mail system to route documents to the next person who must take an action (e.g., approve the expense report). The route can be hard-coded, or a rule may determine the routing path based on a specific value (e.g., the amount of the expense) or on a person's role (e.g., the initiator's supervisor). These rules can be very sophisticated and may be able to go to an external application to obtain some data (e.g., a supervisor's authorization limit).

Routing-based workflow is very powerful for a specific set of applications. It can easily include remote users (via E-mail) and generally does not require a server process, because most systems store the rules in the user's E-mail client. The greatest strength of routing-based workflow is that it matches the model of routing paper: The document is acted upon and sent to the next person for further action.

There are two drawbacks to routing-based workflow. First, since the rules generally reside in (and/or are executed by) the client, there is no assurance that the workflow will continue if the user's machine is not on or if the user does not take an action, such as opening the mail. The results may be disastrous when someone goes on vacation, takes his or her laptop/desktop machine on the road, or leaves the company. An important workflow may stall and may not be recovered for a significant amount of time. In addition, the fact that the rules are generally stored at the client makes administration of the workflow application difficult, because any changes in the process may require the updating of dozens of individuals' mail applications.

A more significant drawback to the routing-based workflow model is that, as the document is being routed, it becomes unavailable to anyone other than the person in whose inbox it currently resides. This may be fine for some applications, but for others it could result in serious problems. Let us look at a hypothetical example.

In a contract-tracking application, a contract is being negotiated with a customer. In order to be signed, it must be internally approved by several people. A workflow is set up to route the contract to each person in turn to have him or her approve, reject, and/or add comments. Under most conditions, the contracts are routed and approved, and everyone is happy.

However, what happens when, during the approval process, the customer calls up and requests some changes? Where are these changes made, and what happens to the approval process? The document is in someone's inbox (it may be possible to determine whose, but it may also be impossible to retrieve it—it could be in the inbox of a remote machine). It may also be difficult to explain to the customer that the changes cannot be made or even proposed until someone connects remotely or comes back from vacation.

Anticipating some of these problems is possible (perhaps rewriting the rule or adding a new rule when the person goes on vacation), but building strategic applications on patches such as this is uncomfortable for companies, and anticipating all conditions and exceptions is impossible.

SHARED DATABASE MODEL

The second workflow model is the shared database. In this model, when an action is required, the user is notified and directed to the document (or record) in question. The document remains in the shared database; it is not sent to the user.

The shared database model has three advantages. First, the database sits on a server and is subject to server-based processes (such as RDBMS triggers or Notes Agents) that can initiate action without any specific user activity. In many cases, the action may be the direct result of a lack of user activity (a sales person has not contacted a customer in 30 days, a monthly report has not been submitted, a contract to be approved has been waiting for a specific person for over 24 hours, etc.) or an external condition (inventory has dropped to the reorder point, a client's credit rating has changed, a deadline is approaching, etc.). The shared database also usually contains the rules of the workflow; these can now be maintained at a single point.

Second, the shared database model keeps the document or record in question available for others while the workflow proceeds. In our contract-approval example, the changes could be made to the original document in the database, and, depending on the changes, the workflow could continue or be aborted and launched again.

The third advantage is that the shared database model makes the management and macromanagement of the workflow much easier. The server can both monitor specific instances of the process and keep statistics about the aggregate of the processes, the latter allowing better management and planning of the workflow.

The key disadvantage of the shared database model is that it generally requires all participants to be on the network to access the database. Notes replication, of course, goes a long way toward eliminating this limitation.

NOTES SUPPORTS BOTH WORKFLOW MODELS (AND MORE)

Notes is the only product that natively supports both workflow models equally. Notes provides a messaging subsystem, mail inbox, and conditional routing capabilities. It also provides (in fact, its essence is) a shared database for storing, retrieving, viewing, and managing business processes. The Notes server can run Agents against the database to monitor and control the workflow.

Notes also takes the two models a step further. The Notes Doc-Link feature integrates the two models into a robust system built on both routing and shared database capabilities. It is easiest to explain this by looking again at the contract approval example introduced earlier.

The contract is created and stored in the Notes database (several Notes facilities, such as OLE launching and Notes/FX, allow the contract to be created in the word processor of choice). When it is saved, a message goes to the first approver's inbox. The message is not the contract itself, nor does it tell the approver where to find the contract. The message contains a DocLink to the contract, which, when clicked, will bring up the contract for the approver's use but will leave it in the shared database. Further approvals and routing can be done, but the most up-to-date version of the contract itself is always available.

Notes replication allows this process to occur even if the user is at a remote site (or in another organization). The appropriate database can be replicated to where it is required, and any changes can be replicated back. Selective replication can be used to streamline this process; for example, a Notes Agent could set the value of a Field in a document to "To Be Approved" or "In Process." The selective replication formula would be set to replicate all such documents in specific databases.

BUILDING WORKFLOW APPLICATIONS

Notes includes a set of development features that specifically address the routing and database coordination requirements for intra- and interenterprise workflow. These features include:

- Automatic routing via the @MailSend command
- Agents, which enable the automation of tracking and workflow databases
- Enhanced formula language, which lets data be retrieved from external sources and moved between Notes databases
- Actions and the Action Bar, which provide users direct access to appropriate tasks within a workflow
- Notes/FX integration, which enables users to participate in workflows while in other applications

AUTOMATIC ROUTING

The Notes formula language includes the ability to set up explicit and/or conditional routing of documents. The "@MailSend" command can be used in Field Formulas, Agents, Action Buttons, and SmartIcons to send documents to named users. It can either send the current document or create a new document. In addition, it can include a DocLink to the original document as well as attachments. This functionality allows automatic routing of any document within a Notes database.

AGENTS

Notes offers an advanced Agent facility that can be used to initiate actions and spawn new documents. Agents can be launched explicitly by the user, run automatically at specified times and intervals, or run as a result of a particular action or condition—for example, when a new document is added to a particular database. These Agents enable workflow functionality, such as daily auditing of a project database to see what actions have been taken, notification of upcoming or past due tasks, and alerting a project manager of delays. Agents, which replicate with all other Notes design features, can be created only by those with developer access rights.

Agents run where the database is stored (including a user's mail database). The Notes server runs an Agent Manager hourly, executing all Agents due to be run that hour. Notes clients do not need to be running in order for the Agent to execute. Remote Notes clients can also execute Agents on a timed or explicit basis.

Periodic Agents are the key feature that lets existing Notes tracking databases be turned instantly into workflows. Agents can be run against Due Date, Next Action, and/or Next Actor Fields, and they can be used to notify the appropriate person that something should be done or has not been done on time.

NOTES FORMULA LANGUAGE

The Notes formula language has several workflow capabilities, including the abilities to create user interaction and to integrate data from external sources. Among the most useful commands are:

@Command, which can be used in SmartIcon Formulas or Action Buttons. (See "Action Buttons" below.) This command allows any command in the Notes menu to be executed, and it is the basis of workflow and Agent building. Some of the Notes commands have been parameterized to allow the @Command to emulate user interaction with a dialog box in a command line.

@DbLookup, **@DbColumn**, and **@DbCommand**, which provide the capability of looking up specific values or columns of values from documents or Views in Notes databases. The lookup facility combined with periodic Agents lets information from one Notes database be populated into another automatically. This means that common information, such as role definitions and sign-off authorities, can be shared among workflows. The lookup facility also enables information to be moved from one database to another as the workflow process proceeds.

@Prompt, which can be used in Fields, Formulae, Agents, Action Buttons, and SmartIcons. This command displays a dialog box that prompts the user to input data or select from a list of values. For example, an application could prompt a user to designate the next person to whom the document should be routed.

ACTIONS

A major enhancement in Notes Release 4 is the concept of Actions. This involves both a new user interface element—the Action Bar—and a new workflow-oriented programming element—Actions.

Actions are bound to a Form or a View. Within each Notes Form or View, users have certain Actions available to them. For example, in a Form, users can always close or print the document. And, in a View, users can always open a document or another View. The concept of Actions brings these abilities to the surface and allows them to be manipulated by the developer.

Actions fall into two categories: Standard Actions and Custom Actions. *Standard Actions* are inherent in the existing Form or View—close, print, open, save, send, edit, categorize, and others. *Custom Actions* are created by the developer. These can be commands, formulae, script, or agents, and can contain logic for sequential routing, for conditional routing, for approval signatures, for automatically saving forms to shared databases, or for virtually any other operation.

For each Form or View, the developer designates which Actions are to be made available to the user. The user sees the Actions in the nonscrolling Action Bar (the Action Bar is always available at the top of the screen) or in the File menu. The developer defines which Actions are available to the user at any given point (e.g., upon creation, when editing or reading, or by a formula). Because the Action Bar and menu are sensitive to this context, users see only those Actions that they can take. There are no grayed-out choices.

Custom Actions are particularly useful for presenting users with the current options within the context of the workflow. A good example is a document that needs to be approved, where the user's next Action should be Approve, Deny, or Return with Comment.

NOTES/FX TRANSFERS ACTIONS TO OLE APPLICATIONS

Notes/FX (Field eXchange), introduced in Release 3, enables Notes documents to exchange Field-level data with embedded OLE objects. Notes R. 4 introduces Notes/FX 2.0, which extends this model from exchanging data to exchanging Actions—a key element in extending Notes-based workflow to other applications (Notes/FX 2.0, in fact, was formerly called NotesFlow—a term now being reserved for all Notes workflow features). With Notes/FX 2.0, Actions defined in a Form can be made continually available to the user not only within the Notes document, but also within any OLE object embedded within the Notes document.

Consider again our contract-approval workflow, for example. A contract, created in a specific word processor (e.g., Microsoft Word, Lotus WordPro, WordPerfect), is embedded in a Notes document that is sent for review and approval to a number of users. When the users open the Notes document, the contract is launched within the word processor. The users have access to all of the word processor commands and to the Notes Actions available to the Form from which the document was launched. So the Notes Approve or Reject commands can now be chosen by the user from within the word processing document. Once chosen, the Action could close the word processing document, change the status of the Notes document, close the Notes document, send a notification to the contract author, or perform other functions.

The way in which the user accesses the Notes Action from within the OLE document depends on the OLE application. If the OLE application specifically supports Notes/FX (as do all Lotus applications), the Action Bar will appear above the OLE document. Any OLE 1.0 or 2.0 application that does not support Notes/FX will require the user to go to the File menu to access the Actions (this requires the Actions within the Notes Form to be designated to appear on the File menu).

10

Notes and the Interenterprise

WHY LOTUS NOTES IS A PREMIER PLATFORM FOR INTERENTERPRISE APPLICATIONS

NOTES SPANS INTERNAL AND EXTERNAL APPLICATIONS

Lotus Notes is a platform for developing and deploying many types of strategic applications, ranging from groupware to workflow to interenterprise electronic commerce. Notes is used by a large number of companies to support their key business processes, such as developing products, acquiring customers, and supporting these customers. It is also used to deliver critical information, such as competitive intelligence, to the appropriate people wherever they are.

Notes spans three domains of applications: internal, interenterprise, and extraenterprise. (See Figure 10.1.) It frequently serves as the point of integration among them.

REASONS TO USE NOTES FOR INTERENTERPRISE APPLICATIONS

Notes is highly appropriate for interenterprise applications for four major reasons:

- The need to extend internal Notes applications
- The suitability of the Notes architecture for interenterprise applications

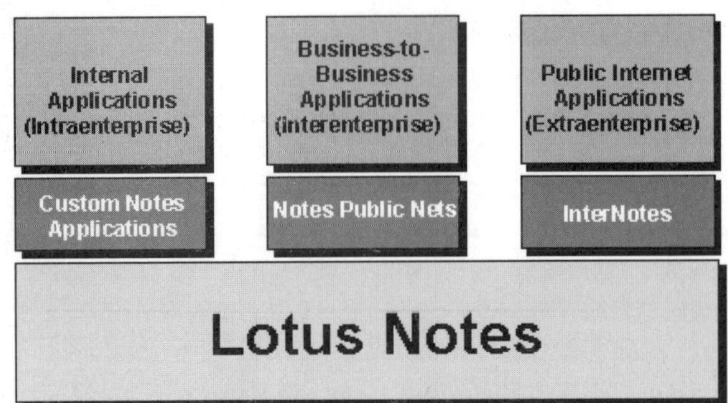

FIGURE 10.1   Notes applications can be deployed internally, between enterprises via a Notes public network, and to individuals on the Internet via InterNotes Web Publisher.

- The development of carrier-grade Notes features
- The availability of commercial-grade public networks for Notes

In this chapter we examine the first of these reasons for using Notes. We will see how companies are using Notes for interenterprise applications ranging from information delivery to creating electronic marketplaces. Chapter 11 discusses the features of Notes that make it a strong platform for interenterprise applications. It includes a discussion of the Notes architecture and the emerging Notes public networks from companies such as IBM and CompuServe.

NEED TO EXTEND INTERNAL NOTES APPLICATIONS

Notes can be used for a wide—almost limitless—variety of applications. However, when one looks at the most strategic Notes applications, they invariably have a direct effect on the supplier–customer relationship. Notes applications are used to automate, improve, and manage all aspects of this relationship, from marketing to prospect tracking to client management to customer support. Even obviously internal applications, such as product development tracking or competitive intelligence, pay off in more quickly meeting customers' needs than the competition can.

For many companies, the next strategic step is to include the customers within the application. This can be done by providing product support information or a help desk, by extending an internal workflow to include customers, or by allowing customers to order products directly and manage their own orders as well as the internal approval processes. Ultimately, the whole relationship can be supported electronically. So far in this book, we have seen examples of all of these, and we will see more.

BUSINESS MUST MOVE OUT TO THE CUSTOMER

In the Introduction, we looked at how one small company has used Lotus Notes to transform its relationship with its primary customers. Jim Wilcoxon is just one example of the way businesses are redefining themselves in the 1990s. The business of today, and even more the business of the twenty-first century, will be driven by the need to reduce cycle time for delivery of products to customers, improve responsiveness to customer needs, and above all, get closer to customers. This is being done by redesigning and better managing internal processes, particularly those relating to product development, customer acquisition, and product support. Not surprisingly, these areas constitute some of the most critical areas for Lotus Notes applications.

The next major step is to expand these processes to actually include the customer. Companies doing this are now finding that bringing down the wall that has always existed between the supplier and the customer can have an impact much greater than anyone had anticipated. Far beyond the increased communications and decreased delivery time, the result is frequently that the customer takes some responsibility, if not ownership, of the process. This creates a bond that is not easily broken. It can truly transform suppliers and customers into type partners.

Lotus Notes and Notes public networks are rapidly becoming critical platforms for the development and support of these new and enhanced relationships. Notes-based applications are distinguished from other electronic platforms, such as the World Wide Web, because they focus specifically on interenterprise applications that enable business-to-business commerce. Notes is uniquely capable of supporting the trading-partner customer/supplier relationship—creating a sort of rich 1990s version of electronic data exchange (EDI).

BUSINESSES EXPLORE NEW SERVICES
AND OPPORTUNITIES

The availability and power of platforms such as Notes and Notes public networks present companies with almost limitless opportunities for new services and businesses, involving not only current customers but also a completely new set of customers, suppliers, partners, regulatory authorities, and others. Some of the areas now being exploited include:

- Information delivery
- Interenterprise workflow
- Electronic marketplaces

DELIVERING INFORMATION TO THE CUSTOMER

Some of the first interenterprise Notes applications are one-way or interactive information delivery between suppliers and customers. Information delivery ranges from free delivery of new product or customer support material, such as that being implemented by Ingram and Lotus, to revenue-generating, subscription-based publishing services of the Patricia Seybold Group.

CASE STUDY

INGRAM DELIVERS INFORMATION
TO RESELLERS

Ingram Industries (Nashville, Tennessee) is the largest aggregator and distributor in the world. It is a 100-year-old company with one vision: to be the preeminent worldwide distributor. Ingram is the largest book distributor and the largest video distributor in the United States, as well as the largest distributor of computer hardware and software.

Ingram Micro (Santa Ana, California) is the channel between software, hardware, and peripheral vendors and resellers. Ingram Micro is Lotus's, Microsoft's, Novell's, and most other vendors' largest customer. Ingram Micro deals with over 850 manufacturers, 50,000 reseller outlets, and 30,000 stock keeping units (SKUs).

THE PROBLEM IS NOT PRODUCT DELIVERY
BUT INFORMATION DELIVERY

The key problem facing the computer software and hardware industry is getting usable information in the resellers' hands, that is, keeping resellers up to date with product information they need in order to sell products and help buyers make purchasing decisions. The ability of vendors and the channel to deliver products quickly has reached new heights, but the ability to deliver the documentation and collateral material for the products has not kept pace. And the cost of producing and delivering these materials is increasingly becoming a larger component of the cost of producing and delivering the product itself. Gina de Miranda, general manager for Ingram Industries' new InfoWare I.T. service, notes, "The people in this industry are producing information the same way they did 20 years ago, only they use a computer rather than a typewriter. There is a large lag between the ability to produce a product and the documentation as to what it does. This is exacerbated by distance and language. Resellers are particularly affected: Vendors announce products and don't explain them well to the market, and then they need to explain them to customers."

The information that the reseller needs may be in many forms, including data sheets, spec sheets, brochures, white papers, bug fixes, press releases, and many, many more.

Ingram Micro is as much in the middle of the information flow as of the product flow. Currently, Ingram Micro handles 20,000 tech-support phone calls per week from resellers, and up to 40 percent of these are product-oriented in presales situations. Gina de Miranda points out that this is not only very costly (the cost is estimated across the industry at $40 per call), it is slowing down purchasing significantly and thereby directly affecting the bottom lines of resellers, distributors, and vendors alike. She cites a 1993 study that looked at all of the information resources available to resellers and how they affected Ingram's and the resellers' business. The clear result is an increased sales cycle attributed to not having the right information at the right time. In addition, customers frequently make the wrong purchase choice because of a lack of proper information. This leads to the many millions of Return Material Authorizations (RMAs) issued every year.

Ingram Micro has now reached the conclusion that, because delivering products without enough information is counterproductive, any electronic application to help order and deliver products must include a method for delivering the information that enables the purchase of the product. According to Gina de Miranda, "Our greatest need is to deliver products and the information about the products. An electronic ordering system is not enough—you need to know what you are ordering, whether it meets the need or not. Our goal is to create strategic advantage with an electronic ordering system [Ingram Micro currently offers this via IM On Line] by adding a customer information system. Ultimately, the pipeline is only as good as the information being supplied to the resellers."

INFOWARE I.T.

Ingram Industries is now investing heavily in building a service to supply resellers with the information they need to sell products more easily and to allow customers to buy products more easily. In fact, Ingram is creating a separate company to run this information service. This company is a subsidiary not of Ingram Micro but of Ingram Industries, the parent company, because Ingram sees the possibility of using the same information distribution services in other sectors, such as its book and video distribution subsidiaries.

InfoWare I.T. is the name of the application and the service Ingram provides. The InfoWare I.T. application is licensed from InfoWare Development L.P. (Los Angeles, California), one of the first companies to recognize Notes as a platform for interenterprise information distribution. InfoWare I.T. is intended to be a multivendor repository for all kinds of information relative to computer products and peripherals. The information delivered crosses manufacturers and product lines, and it is designed to allow resellers to answer their own and their customers' questions quickly, easily, and accurately. Ingram sees InfoWare I.T. as a "magic filing cabinet" containing all, or at least most, of the answers. Using Notes replication, this information will be continually kept up to date.

InfoWare I.T. presents the information to the user (reseller or customer, technician or LAN manager, etc.) in a highly customized manner. The material is presented as a set of virtual file cabinets and folders, each containing a set of documents. Using Notes views, these drawers can "contain" documents of various types, categorized in various ways. The categories include:

- Manufacturers.
- Product groups.
- Topic groups. The three topic groups are Technical (e.g., release notes, bug fixes, etc.), Product & Vendor (e.g., marketing collateral), and Channel Support (i.e., information for reselling, supporting, and recommending products).

The user can also access the Notes full-text search engine to find specific documents.

The InfoWare I.T. Application has three specific parts:

- InfoWare I.T. Author & Editor
- InfoWare I.T. Publisher
- InfoWare I.T. Viewer

The InfoWare I.T. Author & Editor goes to content providers, that is, software and hardware vendors. It is a Notes application that automates the process of publishing a document. This includes adding the categorization, making sure that the document is approved and ready for submission, and attaching the document to the Notes document. The provider can also set configurations, such as when information expires. The file, including the Notes document and attached information file, is E-mailed or replicated to Ingram.

The InfoWare I.T. Publisher is used by people at the service to convert the attached document to an Adobe Acrobat .PDF file. This provides compression and, more important, the fully graphical presentation environment required for people to use the information. The file is then automatically grabbed and placed into Notes databases. (There are actually several Notes databases for each vendor; this number has been optimized for storing and delivering large amounts of data.) These databases are then replicated to a Notes public network site.

Who can access the documents—that is, the security and distribution levels—is defined in the Notes Name & Address Book at the Notes public network server complex. The groups and access control lists (ACLs) are managed with the input of the vendor. Each reseller subscribes to information from one or more vendors and decides which Topics to subscribe to. This material replicates each night and delivers updated information. Resellers can decide whether to replicate the documents or receive just the titles of the documents. To see a document, resellers can click on the title and, at their request, the document will be sent immediately or at the next replication. The document can additionally or alternatively be sent to a third party at an E-mail address.

The InfoWare I.T. Viewer is a C++ developed front-end browser to look at the Topics, Cabinets, and Folders (see Figure 10.2). It allows high customization and personalization of the browsing process.

INFOWARE I.T. BUSINESS MODEL

The InfoWare I.T. process has three parties: the computer product vendors who create the information; Ingram Industries' InfoWare

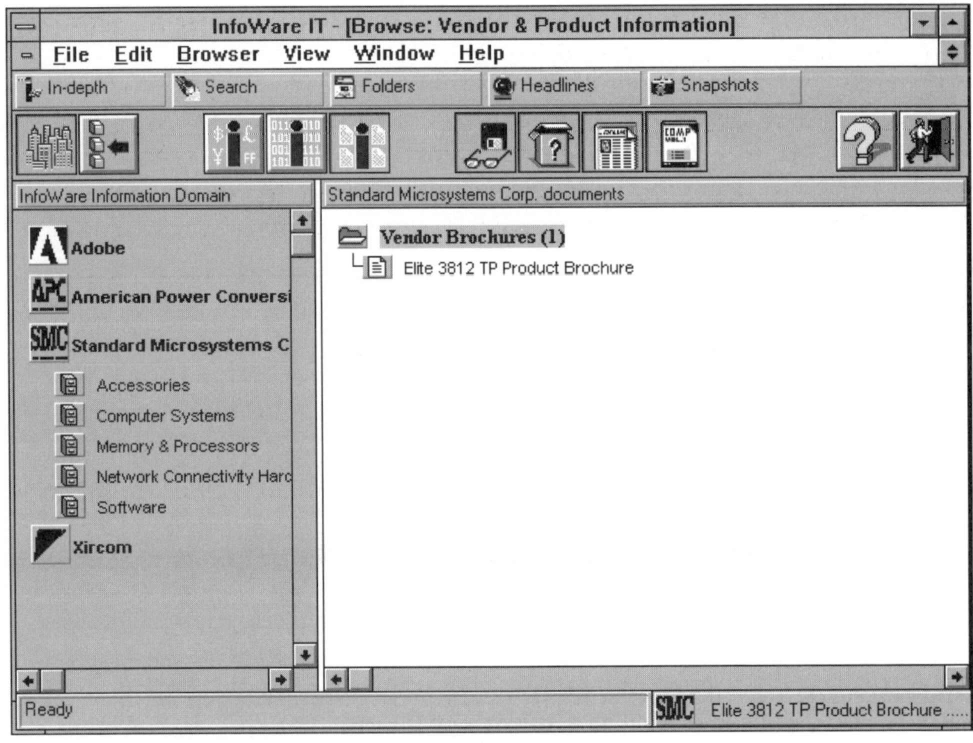

FIGURE 10.2   **The InfoWare I.T. Viewer** allows resellers direct access to technical information from multiple vendors.

I.T. service, which hosts and delivers the information; and the resellers who use the information. The business model is as follows: The computer product vendor pays a certain fee to sign up for the service and receive assistance in preparing its information. The vendor then pays an annual fee for each reseller that subscribes to the information. The resellers pay only for their Notes licenses and connect time to the Notes public network service.

The InfoWare I.T. service was introduced in 1995. The company expected that within three months there would be at least five vendors, with more than 10 by the end of the year.

InfoWare I.T. is also getting very strong support from resellers. In fact, Ingram believes that the success of this application will be reseller driven. The company cites a specific example: Upon seeing a demo for the first time, Bob Din, president of InfoTech, came into the Ingram Micro headquarters the next day and convinced a major PC vendor to sponsor InfoTech for the service. It was expected that 1000 resellers would be signed up by the end of 1995.

Although the initial model for InfoWare I.T. is vendor information to resellers, Ingram is looking past the reseller-only model to one that would allow resellers to connect to their own end users. This, in fact, was driven by the resellers and was surprising to Ingram. However, it does support Ingram's long-term strategy: to bring the information from the headquarters of these companies to the end point, the customer, who is actually implementing the system.

EFFECT ON THE INDUSTRY

Ingram's vision goes even further. The company is aware that, although many providers are building their own electronic infor mation delivery systems, from the resellers' and customers' perspective, the need is a single point of information, a single user interface.

Gina de Miranda believes that resellers have the clout to force the computer industry to subscribe to and live with a standard set of definitions and to converge on a specific service. With this service, InfoWare I.T. plays the role of trusted middleman, and the Notes public network provides a neutral carrier for all software/hardware vendors. The goal is to link the whole IT sector—users, consumers, resellers, consultants, distributors, aggregators, and the like—by building a cross-industry service à la the American Airlines Saber reservation system, which will benefit all.

CASE STUDY

LOTUS BUILDS CONNECTIONS TO ITS PARTNERS AND CUSTOMERS

Lotus Development Corporation (Cambridge, Massachusetts) has been connecting to its customers and partners for a number of years. Lotus Notes Network (LNN) is Lotus's worldwide business partner and customer network. LNN provides partners and customers with access to information from Lotus—KnowledgeBase, product updates, lists of partners, and similar information. LNN also allows Lotus customers and partners to communicate with each other. In addition, LNN hosts a publishing marketplace called

Lotus Newsstand. Newsstand provides a development environment for publishers and a central delivery and management point for Notes-based and World Wide Web-based subscriptions to more than 50 services, such as *PC Week,* the *Notes Report,* and the Patricia Seybold Group's *Notes on Information Technology.*

CASE STUDY

PATRICIA SEYBOLD GROUP CREATES NOTES-BASED INFORMATION SERVICE

In 1991, the Patricia Seybold Group (Boston, Massachusetts) was the first company to deliver Notes-based publications to its customers and provide an interactive electronic information service. Since then, many other information providers have also added Notes-based publications and services. For the Patricia Seybold Group, Notes-based publishing has had a major impact on its relationship with its customers. The level of interaction with them has increased many-fold, and they now work cooperatively on many projects via Notes. Perhaps most significantly, *Notes on Information Technology* now generates greater revenues than any of the Patricia Seybold Group's paper-based subscriptions or services, and it has greatly expanded the group's reader base.

The Patricia Seybold Group has also brought this Notes-based service to the Internet, using the Lotus InterNotes Web Publisher for automatic publishing onto its World Wide Web site (www.psgroup.com).

SUPPORTING INTERENTERPRISE WORKFLOW

Just as workflow is becoming a key building block for internal applications, interenterprise workflow is also emerging. And just as it is the basis for many internal coordination, workflow, and business process management applications, Notes is a strong platform for extending these processes across enterprises. Many, if not most, of the applications in the electronic commerce or electronic marketplace categories contain Notes-based workflow, and some applications, such as DATA Clearinghouse Corporation's automated legal payment service, are themselves interenterprise workflow.

CASE STUDY

DATA CLEARINGHOUSE PLAYS NETWORK-BASED TRUSTED THIRD PARTY

Bill O'Malley, president of DATA Clearinghouse Corporation (South Pasadena, California) says, "We're a small company with big plans." O'Malley sees his opportunity in the problems that companies have in managing the payment of their professional service suppliers and the difficulty that professional service companies have in collecting their bills.

DATA Clearinghouse has initially targeted the insurance industry and its legal services. The company is offering a service that ensures that the majority of legal invoices will be automatically paid overnight. This is done by grabbing data from the lawyers' billing systems and matching the data against a set of rules that define "reasonable and customary" fees (no depositions for this case, no out-of-town travel, use of paralegals for this process, first-class hotels OK, etc.). The majority of the invoices (those that fall within the rules) are paid immediately. Where additional intervention is required, a workflow process is launched.

The benefits of the system are as follows: The attorneys receive payment in a matter of hours rather than months. Because of this, the insurance company can negotiate a rate reduction for fees paid promptly. This tends to average 3 percent to 8 percent of the invoice. The company also has better control and management of the payment process, and there is reduced likelihood of conflict with its legal firm over billing and payment.

DATA Clearinghouse is positioning itself as the trusted middleman that can make this happen less expensively than any of the parties doing it internally or on a bilateral basis. It sees itself becoming the ADP of professional service payment.

DATA Clearinghouse is building this system on Lotus Notes and a Notes public network. Notes was chosen for its support of the electronic submission process, Notes E-mail connections, and what O'Malley terms "Notes's elegant, customizable client software." The Notes public network was chosen to offload the investment and expertise required to run an interenterprise network. According to O'Malley, "I don't want to build my own network. I don't want to handle routine customer care. Just as we're presenting ourselves as the best and the brightest to help our customers do things that they should need to own, we also looked for the best and the brightest to handle those things that we don't need to become experts in."

CREATING AN ELECTRONIC MARKETPLACE

At the highest level, interenterprise applications cease to exist solely between a single supplier and its customers, and the network itself becomes an electronic marketplace in which many suppliers and customers can sell, buy, or barter goods and services. Enabling this many-to-many relationship, along with strong elements of workflow, security, and management, has produced some of the highest-leverage applications to date. EnviroNet provides an excellent example.

CASE STUDY

ENVIRONET TURNS TRASH INTO GOLD

Bob Curry, president of GroupVision (Brookfield, Wisconsin), is keenly aware of the value of trash, specifically, recyclable waste. In Wisconsin, as in many parts of the country, the collection and sale of recyclable waste is an active market, with sellers of recyclables (landfills, municipalities, large manufacturers) connecting with hungry buyers (paper mills, metal processors, box and container companies). These buyers are becoming more and more hungry as federal and state regulations "encourage" manufacturers to make a certain percentage of their goods from recyclable material.

At the same time, those with recyclables are being "encouraged" by public opinion, state legislation, and economics to sell them as recyclables rather than send them to landfills. For example, Wisconsin recently enacted a law prohibiting the dumping of any recyclable into a municipal landfill. This law went into effect in January 1995, with fines for noncompliance beginning in January 1996. Interestingly, this law was expected to "glut the market" and depress prices for recyclables. In fact, since the law was enacted, the value of recyclables has increased, on average, by threefold.

If there are people actively seeking recyclable material and others trying to get rid of it, what is the problem?

Actually, GroupVision has identified the following specific problems with the current system:

Using Landfill as the Waystation. Currently, much of the recyclable material is first sent to a landfill, where the recyclable material is held for potential sale. This places a large burden on the landfills and increases the costs to municipalities, because the value of the salable recyclables is lower than the cost to transport them, store them, and manage the sale.

Buyers and Sellers Finding Each Other. Currently, there is no efficient way for sellers of recyclables to find buyers who need the material. The methods sellers use range from cold-calling a previous customer to a physical company visit to such a customer to sending written requests or faxes to a set of predetermined companies. This all assumes that the company or landfill knows these companies and is trying to determine their current needs. Much of the contact is actually made by the seller or buyer calling the district recycling specialist for the Department of Natural Resources or the county extension agent to see if he or she knows anyone who wants or has specific material.

Pricing: Setting Fair Market Value for the Materials. Once the seller and buyer find each other, there is the matter of setting the price. Currently, to set a price from a municipal landfill, one of the parties has to call the district recycling specialist to get a base price.

ENVIRONET BRINGS BUYERS AND SELLERS TOGETHER IN AN ELECTRONIC MARKETPLACE

Understanding this opportunity, GroupVision is creating an electronic service called EnviroNet whose purpose is to bring those with recyclables together with those who have a demand for them. The initial target includes the 2000 landfills in the state of Wisconsin (Wisconsin is providing early funding for EnviroNet) and the companies within the state that create and buy recyclable material.

EnviroNet will soon expand to include suppliers and buyers nation-wide. Eventually, a landfill or buyer anywhere in the country will be able to purchase a shrink-wrapped package and be up and running within 20 to 30 minutes with the software and a connection to EnviroNet.

EnviroNet is built on a set of Notes databases hosted at a Notes public network server complex. The major database is a bidding database, where recyclables are offered and bid upon. The process is as follows. A company with recyclable material to sell makes an offer. The offer includes the type of material, its location, the amount, the minimum price, and the close date. The company also designates the type of bidding process: open, closed, or limited. With an open bid, anyone can see the bids and raise them; with a closed bid, no one can see the bids; with a limited bid, anyone can see the amount of a bid, but not who made it. Bids are made until the close date, when no more bids are accepted. The seller then has a deal with the highest bidder.

Bidders can browse the database for material they might need. They can use Notes Views to see the offers in any way they want (e.g., by material, by region, by price). Suppliers and bidders replicate the bidding database as often as they want with the EnviroNet database. Notes also provides additional functionality. For example, using Notes Agent capabilities, bidders can have their servers notify them via pager gateway when someone else raises the bid they have put in.

OTHER ENVIRONET SERVICES

EnviroNet is adding more services to the offer/bid marketplace. For example, EnviroNet plans to take the closing prices on the bid documents, put them into another database, and use this for price trending information. EnviroNet will also provide a database on environment legislation, discussion databases in certain focused industry segments, electronic catalogs of material made from recycled material, industry newsletters, and recycling-oriented news feeds.

In addition, EnviroNet is planning to address the issue of buying and selling EPA pollution credits. The EPA grants pollution credits to companies that do something that is particularly environmentally sound, such as reduce emissions or close down a plant or facility. These credits are transferable. They are valuable. The EPA has also mandated in certain areas that there is a finite amount of pollution that a company can put out. Companies that need to exceed these limits can use pollution credits to do so. They can use their own credits, or they can use credits issued to other companies. There is no clearinghouse for pollution credits, and companies needing them have to find companies owning them. A future EnviroNet service will enable the electronic trading of these pollution credits.

ENVIRONET CHOOSES A NOTES PUBLIC NETWORK

EnviroNet is being hosted on a Notes public network because, according to Bob Curry, "The ramp-up of this thing could be incredible." He is, admittedly optimistically, projecting over 200,000 users nationwide after the first year. Curry explains, "This is an example of a small company that does groupware very well and understands a market partnering with a company that understands communications and can manage server complexes. We need the security and reliability. This is market-sensitive information."

THE FUTURE FOR NOTES-BASED INTERENTERPRISE APPLICATIONS IS NOW

Lotus, IBM, Ingram, Compaq, and many, many others are investing heavily in building the infrastructure and content of interenterprise applications. They are not doing this out of altruism or on a speculative whim. They are all very well aware that, by the turn of the century, they will have to be major players in this space or they will not be players at all. They have seen, and in some cases participated directly in, the first wave of applications that exploit the new technologies and address the key business issues of our time.

The range of interenterprise applications and the opportunities presented are unlimited. Companies large and small are jumping in and taking the leadership that they plan to hold as their competitors try to catch up. Two such companies that provide powerful insights into the potential of interenterprise applications are TitleLink, a startup that has a business only because of the public network and application-hosting services, and Egghead Software, the largest commercial software supplier in the United States.

CASE STUDY

TITLELINK AUTOMATES THE INTERENTERPRISE REAL ESTATE CLOSING PROCESS

Millions and millions of real estate transactions are executed in the United States each year. Each of these transactions involves many participants (applicants, lenders, title companies, lawyers, real estate agents, etc.). And each of these transactions involves piles of papers (loan documents, applications, credit reports, surveys, plot plans, appraisals, flood reports, title searches, etc.) that travel among the participants. In some cases, these may travel many times to each of the participants. Today, this is done through faxing, mail, delivery services, and phone calls. It is a very costly process, both in terms of actual delivery and, most important, in the time it takes to get a loan completed. For most of the participants (certainly the sellers, lenders, title companies, real estate agents, and attorneys), this time is money. They do not get paid or start accruing revenue until the process is completed. Though this problem is well known, most see it as endemic to the real estate loan process.

Jody Lane sees the situation not as a problem but as an opportunity. Lane formed a company and service called TitleLink to automate and expedite the process. He is initially aiming the service at banks, lenders, and title companies. The title companies are key, because they put together the whole arrangement—making sure the title transfers from seller to buyer, making sure all moneys are accounted for, and providing title insurance for the lender and buyer. Lane plans to bring in the other parties (attorneys, real estate agents, etc.) as the service expands.

The goal of TitleLink is simple: to deliver documents electronically that have typically been sent by courier services and faxing. Meeting this goal will automatically eliminate redundancy and compress the time of tasks within the process. Additional savings are possible. For example, several lenders who are piloting TitleLink think that they could cut their processing staff in half with the system.

TitleLink centers on a secure Notes database where the lender chooses the title company (see Figure 10.3). Once the order is initiated, a real estate agent and attorney can be brought in by the

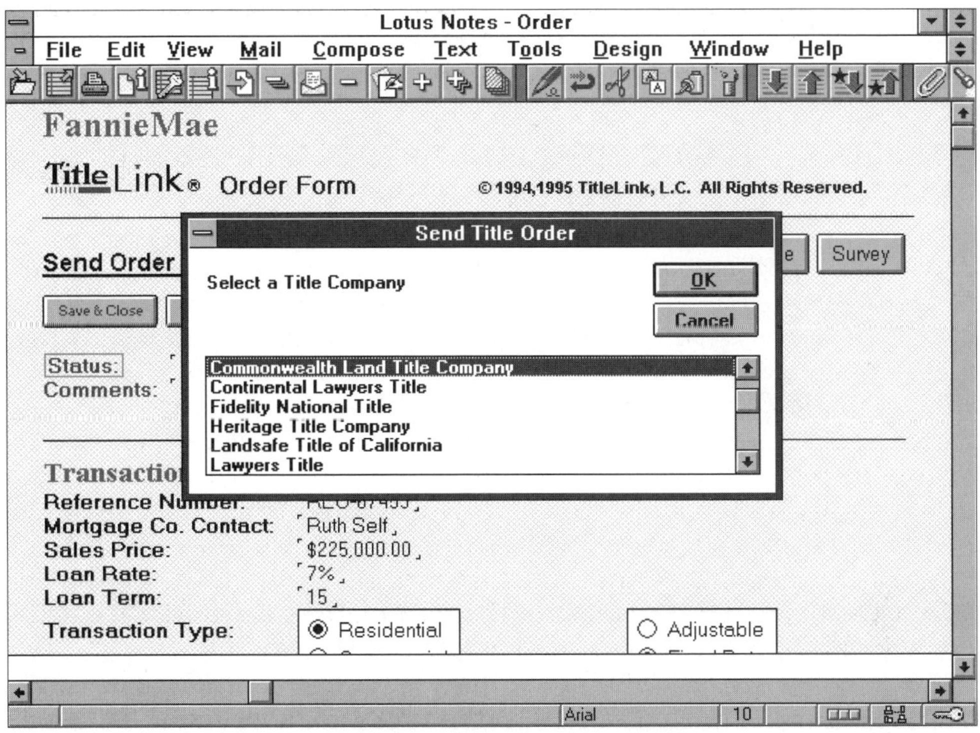

FIGURE 10.3 **Initiating the TitleLink process.** The lender begins
the TitleLink process by selecting a title company.

lender or the title company and given access to the appropriate
documents for that transaction. The following document types can
be added:

- Electronic forms.
- Faxed or scanned-in files.
- Electronic transfers via a custom interface with existing systems at the title company and lending agency. TitleLink supports EDI as well as other formats for this process.

These documents are all available to each of the participants
via a set of Notes Views (see Figure 10.4). The Notes database is
housed in a Notes public network server complex, and each of the
participants replicates it on a scheduled basis.

As the process continues, more information is added (see Figure 10.5). Security is strictly maintained. For example, a lender can

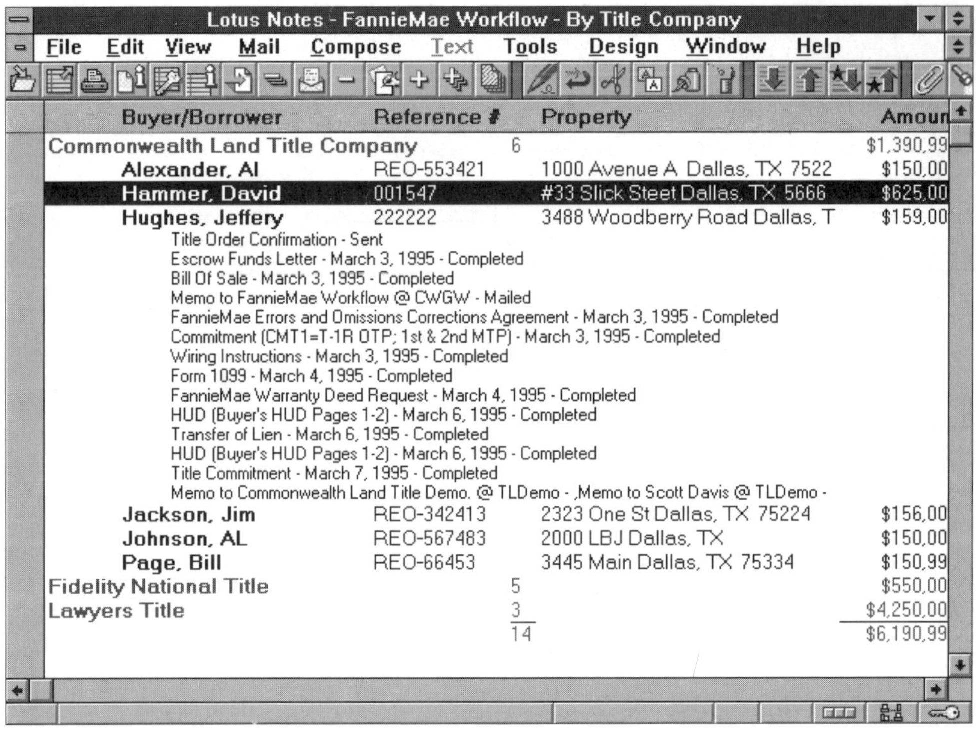

FIGURE 10.4 **Tracking the loan process.** The process can be tracked via Notes Views.

comment on and ask for changes in the title company's documents, but it cannot edit them. As the loan is in process, the status is changed by simply pressing the appropriate button in the Notes form. The process ends with the lender approving the title company's documents and electronically sending the lender's documents to the title company for closing (see Figure 10.6).

In addition to its interenterprise benefits, the TitleLink application also has internal applicability. Because a lender may have as many as 200 different processors using the information, Notes meets the need to view and work with this information in different ways. Notes also allows the lender or title officer to manage the process using all of Notes's capabilities—tracking, sorting, mailing, and workflow.

Jody Lane claims that "Notes, to date, is the only program that provides the security that's necessary in this industry. We've taken the groupware idea and tried to take it to a whole industry. We

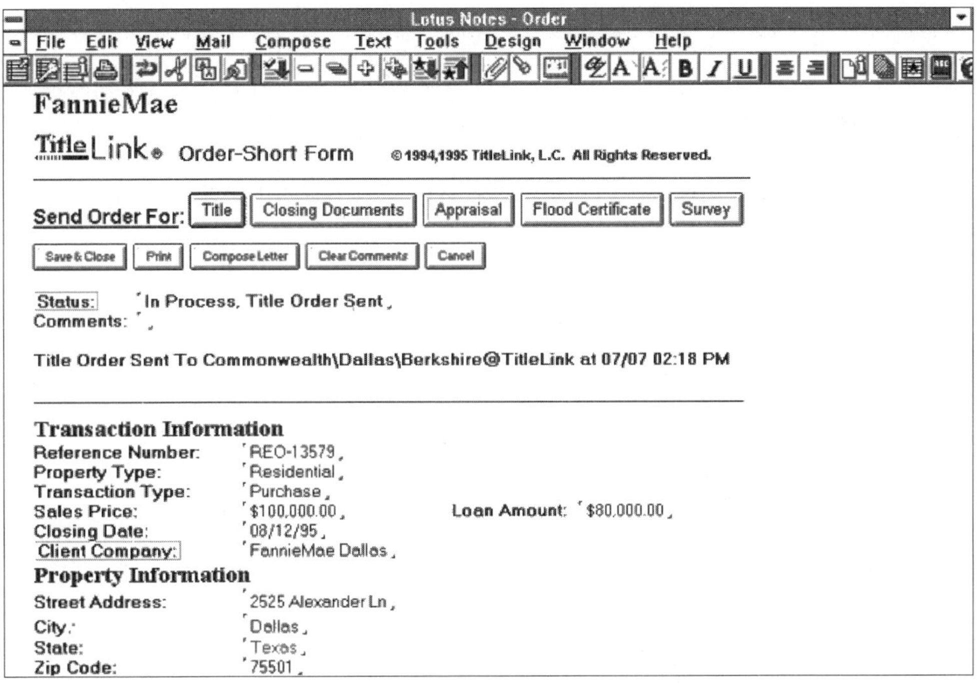

FIGURE 10.5 **TitleLink processing.** As the application is processed, additional documents are added.

allow the lender to interface with all of these different title companies' proprietary systems using one system and allowing all of the title companies to interface with many lenders using one system."

Jody Lane sees TitleLink's neutrality as the key to success. "We are a neutral third party to the transaction. This will not work if it is owned by one of the banks or one of the title companies."

The Notes public network is also crucial to the success of TitleLink. According to Jody Lane, "The title industry is vast. There are eight major title companies, and each has thousands of local offices. Likewise, there are a vast number of lenders, attorneys, real estate agents, etc. We plan to grow this to 100,000 to 500,000 endpoints."

Lane is not modest about his goals: "With the acceptance of electronic signatures, we could allow the lender and the title company to process a paperless transaction. We really think that we are going to change the way the real estate business is transacted across the country."

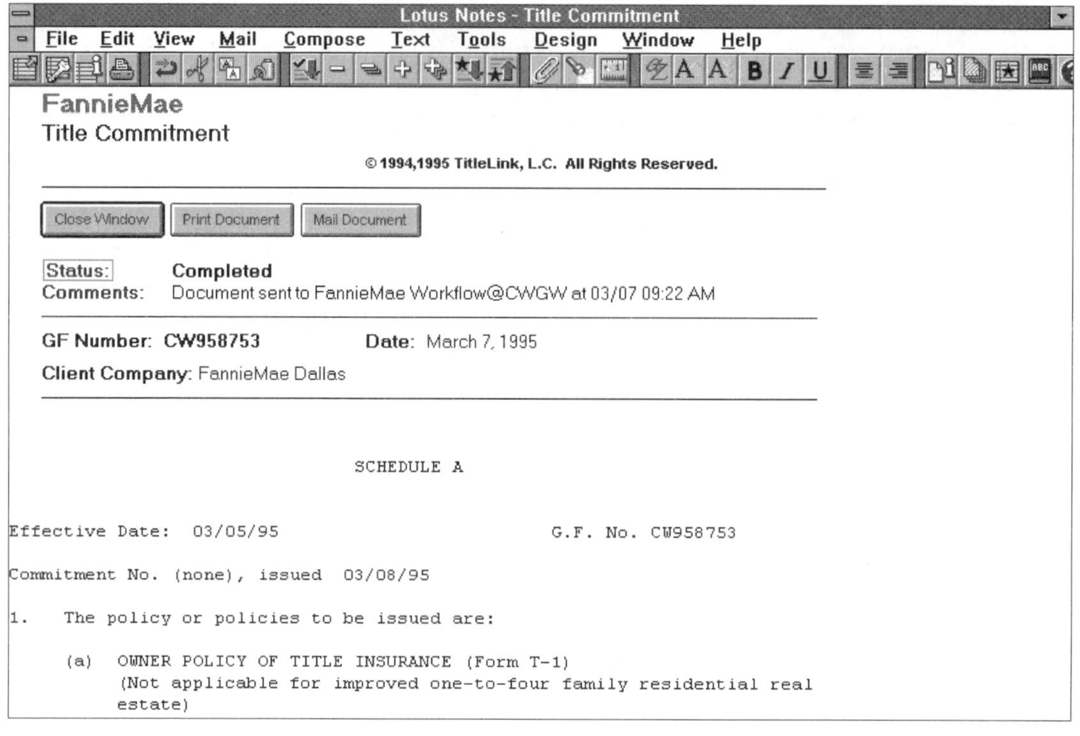

FIGURE 10.6 **Completing the process.** The process ends with the lender approving the title company's documents.

CASE STUDY

EGGHEAD SOFTWARE'S ELECTRONIC COMMERCE APPLICATION

Egghead Software (Spokane, Washington) is best known for its retail stores and its logo of a funny little professor. In fact, Egghead claims to be the leading commercial software reseller in the United States, and these sales account for over 50 percent of its revenues. Egghead also provides a number of business-oriented services, including consulting and integration, education, and training.

Egghead Software is building a Notes-based electronic commerce system to allow customers to browse its product catalog and to place orders interactively. According to Kirk Lockhart, Egghead senior vice president in charge of electronic commerce, this system is being designed from the beginning as a multivendor system, allowing other suppliers to participate and present their products to Egghead customers.

The electronic commerce system is the first step in Egghead's plans to evolve to a value-adding partner for its customers. Key additional areas of added value include services around workflow management and groupware applications. Egghead plans eventually to play the following three roles:

- Product/information supplier
- Product/information concentrator or conduit
- Consultant to suppliers and customers

EVOLUTION OF THE ELECTRONIC CATALOG

The Egghead Electronic Commerce application evolved out of its existing electronic customer order system. In the early 1990s, Egghead introduced Egghead Express, the first Windows-based electronic order system. When the time came to update this system, Egghead surveyed its customers to learn the required features for the next generation. According to Todd Ostrander, director of business development for electronic commerce, three key requirements emerged:

- Users had to have direct access to product information. It was not sufficient for purchasing agents to have exclusive access, because most purchase decisions were now being made by the departments themselves.
- The catalog had to be multivendor. Purchasers were not willing to use different applications to find and order material (software, hardware, office supplies, maintenance supplies, etc.) from different vendors. They demanded a single interface to all of their suppliers. (This, of course, is the Saber model for airline reservations.)
- Purchasers wanted direct support for the purchasing process. This would include both the tracking of orders between their companies and suppliers and management of the internal purchase-approval system.

It soon became clear that updating the proprietary Egghead electronic ordering application would not be sufficient to meet these needs. After learning of the Notes public networks initiative, Egghead realized that the combination of Notes (which the company was already using extensively for internal applications such as sales force automation) and a Notes public network could solve the needs of Egghead customers and provide additional opportunities for Egghead in the future.

Egghead thus embarked on a threefold strategy to provide added value based on its next-generation electronic commerce systems. Egghead saw that it could play three distinct roles in the electronic commerce process.

The first role is as a supplier of information and products. This is the core of the electronic commerce process—Egghead supplying information about products to its customers and enabling these customers to order its products directly. Using Notes, Egghead saw that it could meet the first requirement by allowing users throughout a customer organization to have access to its product information. Egghead also decided that it did not want to limit the information to those familiar with Notes, so it developed an alternative interface that more directly reflects the way users approach catalog shopping. The Notes public network also plays a key role in Egghead's ability to connect its customers quickly without having to build its own WAN infrastructure and server complex.

The second role that Egghead plans to create is that of information integrator. It plans to allow other suppliers (of office supplies, computer hardware, office equipment, etc.) to use its infrastructure to offer their own catalogs to customers they have in common with Egghead. This, of course, is designed to meet the second customer need: a single interface to multiple suppliers. Egghead also sees a distinct consulting opportunity in helping these suppliers build their own catalogs and ordering systems and integrating these into Egghead's. Here, again, the Notes public network will play a key role in isolating all suppliers' proprietary information from Egghead and from one another.

The third opportunity is to use the electronic commerce application as an entrée to customers to provide additional products and services. Initially, Egghead plans to help customers automate their internal purchasing workflow, addressing the third customer need for direct support of the purchasing process. Eventually, Egghead would like to provide application templates and participate in building customers' nonpurchasing workflows and workgroup applications.

EGGHEAD'S PLAN

Egghead plans to attempt the three roles sequentially over a period of time, during which it will roll out its service plan in three steps:

1. Electronic catalog
2. Electronic catalog + workflow
3. Electronic catalog + workflow + workgroup

The first step is the electronic commerce application (see Figure 10.7). This involves delivering the Egghead electronic catalog and delivering the catalogs of selected suppliers soon after.

The second step is to provide consulting and integration services for customers, focusing specifically on the customer's procurement process. This ties one of the customer's internal processes directly to the external purchasing process from Egghead and the other suppliers (see Figure 10.8).

The third step is for Egghead to provide application templates and services for workgroup applications that do not connect directly to its electronic commerce application (see Figure 10.9.) This will not only position Egghead as a value-added applications supplier, it will also position the companies with large consulting practices (such as the Big Six or computer systems vendors) and the many small to mid-sized Notes integrators that have emerged over the past few years. Egghead believes that it can play in this arena because of its knowledge of its customers from the first two steps, its knowledge of Notes and other client/server products, and its nationwide presence.

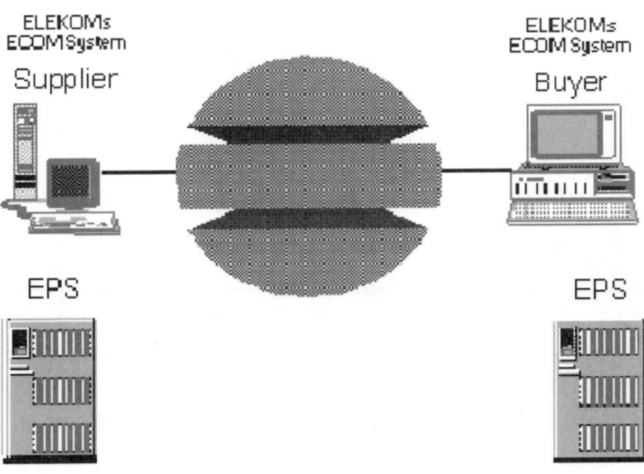

FIGURE 10.7 **Step 1: Electronic commerce.** Egghead's electronic commerce system connects suppliers and customers to each other via a Notes public network. The system also connects to the suppliers' and customers' electronic purchasing systems (EPSs).

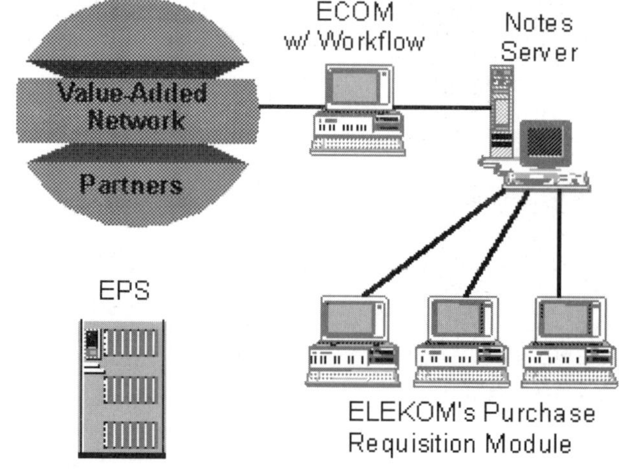

FIGURE 10.8 Step 2: Electronic commerce + workflow. In the second phase, workflow processes are added that link the customer's internal purchasing and approval processes to the electronic commerce system.

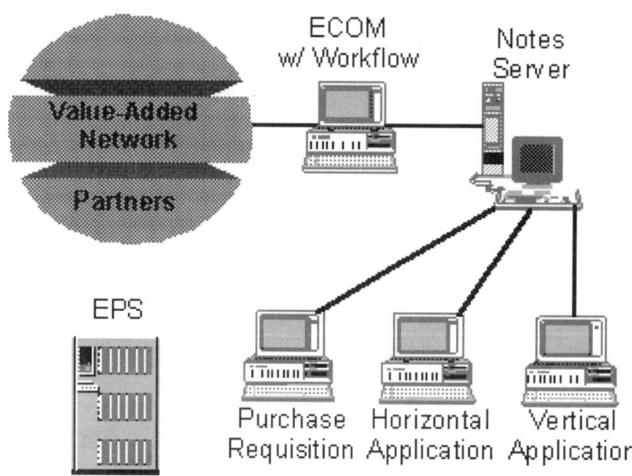

FIGURE 10.9 Step 3: Electronic commerce + workflow + workgroup. In the third phase, Egghead will provide support for its customers' internal workgroup applications via sets of templates and consulting services.

EGGHEAD ELECTRONIC COMMERCE ARCHITECTURE

The electronic commerce system has four components, shown in Figure 10.10:

- Notes databases, which hold the product and order information
- Visual Basic front end, which allows customers to browse and order from the product catalog, containing Egghead and other suppliers' products

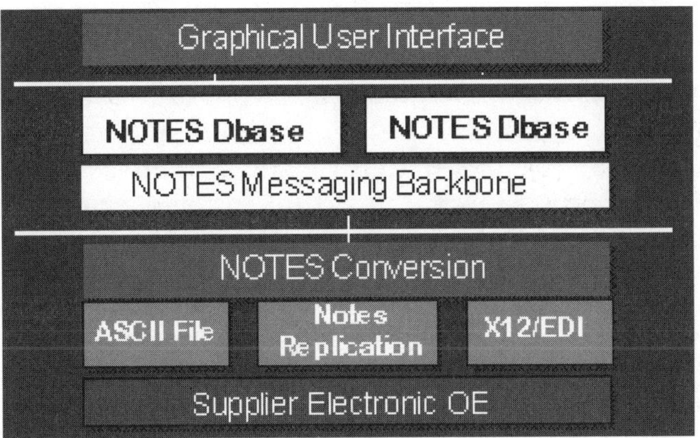

FIGURE 10.10 Egghead electronic commerce architecture. The Egghead electronic commerce application has three levels. At the top is a customized graphical user interface for browsing and ordering from the catalog. In the middle are the Notes databases and E-mail system, which communicate with each other via AT&T Network Notes. At the bottom is the connection to the suppliers' electronic order entry systems.

- EDI interface, which moves information between Notes and Egghead's and the other suppliers' accounting and billing systems
- A Notes public network, which is the delivery mechanism for orders between customers and Egghead

Notes Databases

There are two types of Notes databases: general databases, which replicate to all customers, and customer-specific databases, which are different for each customer site.

The general databases include the product information (which gives graphical access to product features and specifications) and supplier information (which gives addresses and other information about product suppliers). These databases are housed on Egghead servers, customer servers, and/or the Notes public network servers, and all updates are replicated to all copies.

The customer-specific databases include a catalog database, which contains any special pricing arrangements negotiated between the customer and Egghead; user profiles, which contains static customer information, such as "ship to" and "bill to"; and orders, which contains a record of all current and past electronic orders that the customer has made.

Visual Basic Application

According to Bruce Hitchcock, Egghead director of development, Visual Basic is being used as the front-end application because of its ability to create graphical screens for customers to navigate through the product list and to create order forms that are familiar to users.

The process is as follows. Customers can browse through the Egghead electronic commerce catalog by category (see Figure 10.11). These categories, of course, are generated by the categories in the Notes database. The user may select a product category or may click on a button to view the status of current orders or to do some maintenance on other information (e.g., put in a change of address).

Once the category is selected, the customer can scroll through the products on a screen that displays the SKU, description, and price (calculated using the prices from the customer-specific price database). As the customer stops on an item, specific details about that item are shown in the lower part of the screen. The customer can then insert a quantity to be ordered in the quantity column (see Figure 10.12). The Visual Basic application calculates the items, prices, and quantities and presents the customer with a subtotal (the total, including taxes and shipping, is actually calculated later

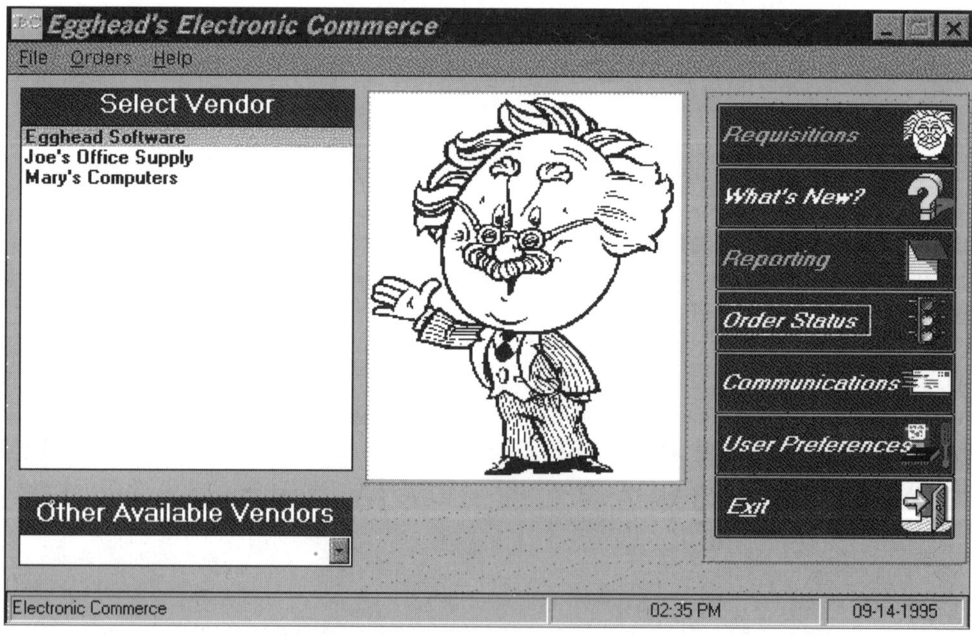

FIGURE 10.11 **Egghead electronic commerce main screen.** This screen allows Egghead customers to browse through product categories before ordering products.

by Egghead's billing system). This information may be viewed through an order form (see Figure 10.13).

Once the customer places the order, the document is both saved into the customer's order database and mailed directly into the Egghead orders database. At any time, customers can look up the status of any order placed with Egghead or any of the other vendors from which the company is purchasing (see Figure 10.14).

EDI Interface

Once the order is mailed into the Egghead orders database, a Notes process moves the order into the Egghead order system via an EDI interface. The order system does the final pricing and invoicing and then logs the order for fulfillment. It also creates an order acknowledgment, which is E-mailed back to the customer's own order database. The customer can now use the main screen of the Visual Basic application to see the status of that order.

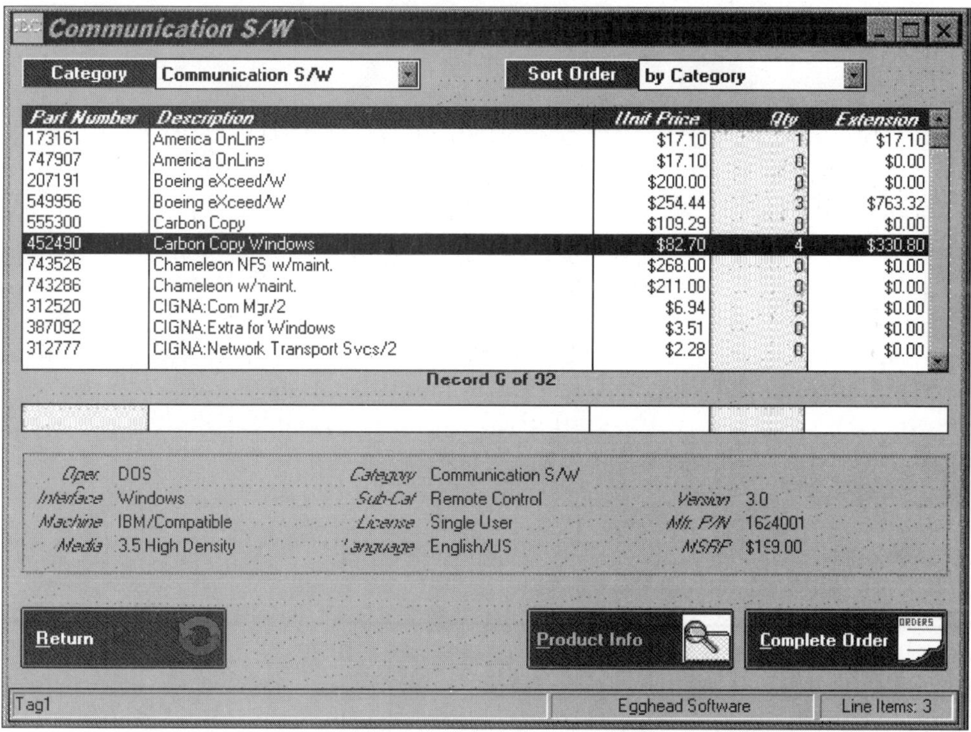

FIGURE 10.12 Egghead electronic commerce catalog. Customers can enter product quantities directly on the Egghead electronic commerce order form.

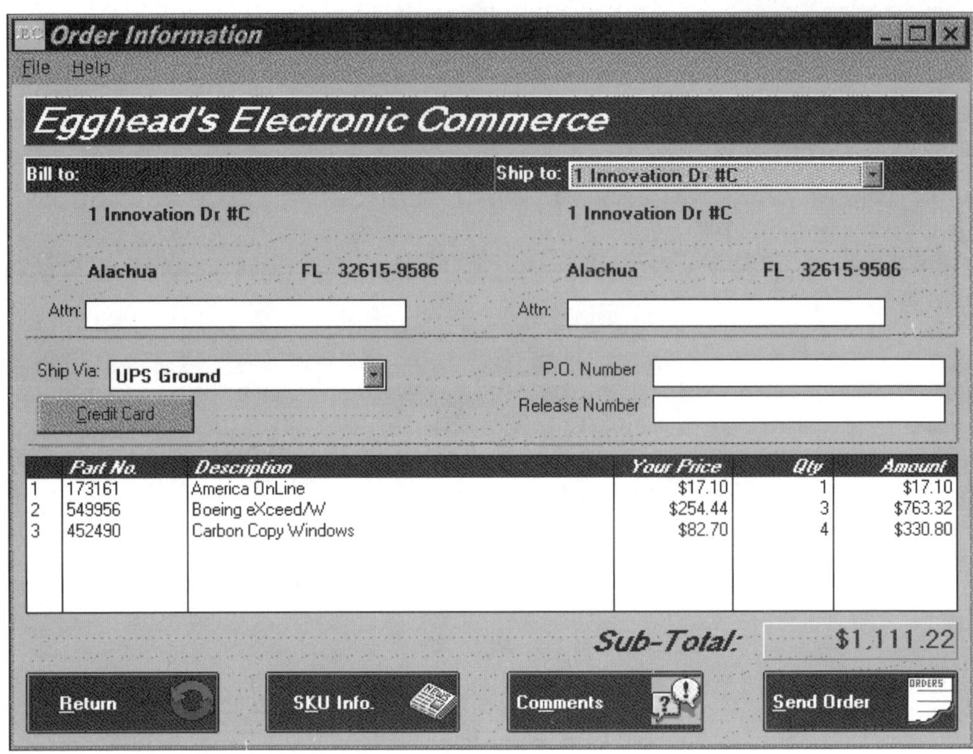

FIGURE 10.13 **Egghead electronic commerce order form.** The order information is viewable in an order form.

As Egghead moves to become a conduit for other providers to deliver their product catalogs and take orders, it has had to focus on integrating with additional systems. Using tools from Lotus and third parties, Egghead has successfully integrated the electronic commerce application with all the internal systems of its partner suppliers.

The Role of the Notes Public Network

The Notes public network plays a key role in the Egghead application: It provides the connection between Egghead and its customers. This connection supports two distinct functions. The first is mailing orders and order confirmations back and forth between Egghead and its customers. The second is the replication of changes to the general databases across the customer base. The use of the Notes public network takes the burden off Egghead of establishing and maintaining these connections. In addition, it lets customers have the option of storing their copies of the databases

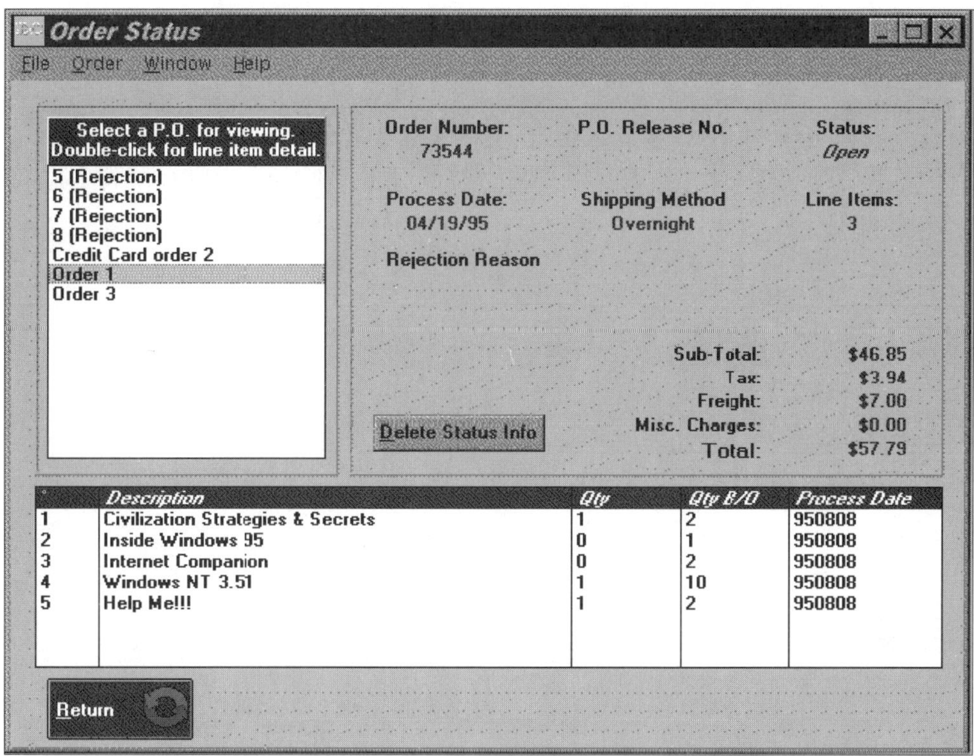

FIGURE 10.14 **Egghead electronic commerce order status form.** At any time, a customer can look up the status of a specific order from any supplier.

in a Notes public network server complex, relieving them of much of the administrative burden.

BENEFITS OF THE EGGHEAD ELECTRONIC COMMERCE APPLICATION

Tom Leach, Egghead director of sales and marketing for electronic commerce, lists a set of benefits already being accrued from the system:

- Single, friendly user interface for browsing and ordering from all suppliers
- Contracted/customized pricing from all suppliers directly to the desktop of the company's staff
- More efficient order tracking
- Order status delivered directly to the user's desktop

- Better asset management and tracking
- Reduced purchasing/processing costs—for example, in Egghead's experience, an average intercorporate EDI transaction ranges from $50 to $200; Egghead's electronic commerce system runs at less than $5 per transaction.

Overall, according to Kirk Lockhart, the key benefit of the system is to help transform Egghead in its customers' eyes from a supplier to a strategic partner.

EGGHEAD ELECTRONIC COMMERCE BECOMES ELETRADE

At the end of 1995, Egghead split out its electronic commerce business into a separate, wholly owned subsidiary of Egghead Inc. called ELEKOM. ELEKOM is charged with commercializing Egghead's electronic commerce efforts under the new product name EleTrade. (As this book went to press, Egghead was in the process of selling its commercial division to Software Spectrum in Garland, TX. This sale is not expected to affect Egghead's electronic commerce plans.)

11

Notes as a Platform for Interenterprise Applications

Chapter 10 focused on how companies are creating new businesses and transforming their current businesses by creating tight links to their customers using Lotus Notes. This chapter examines why Notes is a particularly strong platform for these interenterprise applications, taking an in-depth look at three specific areas:

- The suitability of the Notes architecture for interenterprise applications
- The development of carrier-grade Notes features
- The availability of commercial-grade public networks for Notes

SUITABILITY OF THE NOTES ARCHITECTURE FOR INTERENTERPRISE APPLICATIONS

The Notes architecture is inherently designed for building and deploying secure interenterprise applications. For example, Notes runs on multiple platforms, so providers do not have to try to dictate their customers' client operating systems, server operating systems, or networks. And the Notes development environment is optimized for building customized applications in which business process-specific collaboration and coordination take place. Most important, Notes includes a specific interenterprise model for security and communication, the latter being Notes's unique replication model.

Specifically, the Notes architectural features that enable interenterprise applications are:

- Security
- Connectivity
- Replication
- Custom development environment

NOTES SECURITY IS BUILT FOR INTERENTERPRISE APPLICATIONS

Notes provides very powerful security in all of the key areas, including authentication, authorization and access, and encryption. Particularly important in interenterprise applications is Notes's ability to fully authenticate individuals and organizations. In fact, Notes recognizes various levels of organizations and can enable authenticated communications between specific levels of different organizations. This means that Notes can truly support secure interenterprise commerce because it specifically supports the concept of one enterprise doing business with another.

Notes also supports electronic signatures, a security feature that is very important in intra- and interenterprise workflow.

NOTES COMMUNICATION SUPPORTS LAN, WAN, AND DIAL-UP CONNECTIVITY

Notes was born to communicate—communications ability was not an afterthought. Users can access servers, and servers can access each other via virtually any LAN (including IPX/SPX, NetBIOS, and TCP/IP) or WAN (including SNA, frame relay, X.25, and the Internet). Notes also allows dial-up access between servers or between users and servers without requiring any additional software. This means that, once cross-certified, different organizations can instantly connect and do business with one another.

NOTES REPLICATION SUPPORTS OCCASIONALLY CONNECTED ENVIRONMENTS

Interenterprise applications are, by definition, applications between separate businesses and organizations. Frequently, these organizations do not maintain continuous connections with one another. Notes replication enables applications to be used simultaneously in multiple disconnected locations (including remote and mobile users).

NOTES DEVELOPMENT ENVIRONMENT
SUPPORTS CUSTOM APPLICATIONS

Notes includes a development environment that enables the creation of highly customized applications. These applications are also easy to manage. They can be updated, just as the data within the applications can, via Notes replication. Thus, thousands of users can have their applications upgraded from V.1 to V.2 transparently and overnight.

Notes developers can also use other development environments with which they are familiar and comfortable. For example, front ends to Notes applications can be (and have been) built in C, C++, Visual Basic, PowerBuilder, SQLWindows, and other environments. In addition, many other Lotus and third-party products enhance Notes' workflow capabilities and/or integrate Notes with other workflow platforms.

As we saw in Chapters 8–9, Notes is being used to build applications that support and manage strategic business processes. Notes provides several capabilities that specifically support these workflow applications, including the following:

- Automatic and conditional document routing
- Server-based agents launched on a scheduled, or event, basis
- Action buttons for users to select the next action
- Digital signatures
- Integration of Notes and relational data and legacy systems

As we saw in the examples in Chapter 10, these capabilities translate well from the workgroup and enterprise to the interenterprise arena. And what is another term for "interenterprise workflow"? Electronic commerce!

NOTES RELEASE 4 INTERENTERPRISE ENHANCEMENTS

Many of the new Notes R.4 features address interenterprise applications directly. The most important of these features relate to the scalability of Notes applications.

Improved replication model. Release 4 improves replication by enabling multiple replication processes to be initiated simultaneously from a single server. In addition, R.4 replication supports field-level replication. This means that when a field in a document changes, only that field is replicated to other copies of that database. This can reduce network traffic and replication time by several orders of magnitude, depending on which field is changed.

Server pass-through. The server pass-through enables a server or client to dial into one server and access or replicate Notes databases that reside on another server on the same network. This is important for interdomain security, as well as for optimizing server complex resources.

PPP remote access. Adding point-to-point protocol (PPP) support for dial-in users relaxes the limits on the number of dial-in sessions that a server can support under the XPC protocol. Dial-in users appear as network users and can be supported up to the number of total sessions the server can handle.

General scalability improvements. Release 4 improves scalability by fully supporting 32-bit operating systems. This removes most size and performance limitations based on 16-bit addresses and 64K buffer sizes. Release 4 also provides greater support for symmetric multiprocessing systems (SMP), with full support for four to six (or more) processors expected. Each of these enhancements contributes to the ability to support several times more simultaneous users per server, over 1000 per multiprocessor server. In addition, R.4 supports larger Notes databases (up to 4 GB). This is particularly important when it comes to an interenterprise Name & Address Book.

Enhanced management tools. Release 4, along with new versions of the NotesView, greatly improve the ability to administer and manage large Notes networks and internetworks.

NOTES R.4.x CARRIER-GRADE FEATURES

Lotus and some of the public carriers have worked together to define a set of enhancements that will help Notes reach the level of availability and scalability expected from a service provider, such as a telecommunications company, where the number of simultaneous users can reach the hundreds of thousands and millions. These features will be rolled into later versions of Release 4 in time to keep up with the future expansion of interenterprise applications built on public networks for Notes.

The first three *carrier-grade* features to be added are:

- Server clustering
- Partitioned servers
- Asynchronous message queues

SERVER CLUSTERING

Server clustering is designed to ensure higher overall scalability, availability, and reliability of the public network applications. Server clustering works as follows. If a user or external server cannot access a specific database (this could be due to server failure or load balancing), the system automatically and instantly redirects the request to another replica copy of that database. This ensures that all applications are constantly available, whether or not a specific server or database is up and running.

Server clustering will be enabled by near-real-time replication between Notes databases on different servers within the defined cluster. Replication between these databases will be event driven (e.g., addition, deletion, or modification of a document) rather than based on a schedule.

Server clustering and near-real-time replication also enable interenterprise applications to scale to many more connections. Users or servers can connect to what is virtually the same database residing on different servers; each server can handle hundreds, and eventually thousands, of sessions.

PARTITIONED SERVERS

Partitioned servers—or multiserver hosting—provide scalability in the opposite direction by enabling cost-effective, lower-traffic applications. Partitioned servers allow multiple Notes servers in multiple domains to run on a single physical server while retaining all security features. This reduces the investment of setting up a multidomain application or service, because a whole machine need not be dedicated to each server, customer, or domain.

ASYNCHRONOUS MESSAGE QUEUES

Asynchronous message queues are event hooks that are designed to enable business services, such as billing, to be built upon Notes applications. Asynchronous message queues allow event trapping and recording of Notes events outside the normal Notes processes (e.g., writing to the server log). These processes include such events as opening a document, closing a document, mailing a document, and the like. Service providers will be able to use the Asynchronous Message Queue API, provided in a future version of Notes Release 4, to build billing or monitoring applications that are tailored to the service providers.

Asynchronous message queues are designed to work without blocking the Notes server task that sent the message. For example, a billing task that receives billing messages runs asynchronously to the Notes server tasks that open documents and send billing messages. If the billing task performs an I/O, then it waits for the I/O to complete without blocking a Notes server task.

AVAILABILITY OF COMMERCIAL-GRADE NOTES PUBLIC NETWORKS

The third major advantage of Notes as a platform for interenterprise applications is the new phenomenon of public carriers hosting Notes applications. As we have seen, many companies, such as Egghead and TitleLink, see the availability of Notes public networks as critical to the success of their interenterprise applications.

Companies that currently offer or are building Notes-based services include IBM, CompuServe, WorldCom, BT, Deutsche Telekom, Nippon Telegraph and Telephone, NTT Data Communications Systems, SNET, Telstra, Telecom Italia, Telekom Malaysia, Unisource, and US West.

Notes public networks take the burden of building and maintaining a Notes internetwork away from the company building the application. For example, consider a supplier that wishes to connect its customers via a Notes electronic commerce application (as in the Egghead Software example). In the do-it-yourself model, the supplier has to cross-certify and establish connections to each of its customers. The supplier has to build its own one-to-many network, where it may have to maintain hundreds or thousands of connections. A Notes public network can provide a one-to-one-to-many model, where the supplier would have to establish and maintain only a single connection to the Notes public network. The public carrier would establish and maintain the connections to all the supplier's customers.

Notes public networks can offer additional services over and above providing broad access to a company's application. The public carrier can "host" the application on its own server complex and then add value in areas such as security, availability, management, hardware costs, mail gateways, and investment protection. It can also add business services, such as customer provisioning and setup, tracking and billing, and help desk services.

Public carriers are not limited to hosting interenterprise electronic commerce applications. For example, they can serve as replication hubs for multilocation and multidomain organizations, effectively outsourcing the management of the network infrastructure. Public carriers can also host cross-organizational collaborative projects, such as between consultants and clients or among members of professional societies.

NOTES PUBLIC NETWORK SERVICES

Notes public networks generally provide specific services in the following areas:

Access. As public carriers, companies are able to provide a variety of access options that are not easily available to individual companies building applications for their customers. These options may include frame relay, ISDN, dial-up, and Internet access.

Availability. Most Notes public network server complexes are designed to support nearly 100 percent availability of applications. Disks are mirrored and constantly monitored. And, with the carrier-grade features of Notes R.4.x, automatic connection to a replica database will be available if hardware or software fails.

Management. On-site management at many Notes public networks server complexes is 24×7. The public carrier can use all of the available Notes and network management tools. Some have developed their own tools and techniques to supplement these.

Security. A Notes public network can add to the inherent Notes security by adding network-based security (such as restricted TCP/IP access and connection log-on) and by instituting strict policies and procedures to manage Notes certification and updating of the Notes Name & Address Book.

Customer setup. A Notes public network can offer a set of customer provisioning services and provide the capability of setting up large numbers of customers, whether they are currently Notes users or not, at any location, quickly and efficiently. Customers can be supported throughout the process until the connection is achieved and the application is working.

Customer service. A Notes public network can provide customer care and help desk functions.

Billing services. Public network providers, particularly those that are public utilities, are well known for their ability to collect billing information (long distance, 800 services, 900 services, etc.) and send invoices. These capabilities can be offered to those hosting applications on the Notes public network.

BENEFITS OF NOTES PUBLIC NETWORKS

The primary benefit of using a Notes public network is its support for scaling an interenterprise application from a small number of participants to a large (and perhaps vast) number of participants. Notes itself makes it very easy to build and deploy interenterprise applications. The chief barriers arise when the application is to be extended beyond a small number of customers and a few Notes servers. The resources required to set up and manage the infrastructure, customer access, and customer support can increase significantly as the number of participants increases to hundreds and thousands.

Using a Notes public network can off-load these requirements as they become too burdensome or too specialized for the supplier. The carrier can also provide for the purchase and care of assets (such as servers, backup tape drives, modems, specialized hardware, trunk lines) that the supplier would otherwise invest in, support, and upgrade when necessary.

12

The Significance of Notes Release 4

1996 marked the debut of the fourth version of Notes, officially called Notes Release 4.0, and most of the technical material in this book is based on this version. Notes R.4 is a major upgrade, with a myriad of new features and functions. This chapter is aimed at those who are interested in how Notes Release 4 changes and enhances Notes. Chapter 15 includes a section comparing Notes Release 4 to its nearest E-mail/groupware competitor, Microsoft Exchange.

WHAT NOTES RELEASE 4 DOES

RELEASE 4 DOES NOT CHANGE THE ESSENTIAL NATURE OF NOTES

Throughout this chapter and the next, we will be looking at the new and enhanced features of Notes Release 4.0. Before doing so, it is important to emphasize, particularly for those who are new to Notes, that Notes Release 4.0 is Notes. It does not change the basic nature of Notes, nor does it change the reasons for deploying Notes. Release 4 is only an enhancement—I would argue from a Notes-centric point of view that it is a tremendous enhancement—to Notes. And although current Notes users, developers, and administrators should concentrate on the enhancements that affect them, those who are considering adopting Notes for the first time should look at the essential nature of Notes as a platform for building and deploying information sharing and business process management applications.

This said, there are two key ramifications of Notes Release 4.0. First, it significantly lowers the barriers to wide adoption of Notes; second, it begins to establish an additional definition of Notes.

RELEASE 4 LOWERS BARRIERS TO NOTES ADOPTION

Without changing the essence of Notes, R.4 makes wide adoption of Notes easier, both by those who have some Notes applications established and by those who are newly considering Notes. Release 4 lowers the barriers to adoption in many ways (this is, after all, a significant design goal of the product). The most important include the following.

Increasing the value of Notes applications. Release 4 enables applications that are more graphical, more action-oriented, and better scaled to the enterprise. This allows Notes proponents to build better applications and to make a better case for Notes as an essential element of a company's information infrastructure.

Lowering the frustration levels. Release 4 enhancements significantly lower the frustration levels of users, developers, and administrators and empower them to do better work.

Lowering the cost of ownership. Release 4 supports wider use of Notes by lowering the costs of servers, administration, training, support, development time, and supporting multiple mail systems. In addition, Lotus has significantly lowered the entry price for Notes Mail and Notes Desktop with R.4.

Increasing the contrast between Notes and enhanced messaging systems. Release 4 continues to emphasize the action-oriented, high-return applications that make Notes a strategic investment.

Providing tight integration with and support for the World Wide Web. The InterNotes Web Navigator and Lotus's plans for Notes to fully support HTML, HTTP, Java, and JavaScript allow the mass adoption of Notes without fear that the World Wide Web will undermine this investment.

RELEASE 4 IS THE NEXT MAJOR EVOLUTIONARY STEP FOR NOTES

In an evolutionary sense, each new version of Notes has added a new centricity to the definition of Notes. And in each case, the new centricity has changed significantly the way in which Notes-based companies do business. Interestingly, there have always been some leading-edge Notes companies that are one or two stages ahead of the mainstream of Notes evolution—companies that have been essential in leading the way. In our view, the evolution of Notes is as follows.

- Release 1 was about *LAN-based conferencing.*
- Release 2 was about *information sharing.*
- Release 3 was about *workflow.*
- Release 4 is about *interenterprise applications* and *integration with the World Wide Web.*

With Notes Release 4, companies will change the way in which they interact with each other. We will see many more virtual companies and the dawn of an era of a new business model based on the electronic marketplace. We will also see Notes as a major component of many companies' Internet and World Wide Web strategies.

MAJOR FEATURES OF NOTES RELEASE 4

LOTUS'S GOALS FOR RELEASE 4

Lotus went about designing Notes Release 4 with three major goals in mind:

Decreased cost of ownership. Release 4 is designed to address key cost-of-ownership issues, including user training and support, development, administration and management, and hardware and software scalability.

Enhanced user experience. Release 4 is designed to enhance the user experience by making it easier, by providing more direct access to Notes functions, and by behaving more consistently within its own environment and with other Lotus applications and other platform-specific applications.

Increased programmability. Release 4 is designed to provide increased power and ease of use to all levels of programming, from user-created agents to the enhanced Notes development environment, and from a new BASIC-level scripting environment to increased power and options for the C-level programmer.

Notes Release 4 is not a bunch of features. Rather, it is a set of enhancements designed to meet the R.4 goals and to create a new, easier, and richer experience for each of the constituencies in the Notes community: users, developers, administrators/managers, enterprises, and interenterprises.

At the same time, it is important to highlight some of the breakthrough enhancements of R.4, including:

- Enhanced user interface
- Enhanced electronic mail
- Agent Builder
- Improved replication and location management
- LotusScript
- OLE 2.0 support
- NotesView[1]

ENHANCED USER INTERFACE

Three-Pane Window

Anyone familiar with Notes will immediately recognize several changes in the Notes user interface (see Figure 12.1). The most obvious feature is a three-pane window that provides easier navigation for the user traversing Notes databases. The three-pane window also provides document preview, which allows the user to find and interact with specific information more easily. The multiple-pane feature is also used within document windows to allow the user to find and interact with DocLinks and document hierarchies (i.e., responses).

Folders

The second new user interface element is the Folder, into which users can drag-and-drop documents for later use. The original intention behind the three-pane window and Folders was to provide the user with a mail experience virtually identical to that of

---

[1] NotesView was actually delivered in the Notes Release 3 timeframe. It is included it in the R.4 analysis because of its significant role in meeting R.4 goals.

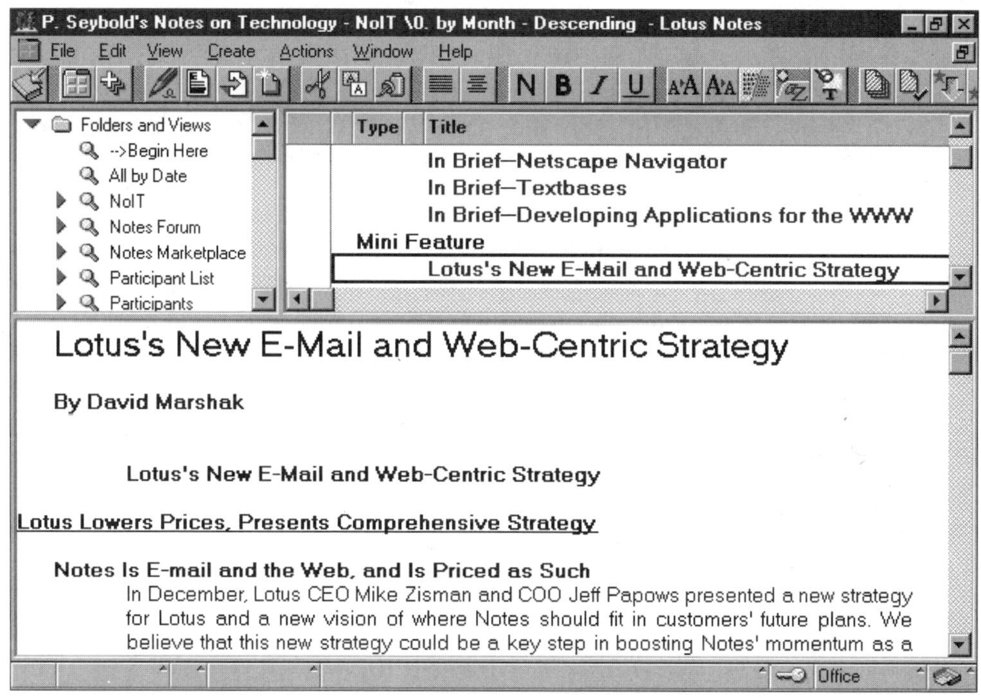

FIGURE 12.1 Notes R.4 user interface. The Notes R.4 user interface provides a three-pane window whose standard configuration shows the Navigator, which presents the View/Folder hierarchy; the specific View selected in the Navigator pane; and a preview of the document selected in the View–Browsing pane.

cc:Mail for Windows. The Notes developers found this user interface so compelling that it has now been extended to all Notes databases, though, because the interface is configurable, it can be made to look very much like the R.3 interface.

Dynamic, Collapsible Sections

A third new element of the user interface is the Collapsible Section. Collapsible Sections let users define expandable sections for easier browsing of large documents. They also let designers define Collapsible Sections in Forms that automatically expand or collapse depending on the reader's user ID. As a document travels through its workflow, it literally expands and collapses, depending on who is reading it and the document state relative to fields in the document.

Navigators

The most exciting new design element is the Navigator. Navigators, which replace the View/Folder hierarchy in the left panel of the standard three-pane window, provide graphical access to Notes data. They allow the user to click on text or a picture and instantly access Notes Views, Notes data, or other applications (see Figure 12.2).

Action Bars and InfoBoxes

Other significant new interface elements include Action Bars and InfoBoxes. Action Bars are nonscrolling regions of Notes Forms and Views that allow instant and continual access to the most appropriate actions that a user could take. InfoBoxes provide users and developers with the ability to manipulate the properties of Notes objects directly without getting lost in the Notes menu structure.

ENHANCED ELECTRONIC MAIL

In addition to its more E-mail-like user interface, R.4 enhances the user's mail experience and capabilities. Notes Mail, which is both a

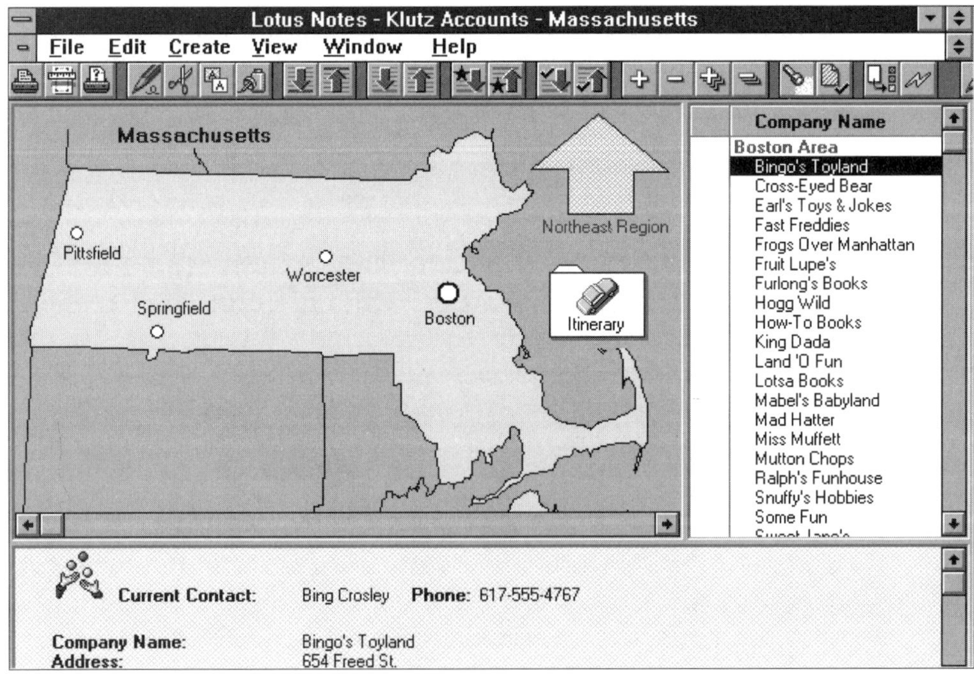

FIGURE 12.2 **Navigator I.** Navigators provide graphical access to Notes data.

separate product and the included mail application in Notes and Notes Desktop clients, has virtually all of the features found in the most advanced mail clients, and some not found in any non-Notes client. Some of the R.4 features include:

- Hierarchical Folders, including default Folders: In Box, Drafts, Sent Mail, Trash, To Do.
- Task management, which allows users to create tasks, assign tasks, prioritize tasks, set due date, and notify of completion. The tasks are stored in the To Do Folder and can be viewed by date, status, person, or priority.
- Automatic archiving of old messages and an archive log View.
- Discussion threading in any folder. This collects and sorts messages and their responses in a hierarchical view.
- Basic serial routing. Enhanced review-cycle workflow is available via the Document Library application template, which provides "canned" workflow whose features include serial review, selection of reviewers from Notes Name & Address Book, collection of responses and edits, definition of allotted time for review, timed reminders to reviewers, and notification by each reviewer or after all reviews.
- Location profile and selective replication (see "Improved Replication and Location Management," below)

Two new delivery options are particularly interesting. The first, For Your Eyes Only, restricts those receiving a message in what they can do: It makes it impossible for them to forward, print, or copy the message to the clipboard. It also limits them to replying only to the sender of the message. This attribute can be placed on any document in any database.

The second delivery option is known as Mood Mail. Mood is a user selection indicating the type of memo being sent. The appearance of the received memo's icon in the selected view depends on which "mood" is selected. Mood choices include:

- Urgent
- Normal
- Personal
- Confidential
- Private
- Thank You

- Good Job
- Joke
- FYI
- Question
- Reminder
- Flame

Of course, Notes Mail has all of the basic Notes R.3 and R.4 features, including the rich-text Notes editor, full-text retrieval, server-based Agents (including some standard Agents, such as "Out of Office"), full and selective replication, and direct access to the World Wide Web via the InterNotes Web Navigator.

AGENT BUILDER

Notes R.4 is designed to put more power in the hands of the user. One of the key features for this is the Agent Builder, which gives users access to Notes's powerful server-based macro capabilities. The Agent Builder walks users through the creation of automated processes. This enables users to build agents that manage their environments and that can be employed by users and developers alike to create automated workflow processes. The Agent Builder is a key element in furthering Notes's original promise as an end-user development environment.

IMPROVED REPLICATION
AND LOCATION MANAGEMENT

One of Notes's greatest differentiators is its support for mobile and remote users. Release 4 enhances the mobile user experience by providing easier tools to manage the replication process, particularly by allowing users' preferences to be automatically tailored for each location from which they access the network. Release 4 also includes technological improvements in the replication process. Two of these that provide a significant benefit to users are field-level replication and server pass-through. *Field-level replication* requires that only fields in a document that have changed be transferred during the replication process. *Server pass-through* lets users dial into a single Notes server and access or replicate databases that reside on multiple Notes servers on the network. Enhanced and easier-to-use selective replication also improves significantly the mobile user's Notes experience.

LOTUSSCRIPT

LotusScript is Lotus's Visual Basic-like language, which Lotus is including in virtually all of its applications. The availability of LotusScript in Notes R.4 provides a significant increase in power and productivity for the Notes developer. Along with other new R.4 design features, such as Navigators, it also reduces the need for Notes developers to use external tools or the Notes API to build complex Notes applications.

OLE 2.0 SUPPORT

Lotus has long been an ardent proponent of object linking and embedding (OLE). The company embraces the OLE container/server model and sees Notes as the preeminent OLE container. Notes R.3 makes significant use of OLE, including the ability to launch OLE objects seamlessly from Notes documents (without the user even having to see the Notes document). Release 3 also introduced Notes Field eXchange (Notes/FX), which extends OLE to allow field-level data exchange between Notes databases and embedded OLE applications.

Lotus has furthered its commitment to OLE by providing wide support for OLE 2.0 in Notes R.4. This includes implementing the three major OLE 2.0 features: drag-and-drop, visual editing (a.k.a. in-place editing), and OLE automation.

In addition, R.4 adopts the standard OLE user interface components, such as Paste Special dialog, Insert Object dialog, Edit Links, Convert, and others. Release 4 also makes use of the optimized OLE 2.0 storage model.

Finally, R.4 OLE support allows any OLE application to be launched directly from the Notes desktop. This lets Notes become the home environment (e.g., workflow manager and document library) for users of Notes and other applications.

NOTESVIEW BRINGS SYSTEMS MANAGEMENT TO NOTES

NotesView, which first shipped with Notes R.3, is a key element in making Notes R.4 an industrial-strength, enterprise-level platform for application development and deployment. NotesView, which is built on Hewlett-Packard's OpenView, the industry-leading management platform, and the industry-standard Simple Network Management Protocol (SNMP) enables Notes administrators to manage their Notes networks as they grow. NotesView provides a real-time graphical view of the status of the Notes network and Notes servers, as well as providing alerts and alarms when conditions require them.

IMPROVED CROSS-PLATFORM SUPPORT

In addition to its new features, R.4 will extend some of its previous capabilities to other platforms where they were lacking, with the goal of providing all Notes functionalities on all Notes platforms. For example, with R.4, Macintosh clients gain the following:

- Local full-text search
- Background replication
- ODBC drivers
- Notes API

Equally important is Notes's support of platform-specific features, such as drag-and-drop on Windows 95 and launching within OS/2 Workplace Shell.

CONCLUSION: NOTES RELEASE 4 RAISES THE BAR

Call it what you want—groupware, workgroup computing, or computer-supported cooperative work—in 1995, Lotus had a wide lead in providing the platform for strategic applications that require communications, collaboration, and coordination among groups and individuals. As many predicted, the year 1996 may indeed prove to have been a watershed, in which Notes was joined by other products in the space, creating severe competition for Lotus and wider choices for customers.

But there is another possibility. With Notes Release 4, Lotus has raised the bar, giving its challengers a much more difficult task. The enhancements of R.4 emphasize the maturity and power of Notes by improving those areas in which the competition currently has only a first-generation product. These areas include:

- Enhanced support for mobile users, with the addition of replication and location management, field-level replication, server pass-through, improved selective replication, etc.
- Increased action and workflow orientation, with Action Bars and user-defined agents

- Improved programmability, from the Agent Builder to Lotus-Script to an increased choice of APIs
- Interenterprise capabilities, with Notes public networks and InterNotes providing platforms for intercorporate applications and electronic marketplaces

NOTES RELEASE 4 IN DEPTH

A more in-depth view of Notes Release 4 is provided in Chapter 13. We recommend particularly "Release 4 for the User," which gives a good sense of how the new release affects what users see and the way they work.

13

Notes Release 4 in Depth

The best way to look at the features and functions of Notes Release 4 is to see how they affect each of the key Notes constituencies:

- Users
- Developers
- Administrators/managers
- Notes enterprises

RELEASE 4 FOR THE USER

The R.4 user interface (UI), which is based partially on cc:Mail for Windows, is designed to increase user access to Notes features and decrease organizational costs of training and support. The R.4 UI enhances user experience in five areas, which could be called the five "-tions" of R.4 for the user. They are:

1. Navigation
2. Manipulation
3. Action

4. Location

5. Integration (with the World Wide Web)

NAVIGATION

The Notes R.4 UI is designed to present more information to the user in a less complex way. This lets the user navigate through information without continually switching contexts among Views, View hierarchies, and documents. User navigation enhancements include:

- Three-pane window
- Navigators
- HotSpots
- Searching
- Linking
- Performance

Three-Pane Window

The key new navigation feature is the three-pane window. The three-pane window is a single operating system (Windows, Macintosh, OS/2, Motif) window that is divided into three panes (at any time, one, two, or three panes may be visible to the user). The panes may have multiple layouts. A standard configuration for the panes includes the Navigation pane, the Folder/View–Browsing pane, and the Document pane (see Figure 12.1).

Navigation Pane. The Navigation pane provides a hierarchical list of the components of the Notes database. The component classes include:

- Folders and Views
- Agents
- Design

Each component class can be viewed collapsed or expanded to show its hierarchy. For example, the Folders and Views class expands to the list of Folders and Views, including public and private; the Agents class shows the agents that can be run; and the Design class expands to show the database's design elements, including Views, Forms, Agents, and others.

Folder/View–Browsing Pane. If the user clicks on one of the Folders or Views in the Navigation pane, the Folder/View–Browsing

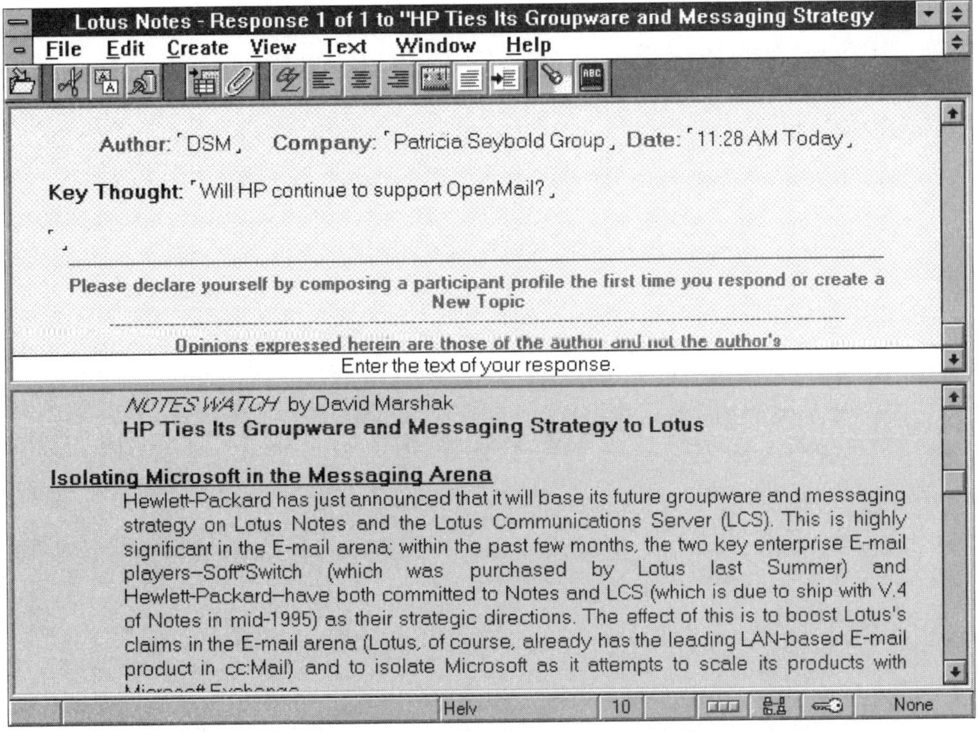

FIGURE 13.1   **Notes R.4 user interface option for responses.** As they create their response, users can preview the document to which they are replying.

pane shows the Folder/View itself, including categories and documents. As the user changes the selected Folder/View in the Navigation pane, the Folder/View–Browsing pane changes automatically as well. In this pane, the user can double-click on a document and open it up into a separate window.

Document Pane. The Document pane appears if the user desires. It is generally empty if the user is selecting an item in the Navigation pane, except when a Navigator HotSpot is designed to retrieve a document. When the user clicks on a document in the Folder/View–Browsing pane, the document is presented in the Document pane. The user can work on the document in this pane or in its own window by double-clicking on it in the Folder/View–Browsing pane. As the user moves through a View in the Folder/View–Browsing pane (using the mouse, cursor arrows, SmartIcons, or short-cut keys), the documents in the Document pane change to reflect the selection. This lets users see quickly if the selected document is the one they want.

Other Uses of the Three-Pane Window. The three-pane window also lets the user preview the parent document when creating a response, as shown in Figure 13.1, and preview a DocLink before opening the linked document in a new window, as shown in Figure 13.2. In these cases, the user sees only two panes.

Navigators

Perhaps the most exciting and certainly the "sexiest" feature of Notes R.4 is the Navigator. A Navigator is a graphical interface element that can appear in the Navigation pane of the R.4 user interface (see Figures 12.2 and 13.3). Navigators can contain text, graphics, and images that, when clicked on, call other Notes functions. These functions can display a different View hierarchy, display a different document, run an agent, run a LotusScript process, or launch an external application.

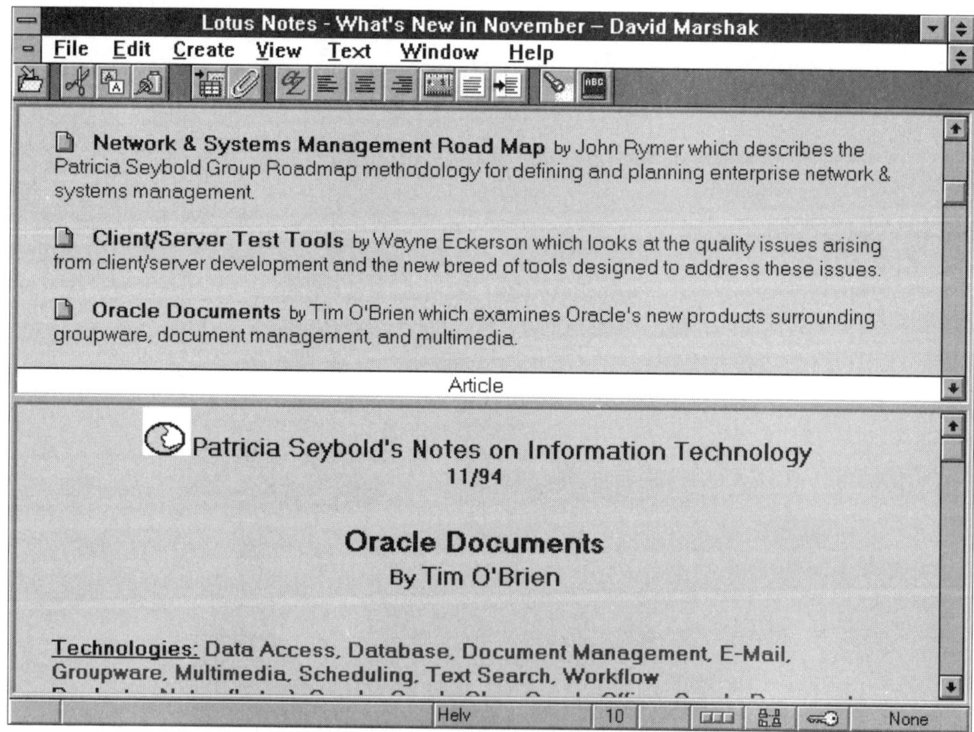

FIGURE 13.2 **Previewing a DocLink.** The user can preview the linked document before opening it.

Navigators let developers deliver a highly graphical and direct navigation experience to users. Examples include using maps (see Figure 12.2) and flow charts (see Figure 13.3).

HotSpots

With R.4, developers can assign HotSpots in any rich-text field or Navigator. HotSpots let a graphic or text section be clicked on. Once clicked on, the HotSpot can take the user to another Notes document, View, or database, or launch an Agent or external application. This capability, in the hands of good developers, will let users, for example, navigate through a sales database by clicking on pictures of territories, products, or salespeople.

Searching

Release 4 enhances the users' ability to employ the Notes full-text searching capabilities. Key improvements include an improved Query Builder and the ability to search attachments and OLE objects in Notes documents.

The new Query Builder provides the consistent interface for Notes searching and agent building. (See "Agent Builder," below.) The

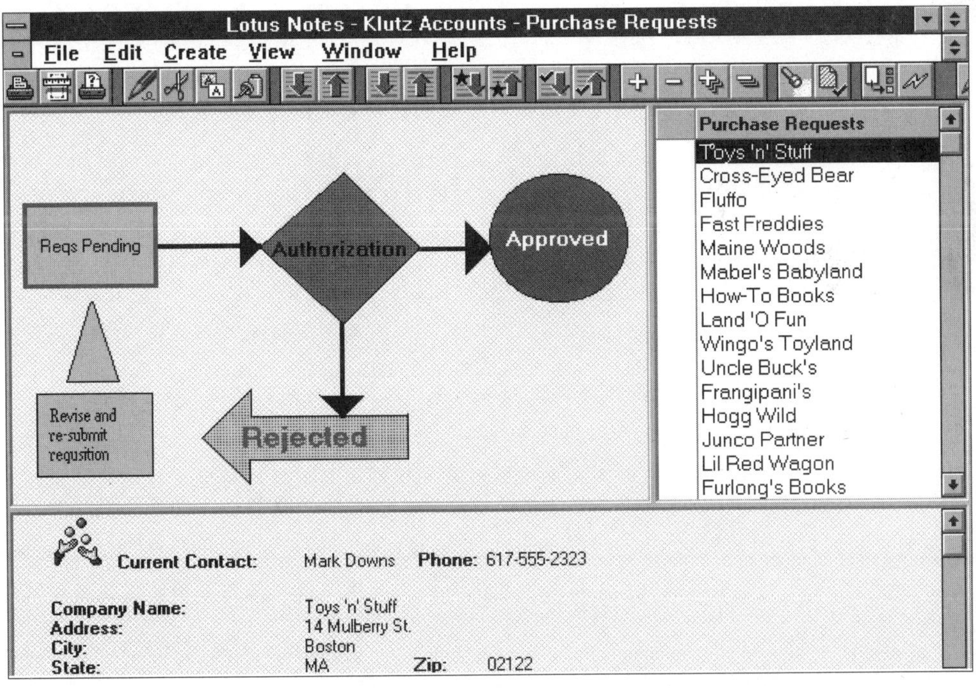

FIGURE 13.3 **Navigator II.** This Navigator lets the user walk graphically through a workflow.

Query Builder gives the user more direct access to the Search functions. The Query Builder allows the combination of searching by Form and also using Boolean searches, which could not be done under R.3. The user can now edit or add conditions to a given query and does not need to have designer access to the database to save the query. Once a query is saved, it can be run against the whole database or against any View or Folder.

Linking

Release 4 provides enhanced linking in two areas. First, users can now link to Notes databases as well as to documents in a database. When users click on a DBLink in a Notes document, they are taken to the default entry point for the database. This could be the last View that the user had open, the Policy Document, or another Notes document. The entry point could also be an external application, which is launched automatically when that database is opened.

The second linking enhancement comes from R.4 OLE Link Server, which lets OLE container applications make DocLinks and DBLinks to Notes documents and databases. This means that a Notes document or database can be linked into an OLE-compliant word processing document, spreadsheet, or mail message. The OLE Link Server also lets Notes and other OLE applications create links to objects that reside in Notes documents.

Performance

It is interesting to list performance as a navigation issue; it could be listed in the manipulation or action categories just as appropriately. The key point is that there are specific R.4 performance enhancements designed to let users find information more quickly, manipulate it, and take action on it, all without the frustration of waiting for documents or Views to appear.

For example, Notes is now designed to fetch the first page of a document while it is retrieving the rest. The user can begin working while the rest of a large document is still loading.

Another example is the user's ability when in Mail (or in any application that accesses the Name & Address Book) to begin typing a recipient's name and have the application fill in the rest once the name becomes unique. This type-ahead addressing, found in most E-mail packages, can run across one or more Notes Name & Address Books. Once the name has been found, it can be dragged and dropped to the To:, cc:, and bcc: areas.

Lotus is working on other performance enhancements in such areas as faster lookup between Notes databases and between Notes and SQL databases, and faster opening of large Views.

MANIPULATION

Notes R.4 gives users much more direct and powerful manipulation of the environment. There is less traversing of the Notes menu structure and less pressure on the user to change work habits to match specific Notes paradigms. Release 4 also provides better ways to manipulate items, such as text and tables, within Notes documents.

Key enhancements to the users' ability to manipulate the Notes environment include:

- Improved View manipulation
- Folders
- InfoBoxes
- Context-sensitive SmartIcons
- Improved document/text manipulation
- Support for OLE 2.0

Manipulating Views

In previous versions of Notes, if users did not find a View that matched their needs, they had three options: Live with the current set of Views, ask a designer to create a new View, or create a Private View. Creating a Private View, though not particularly difficult, required the user to *leave the user role and conceptually become a developer.* This last choice required a leap that most users refused to make. We can call this *Design_Menu_Phobia.*

With R.4, users have a fourth option: Modify an existing View on the fly, with little or no effort and without having to leave the user role. On-the-fly View capabilities now available to users include:

Resizing columns. Users can drag the sides of columns to increase or decrease their size.

Re-sorting columns. Users can sort or re-sort columns by double-clicking on the column heading.

Any revised View that the user creates on the fly can then be saved as a new Private View, or, if the user has designer access to the database, a new Public View.

Folders

Release 4 presents users with a new paradigm, the Folder, for manipulating Notes documents. Folders have their origins in E-mail interfaces and are frequently used for such constructs as Inbox, Outbox, Drafts, and the like. (In fact, the Notes R.4 Mail template includes these Folders.)

Though they seem similar, Folders are quite different from Views. What appears in a View is determined by a formula (any document matching the formula will show up), but items must be specifically placed into Folders. This can be done by users, who can drag-and-drop a document from a View or another Folder into a Folder, or by an Agent that can place items into Folders based on predefined conditions. A good example of the latter is an Agent that takes any incoming mail addressed to the "Editorial" list and places it in my Editorial Folder.

In Notes, items may appear in more than one Folder and in Folders and Views simultaneously. Folders can be nested; that is, there can be a Folder hierarchy. Users may create Shared or Personal Folders. And Folders, of course, replicate. They can be included in selective replication options.

Folders, like Views, are bound to a specific database. We would like to see a sort of personal workspace that is independent of a specific Notes database, where items could be dragged into their Folders. For this author, the Folders might be labeled: "Do today," "Make calls about," "See Patty about," and so forth.

We believe that, for current Notes users, the View/Folder paradigm may cause some confusion. The confusion will be greatest when the user has a lot of experience with Notes but does not understand its structure very well. The basic tenet to remember is: *Formulae put documents into Views; people (or their Agents) put documents into Folders.*

InfoBoxes

The R.4 user interface has also been improved to allow more direct manipulation of Notes elements. The most significant user interface enhancement for direct manipulation is the InfoBox (an element of all new Lotus applications), which is a context-sensitive, modeless control for the attributes of Notes objects. For example, InfoBoxes let the user easily change text properties without going through the Notes menu structure. InfoBoxes can be made to float over the rest of the Notes applications, or they can be minimized for quick access. (For pictures and an in-depth look at InfoBoxes, see "R.4 for the Developer 2: Enhanced Productivity," below).

Context Sensitivity

Lotus provides two interesting types of context sensitivity in R.4. One is object specific; the other, database specific.

An example of object-specific context sensitivity is that when users touch (i.e., edit) rich text, they get:

- A text menu
- A set of SmartIcons that are totally optimized for rich-text editing
- A right-mouse menu that chooses the highest-use items from the context menu
- An InfoBox context change for the selected object

Likewise, when users "touch" a Folder, they get a Folder menu, a Folder set of SmartIcons, etc.

Database-specific actions are actions that the designer can define per View, per Folder, and per Form. For example, Action Bars are database specific and change within the database when the actions available to the user change.

The key is that database-specific actions are an inherent part of the database. They replicate with the database and participate in the inheritance hierarchy.

Document/Text Manipulation

Release 4 also improves significantly the way users can manipulate documents and text. These enhancements include the following:

Named Styles. Named Styles now include font information in addition to paragraph properties. Named Styles appear in the Smart Status bar at the bottom of the Notes screen. The user can cycle through the common styles using the F11 key.

Quick Bullets. Quick Bullets is a new paragraph attribute that automatically formats bulleted lists. R.4 also supports numbered lists.

Permanent Pen. Permanent Pen refers to a user's ability to designate a specific type style (font, size, color) in which to do a series of edits. As users move through a document, they do not have to constantly reselect a particular font or color to show their edits.

This saves the user a lot of time and makes it easier for the author to be sure that all edits show up. A group might, as a matter of policy, consistently assign a given Pen to each member so that comments are instantly recognizable.

Table manipulation. Notes R.4 adds several enhancements to the user's ability to manipulate tables within documents. These improvements include easier table creation, the ability to select rows and columns, the ability to apply properties to tables, and the ability to have zero pad around cells.

OLE 2.0

OLE 2.0 drag-and-drop and in-place editing provide the user with better manipulation and a more consistent UI with other Windows and Windows 95 applications.

In the Notes context, OLE drag-and-drop can be used in the following ways:

- To drag a Notes document into a folder.
- To drag objects from other applications into a Notes document.
- To drop OLE objects or files into Notes Views to create simple object containers, that is, to create a document library application. Since Notes supports the OLE property sets, the Document Summary information properties can be automatically mapped to Notes Fields.

In-place editing, also called "OLE editing" and "visual editing," lets embedded documents—in Notes or any other container—be edited without opening another window in which the OLE server application runs. OLE objects continue to be part of the container compound document. OLE 2.0 also specifies the way the object's user interface (menus and tools palettes) merges with the container UI. This is designed to give the user a seamless editing environment with a minimum of window "context shock."

ACTION

Notes R.3 changed the Notes model from one of searching for documents to an action-oriented, workflow-oriented paradigm. Applications that previously required users to traverse Notes Views, open documents, compose responses (i.e., status reports), and forward messages were replaced by applications that present the user with information, allow the user to click on a button to change the status, and then automatically route the document to the next person who needs to see it. We recently saw a complex R.3 workflow application in which only one document is composed by a user. The rest is done via buttons, prompts to the user, and Macros.

Notes R.4 extends the workflow and action orientation of R.3 in a number of ways. From the user's perspective, three key new elements have been introduced: the Action Bar, the Agent Builder, and Tasks.

Action Bar

The Action Bar is a nonscrolling area of a Notes Form or View that presents the user with the logical Action options (see Figure 13.4). The Action Bar is context sensitive, so only those Actions that are possible are presented to the user.

The Action Bar can present the user with Standard and Custom Actions. Standard Actions are those that are common to all

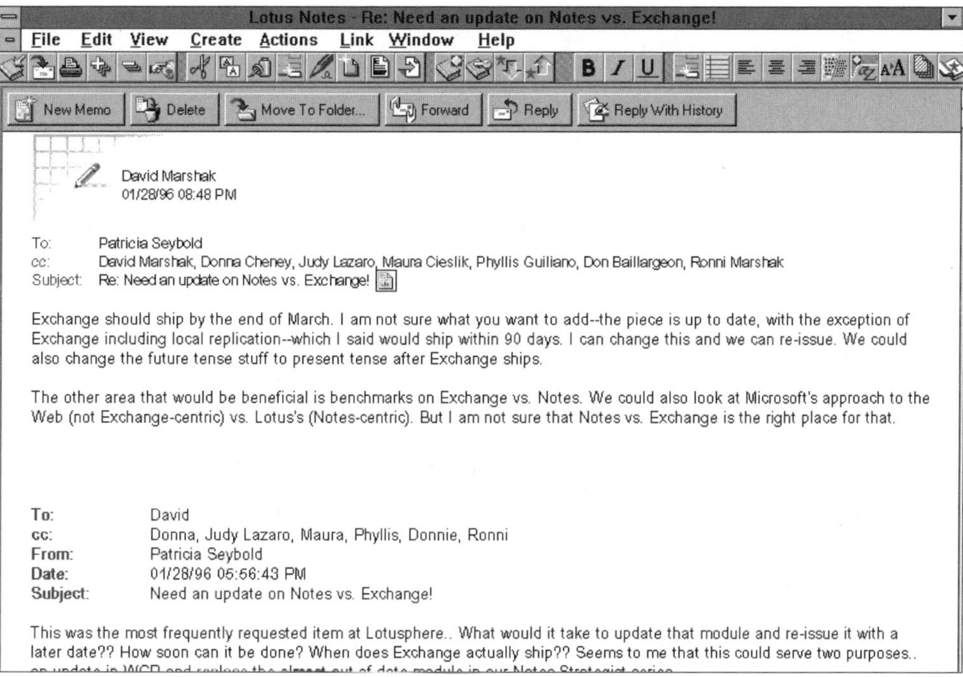

FIGURE 13.4 Notes Action Bar. The Action Bar above the document lets the user create a new memo, delete the current document, move it to a folder, reply to it, or reply to it with its history, with a single click. As the user scrolls through the document, the Action Bar remains in place.

applications—open, close, print, forward, and so on; Custom Actions are defined by the developer. Actions can range from simple tasks (such as closing a document) to functions that change the value of a field (such as Approve or Reject in a status field), to launching complex Agents or LotusScripts to bringing up external applications.

Action Bars are controlled by the database developer, who can create Custom Actions and designate which Standard Action appears in which context. Actions can also appear on the File menu, and they can remain available to the user when an OLE object is launched. (For more on Actions and Action Bars, see "R.4 for the Developer 1: Increased Programmability," below.)

Agent Builder

The Agent Builder extends users' ability to create their own action-oriented environments. In Release 3, users had to use the Notes Macro language, a daunting task even for many developers. In addition, users had to have Designer access to a database to create an Agent. The R.4 Agent Builder lets users and designers easily create Agents that can automatically perform designated tasks on a time- or event-driven basis. Agents can be used for managing personal information or for creating automatic workflows that can be based on a specific value or status of a given business process. Notes Agents (previously called Macros) are particularly powerful, because they can run automatically on the server or on the workstation when the user is disconnected from the network.

The Agent Builder provides a simple interface, shown in Figure 13.5, that enables the creation of Agents based on the user's answers to three questions:

1. When should this Agent act?
2. On which documents should this Agent act?
3. What should this Agent do?

The first question—When should this Agent act?—defines the trigger that launches the Agent at any of the following times:

- When the user makes a menu choice (launched manually from the Actions Menu or Agent List)
- If new mail has arrived
- If documents have been created or modified in the database
- If documents have been pasted in the database

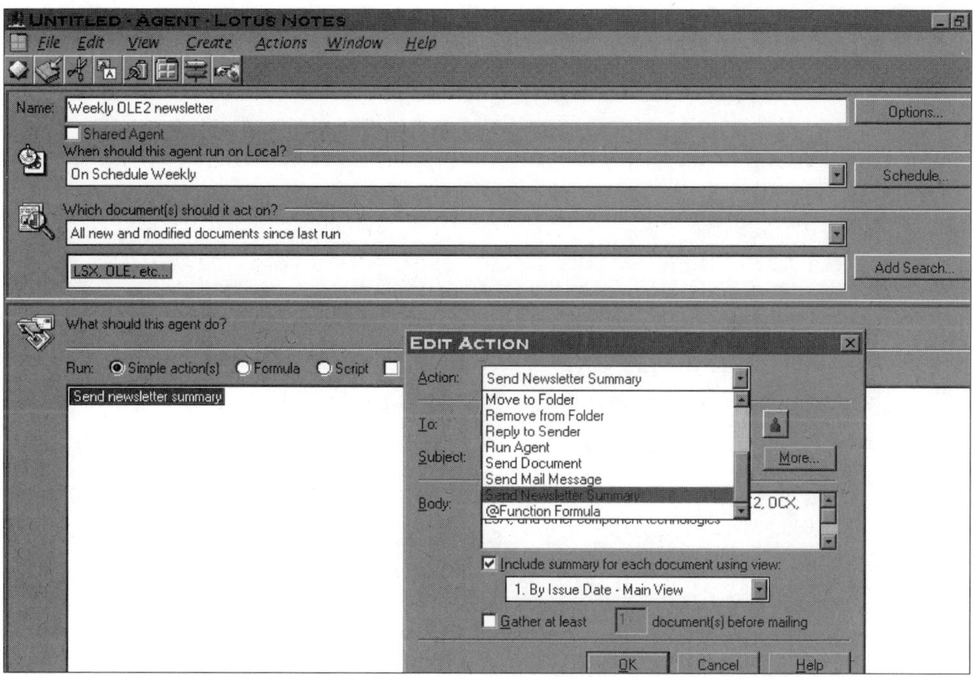

FIGURE 13.5 **Notes R.4 Agent Builder.** The Agent Builder lets
the user define the when, which, and what that make up the intelligence of the Agent.

- On a scheduled basis:
  Hourly (actually, every 30 minutes)
  Daily
  Weekly
  Monthly

The second question—On which documents should this Agent
act?—defines the search and selection criteria for the documents to
be acted upon. The selection can be expressed as a full-text query via
the Query Builder interface (the Agent Builder actually shares code
with the Query Builder) or via a set of predefined controls, including:

- All the documents in the database
- All new or modified documents since the Agent was last run
- All unread documents in View
- All documents in View

- Run once (@Commands may be used)
- Selected documents—this can be selected interactively by the user by formula:

  Search by date—e.g., date created, date modified, or is older than

  Search by author

  Search by Field, where the user is presented with a list of fields in the database and can enter simple or complex search criteria

The database must be full-text indexed for the most efficient use of some of the search capabilities. Other selections can be done directly from field values or through brute-force search of nonindexed documents.

The third question—What should this Agent do?—defines the action the Agent should take upon finding documents that match the search criteria. The Actions can be expressed in one of three ways:

- @Function formula
- LotusScript
- Sequence of one or more canned Actions

Although the first two methods are appropriate for the application developer, the third provides a lot of power to the user as well. The set of canned Actions includes:

- Copy documents to database
- Copy/move to Folder
- Delete from database
- Remove from Folder
- Mark document read/unread
- Modify Field
- Modify Field by Form
- Run another Agent
- Reply to sender
- Send mail
- Send document
- Send newsletter summary
- @Function formula

Significant among these actions are "Run another Agent," which enables the nesting of Agents into a complex workflow, and "Send newsletter summary." The latter takes all the documents in a database that match the criteria, and, in a single mail message, notifies the user of their arrival, summarizes each document using View information, and presents a DocLink back to the document.

Notes R.3 allowed only users with Designer access to a given database to create Macros for that database. There was no Private Agent equivalent to Private Views. With R.4, anyone can create Private Agents (though an administrator can grant or rescind this right on a per-database basis. See the discussion of the Agent Manager in the section "Release 4 for the Administrator/Manager," below).

This, of course, raises the question of security. Release 4, through the Agent Manager, handles Agent security in the following way. All Agents are signed by their owner, using their Notes ID certificate, and each Agent is bound to a specific user. Each runs against any database or accesses any server using the access rights of its owner. For example, if the owner has Author rights, the Agent can create new documents; if the owner has Editor rights, the Agent can modify documents; if the owner has Reader rights, the Agent can copy or send documents. If the reader does not have access rights, the Agent cannot access the database.

The Agent Builder is one of the key elements that make Notes R.4 a platform for action-oriented applications. At the same time, it begins to fulfill the early promise of Notes to be an environment that end users can control and mold to their needs.

Tasks

The ability to compose and assign workflow-related Tasks is another new feature in R.4. The Task Form, along with the associated Task Folder, gives users an organized way of assigning and monitoring tasks with other users. Tasks are launched by default from Notes Mail, although the Task Folder and Task Form can be added to any Notes application.

A Task is launched when Delegator (the user assigning a Task to another individual) composes a Task document and assigns to Assignee (the user to whom the Delegator assigns the task). To do this, the Delegator completes the Task Form, shown in Figure 13.6.

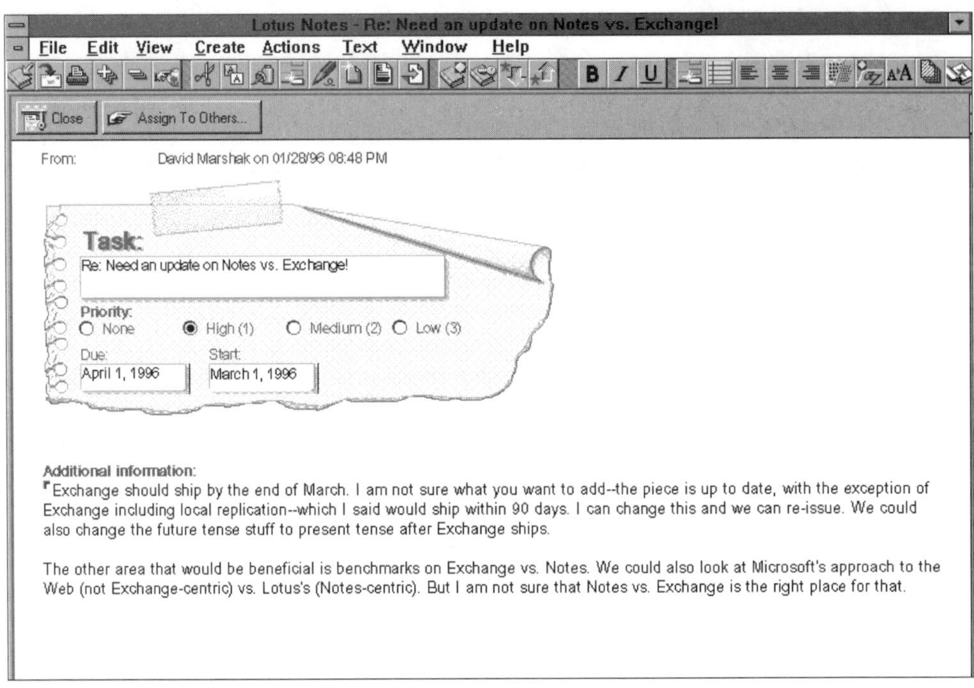

FIGURE 13.6 **Assigning a Task.** Users can assign Tasks to themselves or to others.

The Fields of the Task Form are as follows:

From is the Delegator's name.

Assign to is the Assignee's name. Note that Delegators can assign themselves to tasks, in which case no mail is sent; all workflow occurs within the Delegator's mail file.

cc: is the name(s) of recipient(s) to whom the memo is to be courtesy copied.

Task Title is the subject of the memo.

Due Date is the date by which the Task is to be completed.

Urgent determines whether or not the Task is high priority. Options are Yes and No.

Status is the state of the Task. New Tasks yet to be assigned have a status of New.

Tasks can have the following status classifications:

New—a newly created Task document yet to be assigned

Pending Acceptance—an assigned Task for which the assigned person has not yet accepted responsibility

Pending Completion—a Task accepted by the assigned person, but not yet completed

Completed—a Task completed

Completion Delayed—a Task that, for whatever reason, the assigned person has delayed completion

Rejected—a Task for which the assigned person decided not to accept responsibility

Trashed—a Task the originator decided to "deactivate"

Tasks can be viewed within the Task Folder by Status, Priority, Due Date, etc. Agents can also be created to notify individuals automatically of Status changes, upcoming Due Dates, or late Tasks.

LOCATION

The final area of enhancement to the user experience is perhaps the best thought out of all the R.4 improvements. While Notes has, from the beginning, provided the best support of any product for the mobile user, R.4 takes the support several steps further. With the R.4 enhancements, Notes mobile users are getting very close to true location independence.

The key R.4 features that support the mobile user include:

- Field-level replication
- Server pass-through
- Replication manager
- Location management
- Stacked replicas interface

The first feature is a significant technical breakthrough that has a major effect on the resources required for all Notes replication. The others specifically address the issue of reducing the complexity for the mobile user.

Field-Level Replication

Field-level replication is the major technical breakthrough of Notes R.4. With early versions of Notes, if any part of a document changed, the whole document had to be replicated to all sites and users. As Notes documents become larger and larger—many that contain embedded applications, attachments, graphics, images, audio, or video may be multimegabytes in size—changes in documents have severe implications in replication time, bandwidth, and cost. In our own publications, we have to think twice before making a minor change to a document because the result is likely to be one or many megabytes being transferred to hundreds of locations, many of them overseas. And remote users can come to dread (and, in fact, avoid) replicating a database with large documents that may have to be transferred more than once.

Field-level replication enables only the Field that has changed to be transferred from one copy of the database to another. Although this could be a large Field, it may very well be a small field—for example, a status Field in a document that contains drawings, images, or embedded applications. What may have taken many minutes or even hours to replicate before may now take seconds.

Field-level replication will affect the design of applications. For example, a single Field should not contain more than one large object. If one large object does change, the others do not have to be transferred.

For remote users, field-level replication will reduce replication time and costs and, perhaps more important, will let them participate in applications when before R.4 they could not.

Server Pass-Through

Under R.3, remote users could replicate only databases that were on the server into which they had dialed. Although some companies enabled their remote users to dial directly into the LAN, thus giving them access to all servers, many remote users had to dial into multiple servers to replicate their full set of Notes databases.

Release 4 introduces server pass-through, which lets users dial into a single server and access or replicate databases that reside on any server on the same LAN or WAN as the access server. This greatly reduces complexity for the user.

Replication Manager

The key addition for the remote and mobile user is the R.4 Replication Manager. The Replication Manager provides an easy interface to virtually all replication functions. Compared to R.3, R.4 makes it much easier for the user to create a replica and particularly to define selective replication. Both are now point-and-click, with selective replication on Views and Folders now supported. The user can easily define which databases to replicate (see Figure 13.7) and which documents to receive in full and which to have truncated (see Figure 13.8). Another enhancement in this area is the ability for the user to request the full version of any individual documents that have been truncated due to the selective replication rules.

Other functions controlled through the Replication Manager include the replication schedule, exchange of unread marks (by database), and the order of replication. The last function allows the most important databases to be designated to replicate first, in case users have to abort replication during the process—for example, if they have to catch a plane, have reached checkout time, or have to get to a meeting.

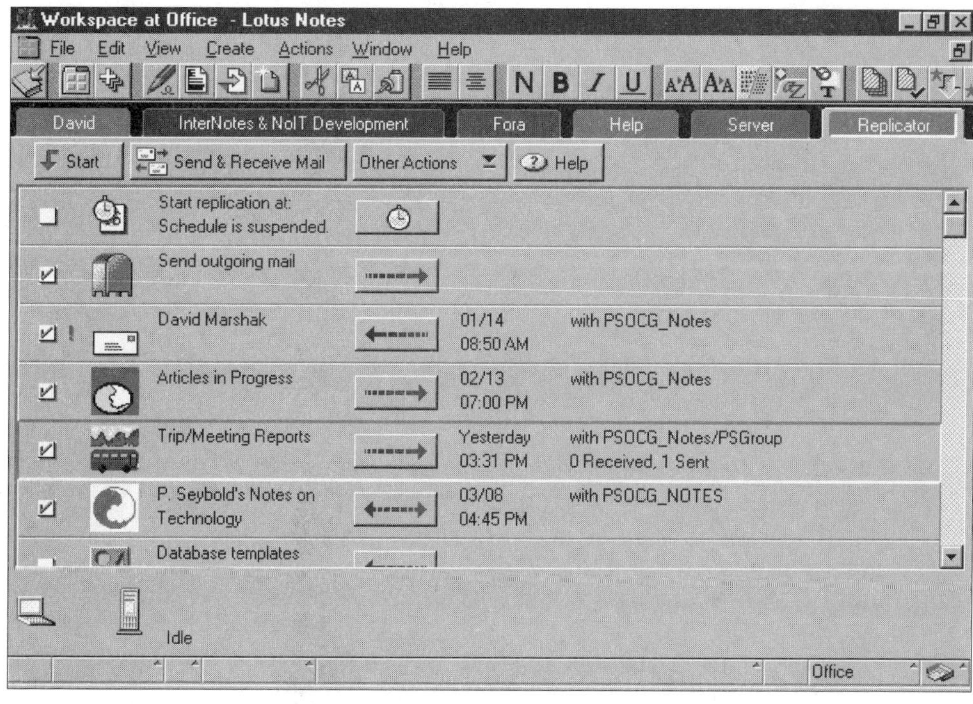

FIGURE 13.7 Notes R.4 Replication Tab. The Replication Tab allows easier access to replication options for each location.

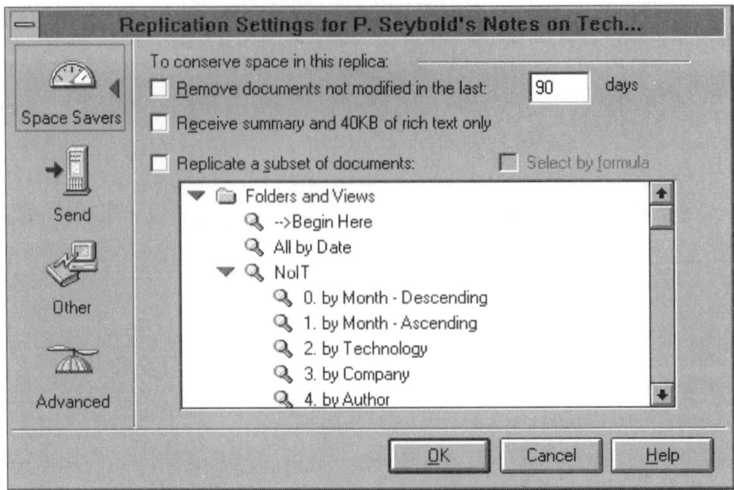

FIGURE 13.8 **Notes R.4 Selective Replication Interface.** Notes R.4 allows the user to easily select which parts of databases are to be replicated.

Location Management

In addition to improved management of the replication process, R.4 adds the concept of named locations. This lets the mobile user designate a set of locations (Home, Office, Hotel, Hotel_Dial_9, Hotel_Dial_8, Plane, etc.). For each location, the user establishes a set of parameters, including:

- Port information
- Phone information
- Replication schedule
- Default home and dial-in server

In addition, virtually any attribute under the control of the Replication Manager can be set by location. This includes:

- Which databases to replicate
- Order of database replication
- Selective replication rules (e.g., truncation)
- Special dialing rules per location

Stacked Replicas Interface

The final enhancement for mobile users is the Stacked Replicas interface, a new interface model for accessing multiple replicas

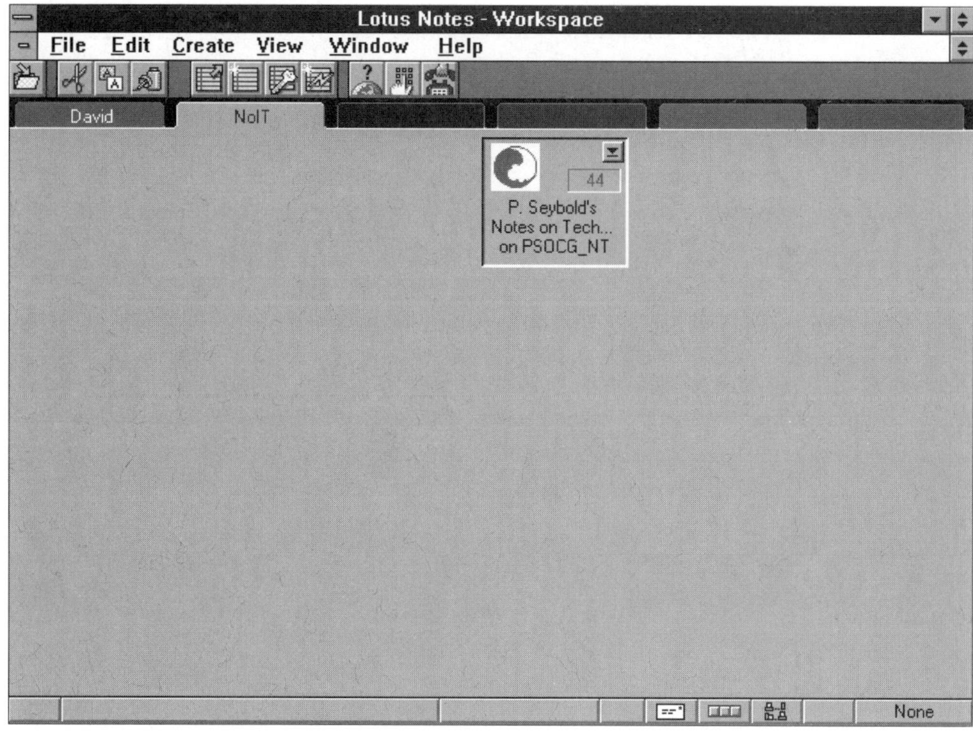

FIGURE 13.9   **Stacked Replicas.** This icon shows that there are other replicas of this database that the user accesses.

of the same database. Most mobile users, particularly those who are on occasion fully connected to the network, have at least two different icons that represent the two replica copies of the same databases (including their mail database). Technically, this makes sense, because one or more of the database copies reside on servers on the LAN, while another is kept locally. However, this can easily lead to "icon confusion," where two, three, or more identical icons appear on the user's desktop, and the user is never quite sure which is the correct one to use.

Release 4 introduces the concept of Stacked Replicas, where each replica of a given database is shown in a single icon that defaults to the most likely database to be accessed: a server version, if on the LAN; otherwise, the local version (see Figure 13.9). Users no longer have to do a setup to change locations; they can now designate their location via the location button on the Smart Status bar. The stacked replica model includes a drop-down interface to show the other locations and lets the user select any copy

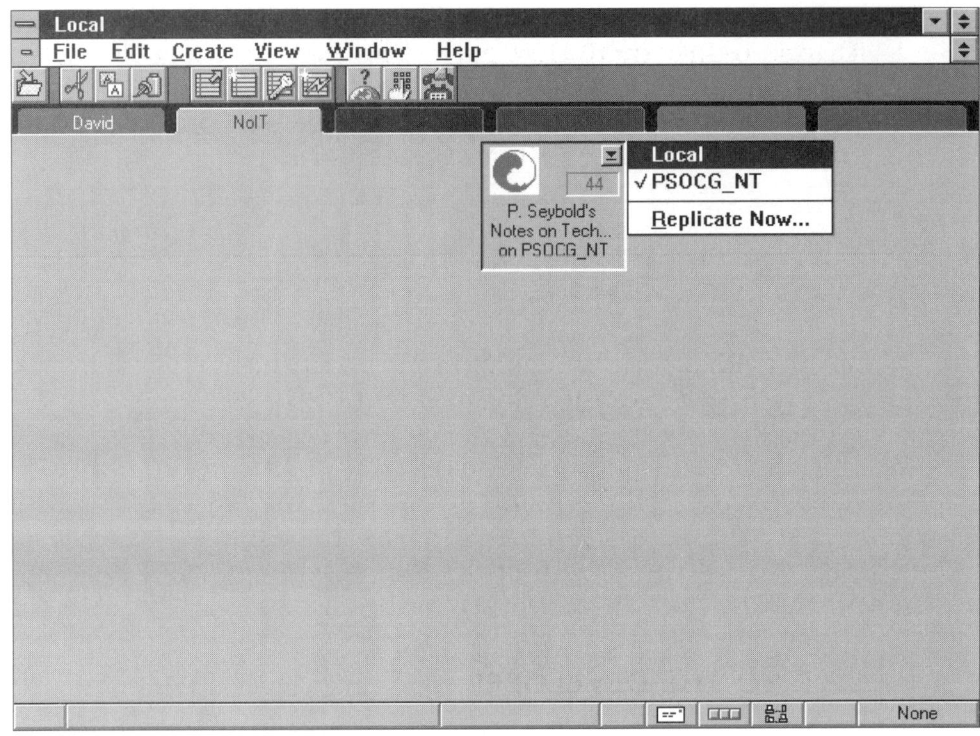

FIGURE 13.10   **Stacked Replicas revealed.** The icon now shows a
local replica and one on the PSOCG_NT server.

desired, as well as initiate replication directly from the icon (see
Figure 13.10).

Most importantly, Notes remembers which replica the user
likes to use most at each location. So, when the user "switches location" via the Status Bar, all the correct replicas bubble to the top
of the stack. The net effect is that users don't even have to think
about it. For example, when a user is at the home office, the
"OurOffice" replica is on top. The user just double-clicks to open.
When the user is on an airplane, the "MyLaptop" replica is on top.
Again, the user just double-clicks. When a user goes to the Los Angeles office, for example, the "LAServer" replica surfaces.

INTEGRATION WITH THE WORLD WIDE WEB

The InterNotes Web Navigator, which ships as part of all Notes R.4
clients, enables users to access HTML pages directly on the World
Wide Web. Users interact with the InterNotes Web Navigator just

as they would with any other Web browser: They can click on a URL and go directly to that page, they can create bookmarks, they can navigate Forward and Back, etc. In addition, they have access to Notes features such as Views and Agents. The InterNotes Web Navigator is discussed fully in Chapter 14.

RELEASE 4 FOR THE DEVELOPER 1: INCREASED PROGRAMMABILITY

Notes provides a rich development environment whose functionality has been extended by other Lotus products and products from third-party vendors. Release 4.0 further expands the power of the Notes development environment. At the same time, R.4 provides enhanced development tools designed to increase developer productivity. This section discusses the *programmability* enhancements, and the next section discusses the *productivity* enhancements.

POWER TO THE DEVELOPER

Key goals for R.4 are to enhance the programmability within the Notes development environment and increase the developer's ability to program Notes from outside the environment.

R.4 increases the developer's power by delivering:

- Enhanced Notes development functions
- Navigators
- Support for OLE 2.0
- Actions and Action Bars
- API enhancements
- LotusScript

ENHANCED NOTES DEVELOPMENT FUNCTIONS

Although much of the discussion of the R.4 impact on the developer centers on the introduction of LotusScript, Lotus has done much to increase the power of the existing Notes development environment. The R.4 enhancements fall into the following categories:

- Improved @Functions
- HotSpots

- Layout Regions
- View presentation
- Text/document control

Improved @Functions

Notes R.4 contains a large number of new @Functions, including @HideWhen, @Picklist, and GURL.

HotSpots

A number of R.4 enhancements (most notable are HotSpots and Navigators) are designed to provide a more graphical environment for the user. In R.3, objects that launch or display other objects (DocLinks, attachments, buttons, etc.) could be inserted into rich-text fields in documents or Forms. The interface to these objects was an object-specific icon.

With R.4, developers can create HotSpots, which can sit over text, images, or any defined area. These HotSpots can then launch DocLinks, buttons, or popups; run a Formula; run an Agent; or run a script. HotSpots can be placed in rich-text fields and in Navigators.

When combined with the Action Bar, Navigators, and Layout Regions (see below), HotSpots give the user direct graphical manipulation within the Notes environment.

Layout Regions

The Layout Region gives designers a graphical interface for laying out text, graphics, Fields, and other components when creating a Form or Subform. In Form design, R.4 designers can insert a Layout Region "frame" paragraph within the Notes Form's rich-text substrate. Within this frame, designers can place text, graphics, and other Fields. These can be created within the frame or dragged into it from other locations within the Form. Multiple Layout Region frame paragraphs can be placed in a Form; they can be adjacent to other frames or "standard" paragraphs.

Layout Regions are intended specifically to:

- Allow Form designers to lay out Notes Fields physically in an X, Y fashion
- Meet users' expectations of "standard" drag-to-locate, drag-to-resize, snap-to-grid behavior
- Preserve advantages of current Notes Form layout: wrap, tables, printability, show/hide paragraphs

Lotus stresses that Layout Region functionality is not intended to reach full feature parity with existing alternative user interfaces, such as Visual Basic or Approach, but instead to demonstrate progress in this area, which will evolve in future versions of Notes.

View Presentation

Release 4 increases the developer's ability to create more readable Views for the user. The View enhancements include:

- Multiple lines per row
- Wordwrapping within a row
- Alternate colors in rows

Text/Document Control

Release 4 gives the developer and the user more control over the contents of documents. Developers now have more direct control of Form layout, including the ability to define Fields visually and pixel-level control of object placement. Other specific enhancements the developer can exploit include better support for Named Styles (which the developer can use in Forms) and Collapsible Sections.

Named Styles now include font attributes as well as paragraph properties.

Collapsible Sections allow different parts of a document or Form to be defined as a section. This section can be displayed in expanded or collapsed form. The collapsed form allows better use of the screen real estate and easier navigation for the user. The developer can control the default collapse/expand/hide status for each section by Formula, access rights, or whenever the document is being created, edited, or viewed.

The developer can also control the mode in which a document opens. Documents that, in R.3, always open in Read mode can, in R.4, default to open in Edit mode. This capability is used in the R.4 mail template: When a message is saved as a draft, it opens up again in Edit mode when the user double-clicks on it.

Release 4 also addresses one of the key R.3 limitations: manipulation of table data. Under R.4, developers can:

- Create tables of a specific size more easily
- Select across cells
- Apply table properties
- Have zero pad around cells

NAVIGATORS BRING A GRAPHICAL USER INTERFACE TO NOTES VIEWS

Along with the three-pane window interface, the Navigator is the most obvious R.4 enhancement to the Notes user interface. Navigators appear in the Navigation pane of the Notes database window, and, for the first time within the Notes environment, provide graphical access to Notes data within Notes. The introduction of Navigators eliminates (or at least decreases) the need to use an external tool, such as ViP or Visual Basic, to create a simple graphical interface to Notes.

Navigators are a new design element of a Notes database that give users graphical access to Notes functions. Navigators are built by developers through a new set of graphic design tools (see Figure 13.11). Although they are functional, these tools do not compete with the leading design tools. Thus, developers can also import bit maps or their favorite designs from tools such as Visio.

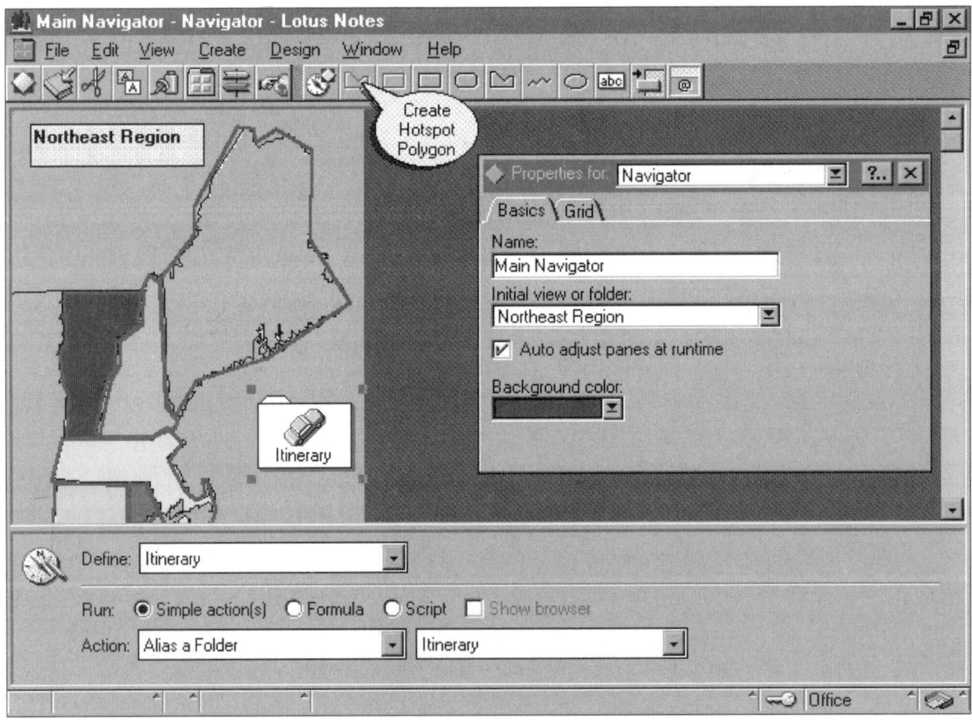

FIGURE 13.11 **Designing a Navigator.** In addition to being able to import drawings and bitmaps, designers have access to basic drawing tools to build Navigators.

The Navigator can contain one or multiple HotSpots. In fact, a HotSpot can be attached to any graphical or textual element in the Navigator. Actions can then be attached to the HotSpots. For example, clicking on a HotSpot can change Views in the View pane. Navigators can also be used to launch external applications, run LotusScripts, or call up other Navigators. This last capability can be used to create a graphical drill-down interface for Notes.

SUPPORT FOR OLE 2.0

The support for OLE 2.0 in Notes R.4 provides additional power to the developer in a number of ways.

OLE In-Place Editing

OLE 2.0 in-place editing lets the developer embed an OLE object into a Notes Form, which looks and behaves like part of the Notes compound document but has all the capabilities of the OLE server.

OLE Automation

OLE automation lets the Notes developer call OLE automation servers from Notes applications, specifically from LotusScripts. This provides Notes-centric control of multiple processes to create a seamless application. Support for OLE automation also enables non-Notes-centric processes to include Notes (specifically Lotus-Script) functions within their applications.

Notes/FX 2.0

Notes/FX 2.0 is an enhancement to Notes/FX, which itself extends the standard OLE capabilities. Whereas Notes/FX 1.x supports two-way, Field-level data exchange, Notes/FX 2.0 is an extension that allows sharing Actions. (See "Actions and Action Bars Enhance Workflow," below, for a further explanation and an example.) Notes/FX 2.0 supports both OLE 1 and OLE 2, and its basic functions do not require any changes in the OLE application.

OLE Auto Launch

Release 4 gives the developer additional OLE launch options. In R.3, an OLE object could be launched when the user created, edited, or read a document. With R.4, the developer has additional options, including launching an application when a database is first opened. This lets the developer provide an alternate interface for a specific database. For example, upon clicking on a Notes database, the user could be presented with a Form from a Forms package, a Visual Basic or ViP screen, or a ScreenCam help movie that is associated with that Notes database. Taking this one step further, the Notes desktop could be used to launch non-Notes applications, thus becoming the user's desktop for all processes, Notes-oriented or otherwise.

Release 4 also offers a facility that provides a stopping point between launching the OLE server and the actual point when the OLE server takes control. This lets the designer inform users that they are entering another application; more important, it lets the designer have users enter values into Fields—values that can then be transferred into the OLE server application via Notes/FX.

ACTIONS AND ACTION BARS ENHANCE WORKFLOW

Actions: What the User Can Do

A major enhancement in R.4 is the concept of Actions. This involves both a new user interface element—the Action Bar—and a new workflow-oriented programming element—Actions. (The Action Bar is discussed more fully on page 161.)

Actions are bound to a Form or a View. Within each Notes Form or View, users have certain Actions available to them. For example, in a Form, users can always close or print the document. And in a View, users can always open a document or another View. The concept of Actions brings these abilities to the surface and allows them to be manipulated by the developer.

Standard and Custom Actions

Actions fall into two categories: Standard Actions and Custom Actions. Standard Actions are those that are inherent in the existing Form or View—close, print, open, save, send, edit, categorize, and others. Custom Actions are created by the developer. These can be a command, formula, script, or Agent—that is, anything that can be put behind a button. Thus, Custom Actions are particularly useful for presenting users with the preferred Action. A good example is a document that needs to be approved, where the user's next Action should be Approve, Deny, or Return with Comment.

For each Form or View, the developer designates which Actions are to be made available to the user. The user sees the Actions in the non-scrolling Action Bar or in the File menu. The developer defines which Actions are available to the user at any given point (e.g., upon creation, when editing or reading, or by a Formula). Because the Action Bar and menu are sensitive to this context, users see only those Actions that they can take. There are no "grayed-out" choices.

Notes/FX Transfers Actions to OLE Servers

Using Notes/FX 2.0, the Actions defined in a Form can be transferred to the OLE object embedded within the Notes document. Consider a contract approval workflow, for example. A contract, which is displayed in a specific word processor, is embedded in a Notes document that is sent for review and approval to a number of users. When the users open the Notes document, the contract is launched within the word processor. The users have access to all of the word processor commands and to the Notes commands available to the form from which the document was launched. So the Notes Approve or Reject commands can now be chosen by the user from within the word processing document. Once chosen, the command could close the word processing document, change the status of the Notes document, close the Notes document, send a notification to the contract author, or perform other functions.

The way in which the user accesses the Notes command from within the OLE document depends on the OLE application. If the OLE application specifically supports Notes/FX (as do all Lotus applications), the Action Bar will appear above the OLE document. Any OLE 1.0 or 2.0 application that does not support Notes/FX will require the user to go to the File menu to access the Actions (this requires the Actions within the Notes form to be designated to appear on the File menu).

API ENHANCEMENTS: MORE POWER, MORE OPTIONS

Release 4.0 provides enhancements to the Notes API. At the same time, Lotus is deemphasizing the low-level C API in favor of several higher-level tools (LotusScript, the HiTest API, and a future C++ API) to be offered in the R.4 timeframe. Lotus's current API direction is to create a common object model for LotusScript, the HiTest API, and the future C++ API.

C API 4.0

The key enhancement to the Notes API is the Extension Manager. The Extension Manager allows a dynamic link library (DLL) to register a callback routine that is called before or after Notes performs selected internal calls. The Extension Manager supports a set of over 60 notification events. Examples of typical events include:

- NSFDbOpen
- NSFDbClose

- NSFNotesOpen
- NSFNotesClose

These events let the developer launch actions when a Notes database is opened or closed or when a Notes document is opened or closed, respectively.

The new Notes API also supports Notes/FX 2.0, which lets Notes share Actions with OLE servers.

In addition to the new extensions, the R.4 API offers a number of new functions, including:

- NSFDbAccessGet, which returns the current access level for an open database
- NSFDbMajorMinorVersionGet, which returns the major and minor version numbers
- NSFDbGetOpenDatabaseID, which returns the unique database ID for an open database
- NSFGetServerLatency, which returns the estimate of time needed to access the server
- REGCrossCertifyID, which cross-certifies an ID from the API
- ListRemoveAllEntries, which removes all the entries in a list

Migrating API Applications

All current R.3.x API applications will run with Notes R.4. Lotus is providing a set of instructions on how to upgrade R.3.x API applications to take advantage of R.4 functionality.

Platform Support

Under Notes R.3, the API was available to run in a limited set of environments—Windows and OS/2. The R.4 API will support all Notes clients and servers.

HiTest API

The HiTest API (developed by Edge Research, which was acquired by Lotus in 1994) is an enhanced set of C-language calls layered over the Notes API. It lets C programmers access Notes services at a higher level of abstraction, requiring significantly fewer calls and commands to execute required functions. The HiTest API objectifies many Notes components—such as ID tables, collections, memory blocks, and composite data—that are cumbersome to handle with the Notes API. It also provides automatic data conversion and access to the built-in scheduler for server or client add-in programs. The HiTest API also creates a protective layer to prevent crashes and provides a number of error-handling methods.

With Notes R.4, the object model of the HiTest API has been merged with that of LotusScript and a new C++ API, providing a constant programming model and syntax for developers across the tools.

LOTUSSCRIPT PROVIDES SCRIPTED ACCESS TO NOTES FUNCTIONS

LotusScript is Lotus's strategic platform for programmability for all of its applications. LotusScript is very much like Microsoft's Visual Basic, and many scripts could be identical. Actually, LotusScript is conceptually more like Visual Basic for Applications (VBA) in that it is application-centric rather than tool-centric. However, LotusScript differs from VBA in that it is multiplatform (Windows, Macintosh, OS/2, and Unix) and has functions that are customized for Lotus products.

Four major implications of LotusScript for Notes developers are the following:

- LotusScript will be used for most of the tasks that currently require the Notes API, giving developers a higher-level interface into the API functions.

- LotusScript enhances the Notes development environment by adding such features as a script editor, debugger, and variable/property inspector.

- LotusScript provides an extensive programming environment, including complex logic constructs (such as looping and subroutines), which will allow the developer to create fuller, more complex applications.

- LotusScript provides the capability for internal developers and ISVs to build server processes that automate tasks and/or manage ongoing applications, such as workflows. Actions that are currently Macro-based, and thus cannot automatically run more frequently than once an hour, can run as ongoing server processes, continually monitoring the status of key indicators or being continually available to external calls, such as a relational database trigger.

LotusScript functionality is described in Chapter 6.

RELEASE 4 FOR THE DEVELOPER 2: ENHANCED PRODUCTIVITY

In addition to giving additional power to developers within the Notes environment, R.4 affects the speed and comfort with which

Notes developers can work. The impact of the R.4 developer productivity enhancements can be felt throughout the product. The
most significant of these enhancements are:

- General R.4 user interface enhancements
- Notes Agent Builder
- Reusable Subforms
- Enhancements to the Notes Macro Editor
- Higher-level APIs for the C programmer
- LotusScript IDE

GENERAL R.4 USER INTERFACE ENHANCEMENTS

Notes developers benefit from all of the R.4 interface enhancements, particularly those that provide direct access and manipulation of Notes functions and features. For example, the developer
has direct access to the Notes database design elements (Forms,
Views, Shared Fields, Subforms, Navigators, etc.) from the Navigation pane. Clicking on an element, such as Forms, presents the developer with a list of the elements that can be modified (see Figure
13.12). Clicking on the element, in this case, the Article Form,
brings up that form for modification.

The Power of InfoBoxes

The most important R.4 UI feature, whose value to developers
cannot be overstated, is the InfoBox. InfoBoxes provide two specific
benefits to developers. The first is more direct access to Notes design elements and their properties. For example, when a developer
selects (or adds) a Field in a Form, an InfoBox pops up (see Figure
13.13). The InfoBox allows the developer access to define the Field
and its properties without having to traverse a myriad of menu
choices. The developer can navigate through and manipulate the
object's properties with dialog boxes, pick lists, and tabbed pages.
In our experience, this itself speeds up Notes Form and View development by several factors. At the same time, the developer can
choose which object will have the current focus of the InfoBox.
Thus, moving between Field definition and database definition is
simply a choice from the Properties for: drop-down list.

As the developer changes the properties in the InfoBox, the
changes are instantly reflected in the actual Form or View. This
means that the developer does not have to go back and forth between developing and checking the results.

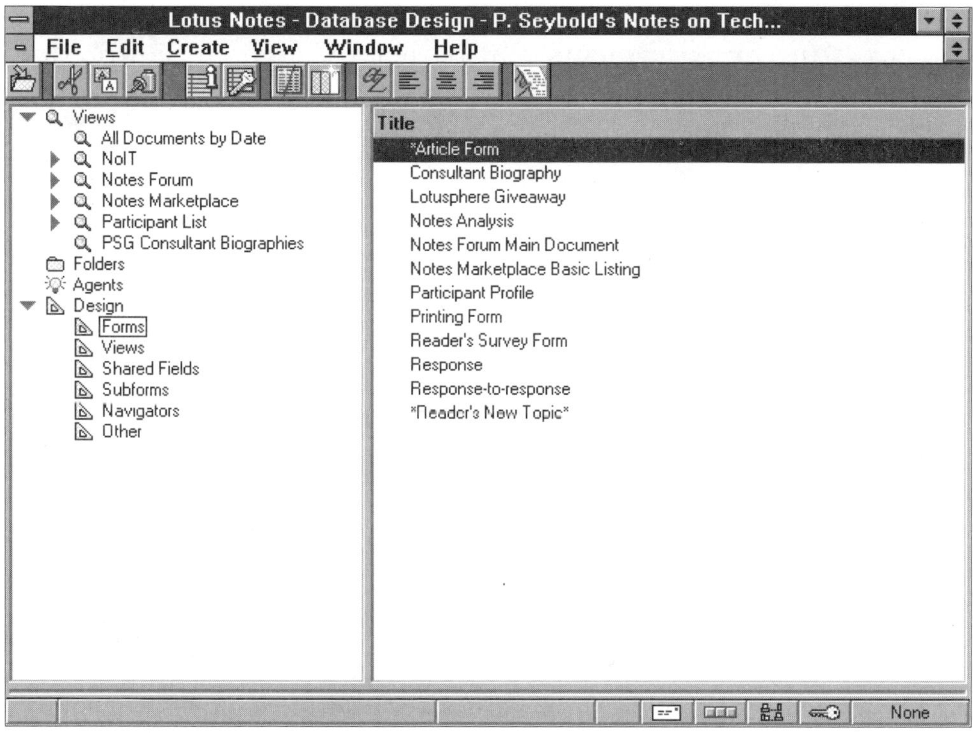

FIGURE 13.12   Notes R.4 user interface. Clicking on the Design hierarchy in the Navigator lets the developer access the design elements directly. The developer could open a third pane to see the actual design element.

The second major benefit of InfoBoxes (and this is a feature that benefits all Notes users as they manipulate Notes objects) is that they are modeless and context sensitive. The modeless nature of InfoBoxes means that they are persistent—they stay on top of the user interface even when the user changes the context to the object below the InfoBox. Thus, a developer can move from one Field to another on a Form, and the InfoBox remains available (in fact, it displays the properties of each Field as it becomes the focus). This persistence can be changed by the user, who can close or minimize the InfoBox with a single click.

The context sensitivity of the InfoBox is not limited to a single object type. For example, when the focus changes (i.e., the cursor is moved) from the Field itself to the name of the Field on the Form, the InfoBox brings up the properties for text (see Figure 13.14). We found that the defaults of the context sensitivity match the user's

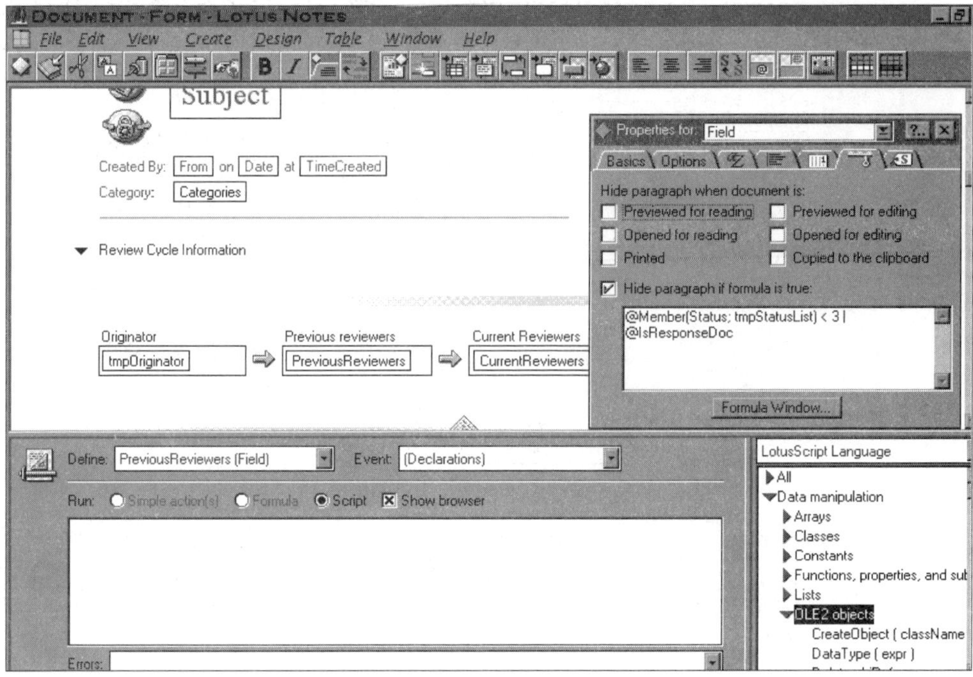

FIGURE 13.13 Defining a Notes Field. The developer can enter values for this Keyword Field and assign it a formula, a style, and security.

desires quite well, although at times we had to change the properties, for example, if we wanted to insert a new Field next to some text. In that case, it took only a simple selection from the Properties for: list to change the focus of the InfoBox.

The InfoBox remains persistent because it can be applicable in virtually every development situation. For example, closing a Form brings back the screen from which the Form was launched (see Figure 13.15). The InfoBox, rather than disappearing, has again changed context, this time to reflect the types of activities available to the developer to set the properties of the database itself. (This set of properties was always available through the Properties for: box.)

The same capabilities are available when defining a View. The developer can create View conditions in the InfoBox, defining conditions and columns via point-and-click. As the View properties change, they are immediately reflected in the View. If they need to be recalculated, the developer can have the update done without losing the context of the InfoBox.

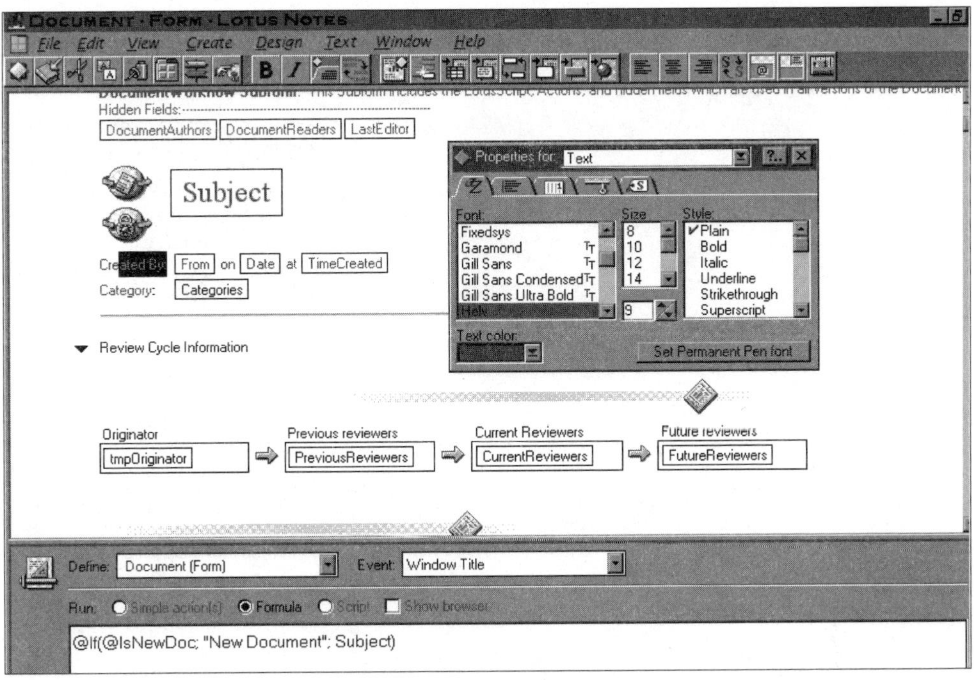

FIGURE 13.14 Setting text properties. Clicking in the text brings up the text-oriented set of properties.

NOTES AGENT BUILDER

Although we have described the Notes Agent Builder in the section "Release 4 for the User," it clearly can be (and will be) used by developers to build intelligence into applications that can be created at a higher level than those created via the Notes Macro language, LotusScript, or one of the Notes APIs. We believe that the Agent Builder will also be used in conjunction with processes created via the lower-level Notes tools, particularly to launch them on a timed basis.

The Agent Builder also lets the developer build Custom Actions, which can then be added to the Action Bar and/or called from the File menu.

REUSABLE SUBFORMS

Notes R.4 introduces a new design element, the Subform. Subforms are shared objects that can be used within Forms or as Forms

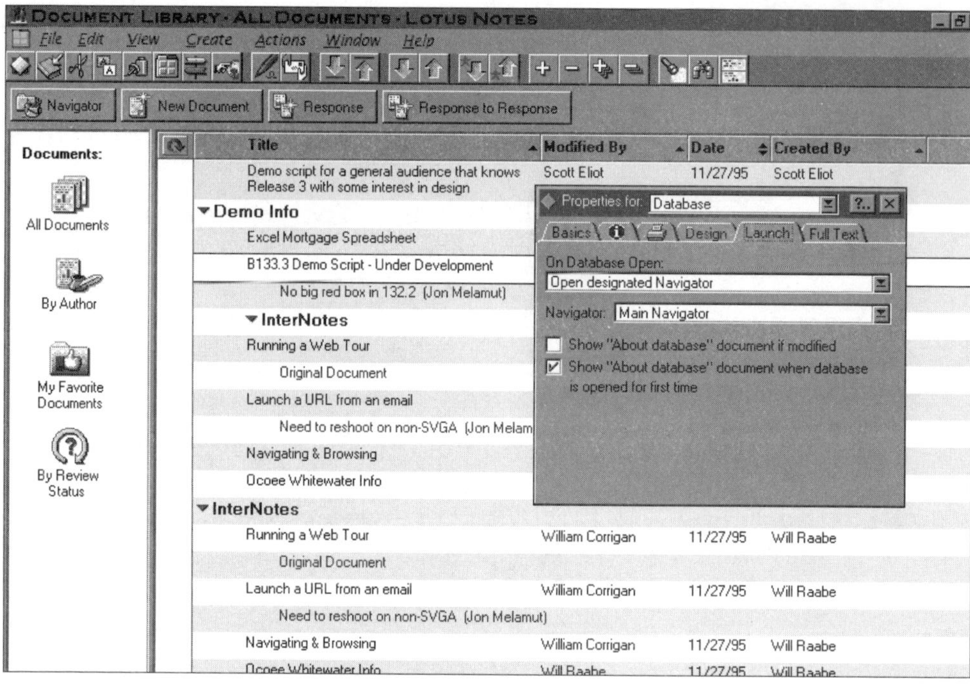

FIGURE 13.15 **Setting database properties.** This InfoBox gives the developer direct access to the database properties, including how it is to appear to the user, whether it should open up to a View or to an internal or external document or application, the security of the database, and the status of full-text indexing.

themselves. They can be as simple as a background with a company logo, or they can be highly complex, containing Agents, Lotus-Scripts, and Action Bars.

Subforms create a new level of reusability in Notes applications. Certain features, such as input Forms, routing rules, Actions, or graphics, can be managed centrally and accessed as needed. An organization can designate a set of Subforms to be used in creating new Forms. This provides both management and efficient use of compound design elements; it obviates the task of re-creating each combination of elements every time it is needed.

Once used in an application, Subforms can inherit all changes to the original Subform. All new and edited documents will then reflect the changes.

ENHANCEMENTS TO THE NOTES MACRO EDITOR

Although most of the industry's attention has been paid to the LotusScript IDE, the Notes Macro Editor has also been enhanced to let developers create a structured look to their macro code. Under R.3, any indenting the developer did to make the structure of the code clearer was removed by the Macro Editor (although some third-party products enable R.3 developers to fool the Macro Editor). The R.4 editor supports and maintains the developer's indenting structure.

HIGHER-LEVEL APIS FOR THE C PROGRAMMER

Lotus's purchase and offering of the HiTest API, as well as its commitment to a future C++ API, should let developers who do not need the lowest-level capabilities of the Notes API build code much faster with fewer lines of code and fewer debugging requirements.

LOTUSSCRIPT INTERACTIVE DEVELOPMENT ENVIRONMENT

Certainly the most anticipated enhancement of R.4 that is designed to improve developer productivity is the LotusScript IDE itself. In addition to the increased functionality it provides, LotusScript specifically addresses key limitations in the R.3 development environment: the lack of an editor and debugger. As already noted, using the R.3 Macro Editor is particularly annoying. LotusScript's integrated editor provides full editing and formatting capabilities to scripts.

Even more significant is the LotusScript debugger. With R.3 Macros, developers had to resort to including Print statements between each command in a Macro to see where it failed. This worked for foreground Macros, but background Macros required an even more roundabout approach, such as that used by developers at MFJ International of New York. These developers inserted SendMail statements between each command in a background Macro. When the message was not received, the developer knew where the Macro stopped.

The LotusScript debugger provides built-in and developer-defined breakpoints, as well as allowing the developer to step through the script one command at a time. At any point or step, the developer can examine the current value of any variable.

RELEASE 4 FOR THE ADMINISTRATOR/MANAGER

With Notes Release 4.0 (and NotesView, which was actually initially delivered for R.3), administrators gain additional control over the Notes environment. Several key enhancements include:

- Administration Control Panel
- Server Pass-through
- Agent Manager

ENHANCED ADMINISTRATION TOOLS

Notes Release 4.0 includes a new set of administration tools designed to provide centralized management and streamlined administration across an enterprise. Lotus's explicit goal for these tools is to allow organizations to reduce training costs, the expertise required by administrators, and the number of administrators who manage a Notes enterprise. Key new tools and capabilities include:

- Administrative Control Panel
- Server Configuration Record
- Server Console Panel
- Name & Address Book and ACL Management Tool
- Delegated Administration

Administrative Control Panel

The Administrative Control Panel is designed to provide administrators with the ease of use of a graphical user interface and a single interface to administrative actions. From the Administrative Control Panel, administrators can control virtually all of the Notes Name & Address Book functions, including maintaining users, groups, and servers. The Administrative Control Panel also provides push-button access to view and edit server systems logs and configuration variables. It also lets administrators look at various statistics, look at the server log, and run the remote console.

In addition, from the Administrative Control Panel, the administrator can access other functions and utilities, including:

- A database analysis tool, which provides information about database-specific activity, including reads, writes, and modifications to documents and design elements
- A recertification tool for automatically recertifying user IDs

- A message trace tool to manage the message routing environment by providing direct access to message queues and mail trace/probe utilities

Server Configuration Record

The Server Configuration Record provides centralized management of server configuration variables via the replicated Notes Name & Address Book. Administrators can make a change at any server within the network and the change will be applied to designated servers regardless of geographic location. The Server Configuration Record also allows generic configuration (i.e., setting the maximum number of mail threads for a group of servers that act as mail hubs) to be completed and applied to all or a certain set of servers. With this new tool, administrators can make global changes to enterprise server configurations from anywhere on the network. The Server Configuration Record also lets administrators fine-tune or troubleshoot servers more easily.

Server Console Panel

The Server Console Panel is designed to provide an easy-to-use, intuitive interface for more streamlined administration. The Server Console Panel groups functions and consolidates administration information into a single panel with graphical buttons for user, group, server, database, and certified administration activities.

Name & Address Book and ACL Management Tool

The Name & Address Book and ACL Management Tool automates the user administration process for renaming and deleting users by making the necessary changes to all server access lists, groups, and access control lists (ACL) throughout the Notes environment in a secure, reliable manner. For administrators, this tool should greatly reduce the amount of time spent maintaining and manually updating user accounts and ACLs. It also allows for a more secure Notes environment by guaranteeing that user accounts are added to or deleted from ACLs on all servers throughout the Notes enterprise.

Delegated Administration

The new feature called Delegated Administration offers administrators the ability to centralize policy making and control while at the same time delegating specific administration tasks by assigning certain administration privileges or roles. For example, a select team of administrators could be responsible for maintaining mail routing and replication topology, while another group could be solely accountable for adding and modifying user records. Because each group has a different set of privileges, neither group can affect the others' administrative assignments, regardless of having access to all administration information worldwide via the Notes Name & Address Book. Without sacrificing centralized control, delegated administration allows for more secure operations of servers, minimizes the chance for error, and increases administration efficiency and productivity.

AGENT MANAGER IMPROVES CONTROL AND PERFORMANCE OF AGENTS

The R.4 Notes server replaces Chronos, the program that launched Macros in Notes R.3, with a new program called the Agent Manager. The Agent Manager increases the performance and efficiency of server-based agents and provides server administrators with more power and flexibility to manage the Agents running on the server.

The Agent Manager is designed to perform better than Chronos. A major increase in efficiency is the Agent Manager's maintenance of a list of agents that must be run during every time period. Under R.3, Chronos had to search each database on the server every hour to see if there was a Macro to be run.

The Agent Manager gives administrators a new set of capabilities to control the impact of Agents running on the server. For example, administrators can designate how much of the server's resources (i.e., CPU cycle time) will be devoted to running Agents. The administrator also controls which users can create Personal Agents that run on a specific server and which users can create Agents that run LotusScripts; the latter potentially has the greatest impact on server and network resources.

NOTESVIEW

Again, it is important to emphasize that NotesView is not part of Notes Release 4.0; the version for Notes 3.x shipped in mid-1995. With the introduction of R.4, it is important not to underestimate the significance of NotesView for Notes administration and management in both Release 3 and Release 4.0.

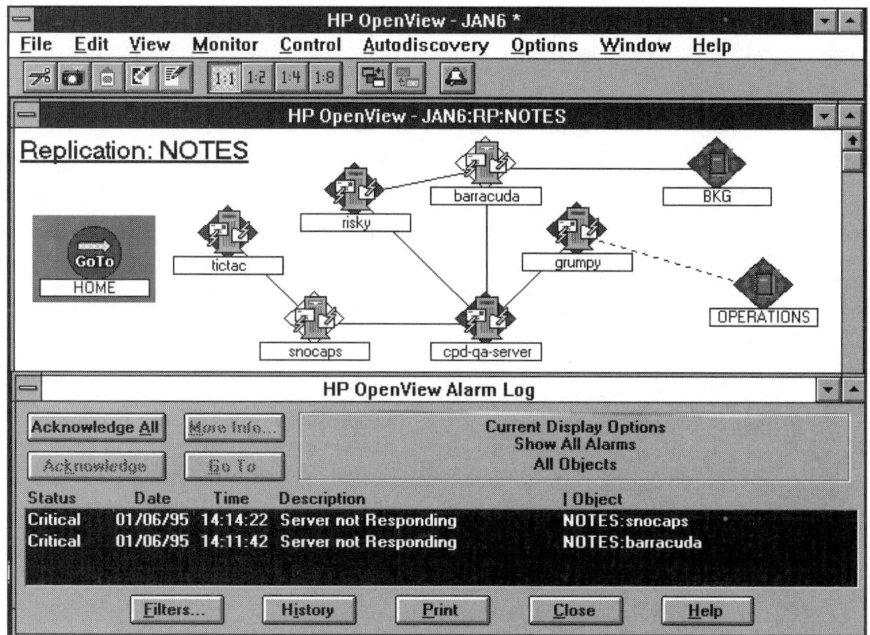

FIGURE 13.16 **NotesView screen.** This NotesView screen provides a graphical view of the status of the Notes network, as well as displaying alarms when conditions require.

NotesView is the first facility to provide a real-time graphical view of the status of the Notes network and Notes servers, as well as providing alerts and alarms when conditions require. NotesView also provides reports on server and network status (see Figure 13.16).

NotesView is built on top of Hewlett-Packard's OpenView for Windows. NotesView is actually a combination of OpenView and Notes facilities. From OpenView, it derives management workstations' SNMP-based real-time and out-of-band facilities. And it uses the robust client/server protocol support and security features inherent in Notes.

NotesView is designed specifically to enable customers to better manage and monitor Lotus Notes servers, server tasks, replication, and mail-routing facilities. It also lets administrators make changes to LAN-based or remote configurations or environmental variables from a management workstation.

RELEASE 4 FOR THE ENTERPRISE

A critical goal for Notes Release 4.0 is to better meet enterprise-level needs. Although Notes is best known as a groupware product, many, if not most, successful Notes implementations quickly burst the bounds of specific workgroups and become strategic elements of an organization's information infrastructure.

Release 4 is designed specifically to better support enterprise-level requirements in the areas of scalability and security.

SCALABILITY

Scalability of the environment is a key factor in enabling Notes to become an enterprise-level platform. At the same time, it is an important element in minimizing customers' cost of ownership and maximizing the return on investment of the Notes decision.

The two major issues addressed by the R.4 scalability enhancements are the ability for servers to handle more simultaneous processes (this translates into more users, more sessions, more replications, etc.) and the ability to create larger Notes applications.

Release 4 improves scalability by fully supporting 32-bit operating systems. This removes most size and performance limitations based on 16-bit addresses and 64K buffer sizes. Release 4 also provides greater support for symmetric multiprocessing systems (SMP), with full support for four to six (or more) processors. Each of these enhancements contributes to the ability to support several times more simultaneous users per server. In addition, R.4 supports larger Notes databases (up to 4 GB). This is particularly important when it comes to large Name & Address Books.

Most of the scalability improvements of R.4 are in the form of enhancements to the Notes server. These include:

32-bit multithreaded SMP support on OS/2, Unix, and Windows NT. Symmetric multiprocessor support in R.4 is designed to pass the R.3 limit of two processors. The goal for R.4 is four- to six-processor support.

Replication enhancements. Replication enhancements include faster replication algorithms and support for multiple simultaneous replication processes on a server. In addition, R.4 replication supports Field-level replication. This means that, when a Field in a document changes, only that Field is replicated to other copies of that database. This can reduce network traffic and replication time by several orders of magnitude, depending on which Field is changed.

More efficient execution of Macros (now called Agents). Chronos has been replaced by the Agent Manager. The Agent Manager runs Agents more efficiently (e.g., it does not have to check each database every hour to see if there is a Macro to be run) and provides administrators with better abilities to manage the impact of Agents on the infrastructure (e.g., controlling who can run Agents on the server and setting the percentage of server processor time that is used for running Agents).

Maximum database size. A consistent complaint of enterprise-level Notes customers was their unhappiness with the R.3 absolute database limit of 1 GB. This criticism goes hand in hand with their frustration about the performance of large Notes databases. Most R.3 Notes applications became unwieldy long before they reach 1 GB in size. Notes R.4 increases the maximum supported database size to 4 GB, while promising acceptable performance for databases of all supported databases.

Initial scalability results are very encouraging. According to Lotus, initial Notes Release 4.0 testing across several multiprocessor platforms has yielded nearly 10-fold performance gains, supporting up to 1000 active, concurrent users per server, compared with approximately 100 users per server on Notes Release 3.x platforms.

SECURITY

Security has always been a Notes strength. However, there have been some idiosyncratic features that can frustrate enterprise-level Notes deployment. The first of these is the fact that in order to do some administrative-level functions, such as compacting a database, the administrator had to have Designer access to the database. Thus, administrators had to have access to the documents and design elements of the database, whether they needed it or not. Although this is probably all right in a workgroup-level application, where the designer also manages the application and the server it is on, it makes little sense across an enterprise. Release 4 adds a new server-access level to allow administrators to take administrative action without being able to see into unauthorized databases.

Release 4 also adds database encryption, which provides encryption of databases on a server, workstation, or laptop. With this in force, only the user who created the database (identified by the user ID) can open the database. This feature is designed to reassure those companies that are afraid to put sensitive databases on laptops because the machine itself could be misplaced. It also enhances security against unauthorized access on the server.

The "For Your Eyes Only" attribute developed for Notes Mail can also be used as a general document-level security feature, allowing users to read the document, but not to print, copy, or forward it.

RELEASE 4 ENTERPRISE ELECTRONIC MAIL

Notes Release 4 is the key product in Lotus's client/server E-mail strategy. The Notes R.4 server is designed to provide all the elements of enterprise electronic mail, including replicating directory services, client/server message routing, and rich-message store. In addition, just as the R.4 client has been enhanced to provide a better E-mail experience for the user (three-pane window, Folders, type-ahead addressing), the R.4 server has been enhanced to better support enterprise electronic mail with such features as the following:

Single-message store. Release 4 provides a single-message store option for E-mail. Under R.3, if someone sent a message to many users on the same mail server, a copy of the message was stored in each user's .nsf file. With R.4, all copies may be stored in a single place on the server, and pointers are put in each user's mail file. This can save significant disk space.

Better mail administration. Release 4 gives the administrator more information on where specific messages were sent, when they were received, the route they took, and other details. This information is available through administrative tools such as the Administrative Control Panel, the mail trace tool, and NotesView.

MAPI and CMC support. Notes R.4 provides support for any client that uses the Microsoft Messaging API (MAPI) or XAPIA Common Mail Calls (CMC). For example, MAPI support allows a client (such as the one shipped as part of Windows 95) to operate with Notes as the messaging infrastructure.

X.400 and SMTP support. The Notes R.4 server can optionally run native X.400 or Simple Mail Transport Protocol (SMTP) as its transport. This can be done between Notes servers, as well as be used to connect to external services, such as value-added networks or the Internet.

INTEGRATION WITH CC:MAIL AND LOTUS MESSAGE SWITCH

Lotus is rolling out a new communications architecture that clarifies its overall messaging strategy and the integration of its three messaging platforms: Notes, cc:Mail, and Lotus Message Switch (LMS, previously known as SoftSwitch Enterprise Messaging Switch, or EMX).

Lotus's messaging strategy is to upgrade the current cc:Mail file-sharing database to support such features as rich text, hierarchical Folders, and, most important, 24-hour/seven-day uptime for the server. This lets cc:Mail customers upgrade their current systems without changing their basic architectures.

Lotus will also introduce a new cc:Mail client that will communicate with the new database via MAPI. This is a significant opening up of the cc:Mail architecture for Lotus: Any MAPI client will be able to use cc:Mail services, and cc:Mail clients will be able to use any MAPI service provider. The new cc:Mail client will also be able to use the Notes server as a client/server messaging infrastructure, again communicating via MAPI.

On the server side, Lotus is adding two pieces to the cc:Mail file-sharing database and the Notes server. The first is the Lotus Notes/cc:Mail Communications Server, a.k.a. CommServer. CommServer is essentially a Notes server with the addition of the cc:Mail router protocol and an enhanced version of the current Notes/cc:Mail gateway. CommServer allows messages to be translated between Notes and cc:Mail formats (and vice versa) and delivered to and from a cc:Mail Router. CommServer also enables the synchronization of the Notes Name & Address Book and the cc:Mail directory.

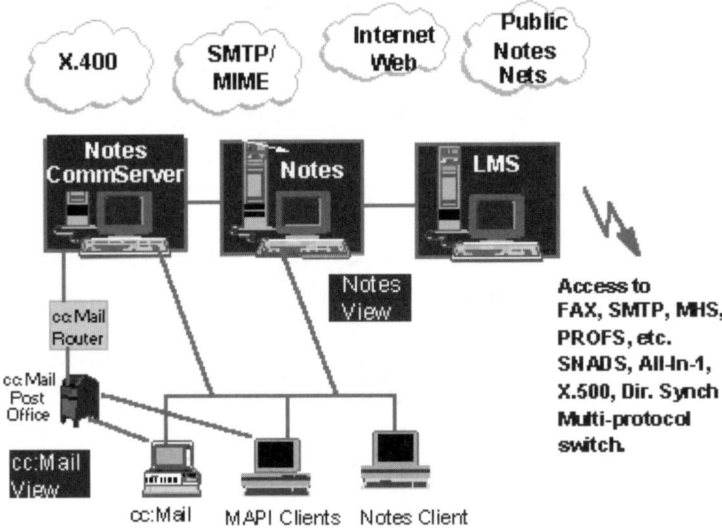

FIGURE 13.17 **Lotus communications architecture.** The Lotus communications architecture supports file-sharing mail, client/ server mail, and enterprise-level switching.

The second addition is enterprise-level switching of messages between Notes, cc:Mail, and legacy formats, such as PROFS, All-In-1, and others by means of the Lotus Message Switch. In addition to message translation and switching, LMS provides directory exchange and has added LMS X.500 support to its directory services (see Figure 13.17).

14

Notes and the World Wide Web

The most frequently asked questions that I hear today revolve around the issues of Notes and the Internet and Notes versus the World Wide Web. There are actually two seemingly contradictory answers to these questions. The first position is that the Internet and the World Wide Web are actually complementary with Notes. This is Lotus's position, and the company is building products that enhance the integration and complementary nature of the two products. The second position asserts that while Lotus was watching Microsoft for a real competitor to Notes (which still has not come and may not come for another generation), it was blind-sided by the emergence of the Web, which itself can be used to build the same collaborative, publishing, and electronic commerce applications as Notes does, in a cheaper, more widely distributed, and open manner.

NOTES AND THE INTERNET: COMPETITIVE OR COMPLEMENTARY?

Although Notes and the Internet (specifically, the World Wide Web) are frequently viewed as competitors, for many companies they are more accurately viewed as complementary platforms for building and deploying applications and services. The Notes-versus-the-Web debate is quite reminiscent of the Notes-versus-RDBMS (relational database management systems) debates of a few years ago. Most companies have now found that this never was an either/or debate, but rather a set of decisions about which platform to build and deploy which applications.

MAKING THE DECISION

With Notes and the Web, the key decisions revolve around the type of application being built. If the application is designed to deliver information—marketing, corporate, or service and support—to a large, previously unknown market, the Web is the obvious platform. And, with recent technology enhancements, this delivery can be turned into one-off transactions between the supplying company and the individual Web user.

If the application involves support of specific business processes that need workflow features, such as notification, triggered processes, customization, multiple levels of security, and mobile user support, then Notes becomes the best choice. Notes, as we saw in Chapters 10–11, is also particularly appropriate for business-to-business applications, where the Notes architecture, security, and the presence of managed, public networks can assure continuous, high-grade service. Notes also supports, via the InterNotes Web Publisher, publishing Notes documents to Web users (see below).

INTEGRATING NOTES AND THE INTERNET

The key lesson from the Notes/RDBMS debate was the need to integrate the platforms—a lesson that is now being applied to Notes and the Internet. This integration currently falls into five areas:

Connectivity. The Internet, as any TCP/IP network, can be used for Notes server-to-server or client-to-server replication and access. Several public networks plan to support Notes replication over the Internet.

E-mail exchange. Lotus offers a MIME-compliant Simple Message Transfer Protocol (SMTP) gateway that allows mail to be exchanged between Notes and any SMTP mail host. Notes Release 4 also supports a native SMTP/MIME connection.

Mail list and news interchange. A number of products are now available that translate Internet mail lists and/or Usenet News Groups into Notes databases. Most of these support bidirectional conversion, allowing Notes users to add to the Internet conversations.

Notes to World Wide Web publishing. Lotus offers a product, the InterNotes Web Publisher, that automatically translates Notes databases into Hypertext Markup Language (HTML) files for use on a World Wide Web server.

Notes user access to the World Wide Web. The InterNotes Web Navigator provides access to HTML documents on the Internet and within Intranets.

This chapter focuses on the last two products.

THE LOTUS INTERNOTES WEB PUBLISHER

Currently, a number of companies, including Lotus and the Patricia Seybold Group, are using Notes databases to manage information that is published onto the World Wide Web. This is being done using Lotus's InterNotes Web Publisher product, which allows the use of Notes to create and manage Web sites. It also allows a single application to span Notes users and Web users while taking advantage of the document management and workflow capabilities of the Notes server.

The InterNotes Web Publisher is a process that automatically takes Notes databases and creates a set of HTML pages on a WWW server (see Figure 14.1). These pages can then be accessed via any Web browser, such as Netscape Navigator or Microsoft Internet Explorer. The InterNotes Web Publisher runs continuously on the Notes server, and it can be set to update the Web pages at the interval of choice, such as every minute, 10 minutes, 1 hour, 6 hours, 12 hours, 1 day, 1 week, or others (see Figure 14.2).

The InterNotes Web Publisher uses Notes Views to present a specific set of documents to the user. The View appears as a list of document titles (actually, this matches the Column information in the Notes View) that are hyperlinked to the documents themselves (see Figures 14.3 and 14.4). The beauty of this arrangement is that, unlike other Web management environments, there is no

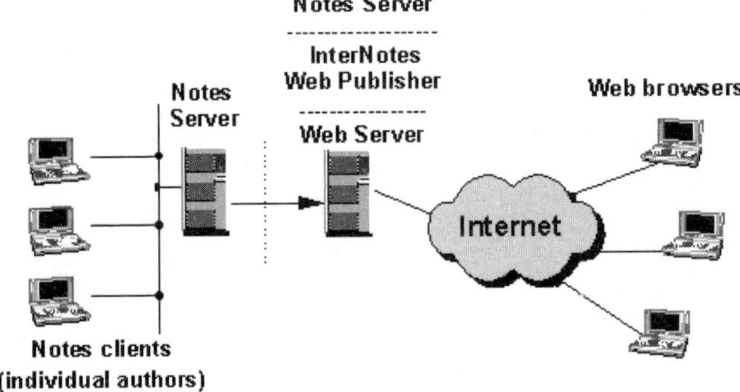

FIGURE 14.1 **InterNotes Web Publisher architecture.** With the Lotus InterNotes Web Publisher, Notes databases that reside on a Notes server are automatically used to create Web sites on a Web server. The documents in the Web site can be made available to anyone on the Internet with a Web browser.

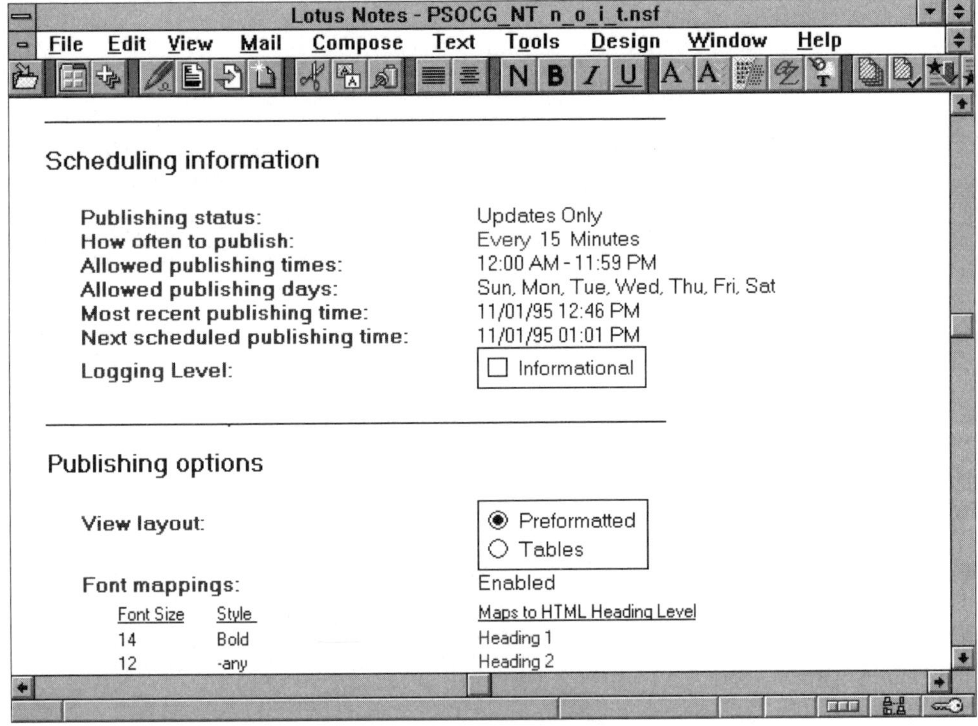

FIGURE 14.2 **InterNotes Web Publisher configuration.** Each Notes database to be published can be configured separately. Options include whether to replace all documents or update changes only, how often to publish, and times to publish. The look of the HTML documents can also be controlled by setting Notes styles to HTML Headings.

need to create these links manually. In addition, these links are automatically added or deleted each time to reflect changes in the Notes database (again, without Notes, HTML link deletion is manual). This makes the InterNotes Web Publisher a powerful Web management tool whether or not Notes is being used for other tasks.

The InterNotes Web Publisher preserves Notes attributes, such as graphics, images, and attachments (see Figures 14.5 and 14.6). Text characteristics are set by the Web browser, and InterNotes Web Publisher enables Notes styles to be mapped to HTML headings (see Figure 14.2). Notes DocLinks are retained, including the ability to link to documents across Notes databases if both Notes databases have been published via the InterNotes Web Publisher.

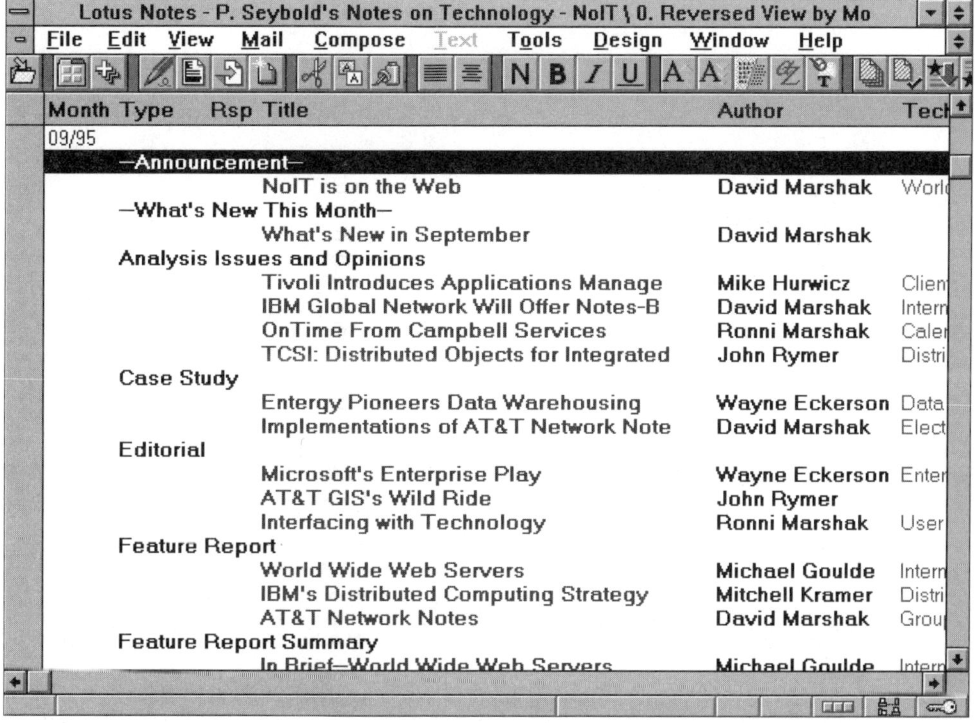

FIGURE 14.3 **A Notes View.** This is a View of the Patricia Seybold Group Notes on Information Technology service, which is delivered in Notes.

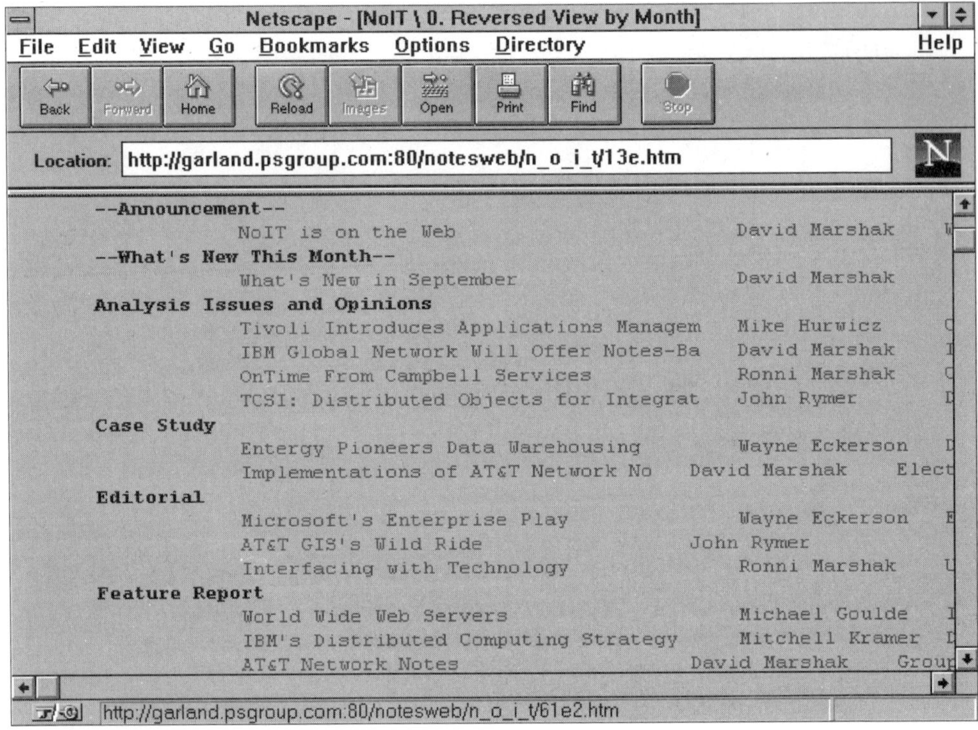

FIGURE 14.4 **A Web Index Built from a Notes View.** This is an HTML page from the Web version of Notes on Information Technology. It is a linked index to the other HTML documents that was generated automatically by the InterNotes Web Publisher.

The InterNotes Web Publisher also supports embedding HTML commands directly into Notes documents, Forms, and Views. This allows the publishing characteristics that Notes does not itself support, such as specific URL links, into the Web pages.

INTERNOTES WEB PUBLISHER RELEASE 2

At the end of 1995, Lotus introduced Release 2.0 of the InterNotes Web Publisher. Release 2 enhancements include the following.

Forms support. InterNotes Web Publisher now allows Web browser users to fill out Notes forms and submit them directly into

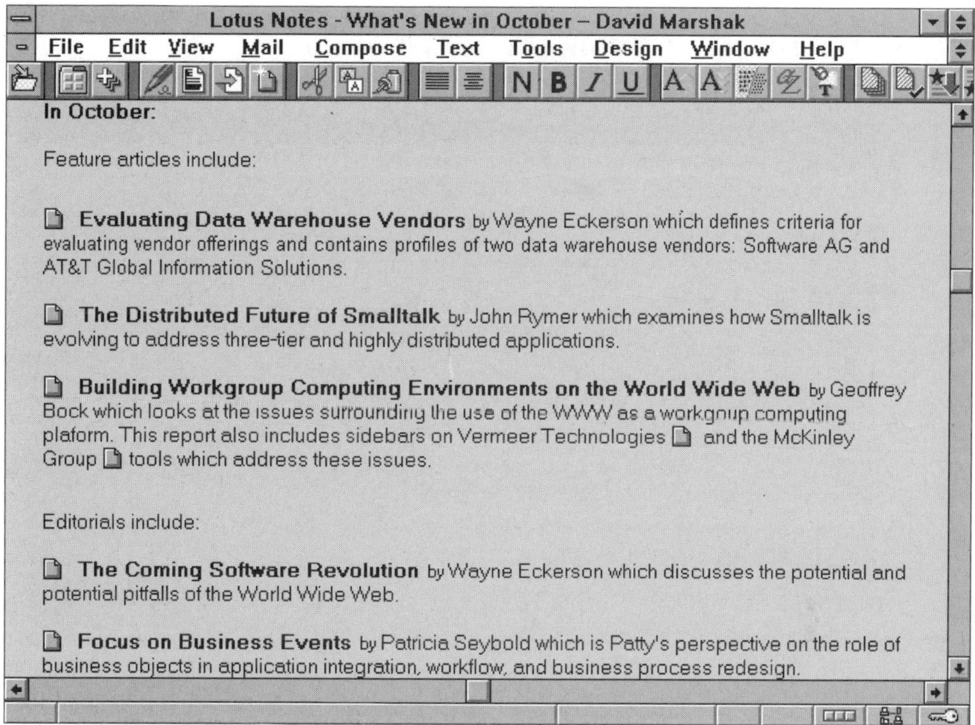

FIGURE 14.5 **A Notes document.** This is a Notes document in
the *Notes on Information Technology* service.

a Notes database. This can be used in a range of applications, from
enabling Web users to participate in Notes discussions to enabling
Web users to engage in Notes-managed electronic commerce.

Enhanced Web publishing. Users of InterNotes Release 2.0
now have the flexibility and discretion to publish only selected
views designed for public use. In addition, InterNotes makes it easier for browsers to navigate large views by separating them into a
series of linked pages.

Notes full-text search. The search enhancement allows anyone with a standard Web browser to search a site managed with
Notes and InterNotes Web Publisher 2.0 to find the information
they need. Users enter their search criteria into an HTML form and
submit it. Web Publisher 2.0 executes a search against a Notes

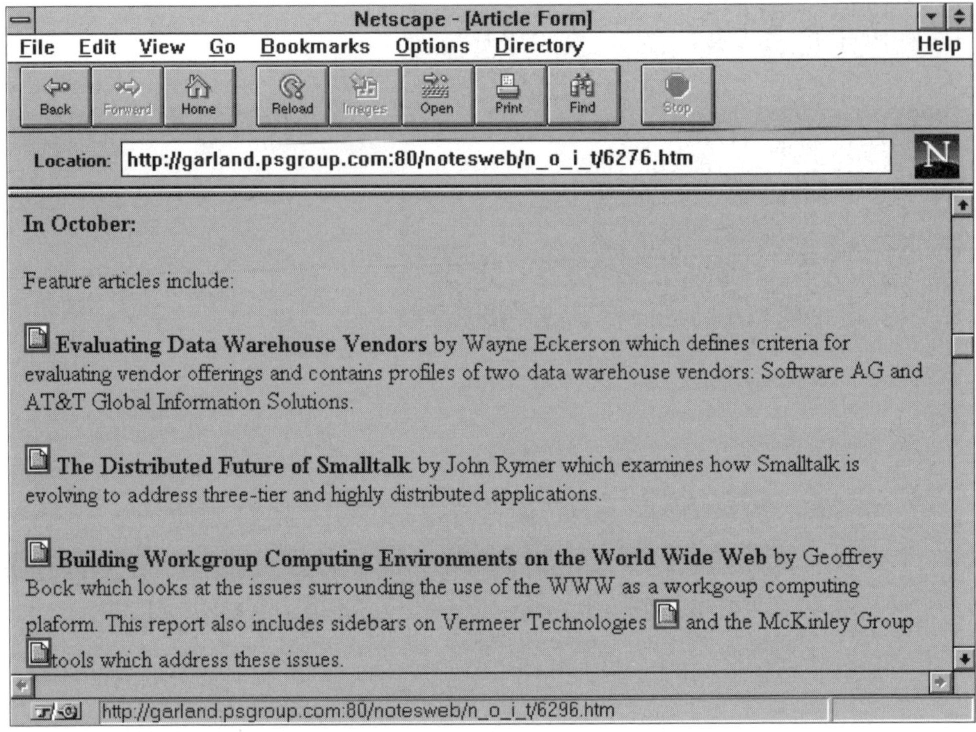

FIGURE 14.6 **A Web document.** This is the HTML version of the same Notes document.

database and returns a list of links to the user. The full range of Notes search options, including a full-search query language, is available to Web browsers.

FUTURE DIRECTIONS

Lotus has recently made two significant announcements about the InterNotes Web Publisher. First, the product, which originally sold for just under $3000 per server, will be included free with all Notes Release 4 servers. Second, Lotus announced that by mid-1996, the Notes server will support direct access from Web browsers. This will be done by incorporating HTTP, HTML, Java, and JavaScript as native protocols (for the implications of this announcement, see Chapter 15).

FIGURE 14.7   InterNotes Web Navigator architecture. The InterNotes Web Navigator runs on a Notes server, which is connected to the World Wide Web on the Internet. Any Notes server or client can access or replicate the InterNotes Web Navigator database from that server.

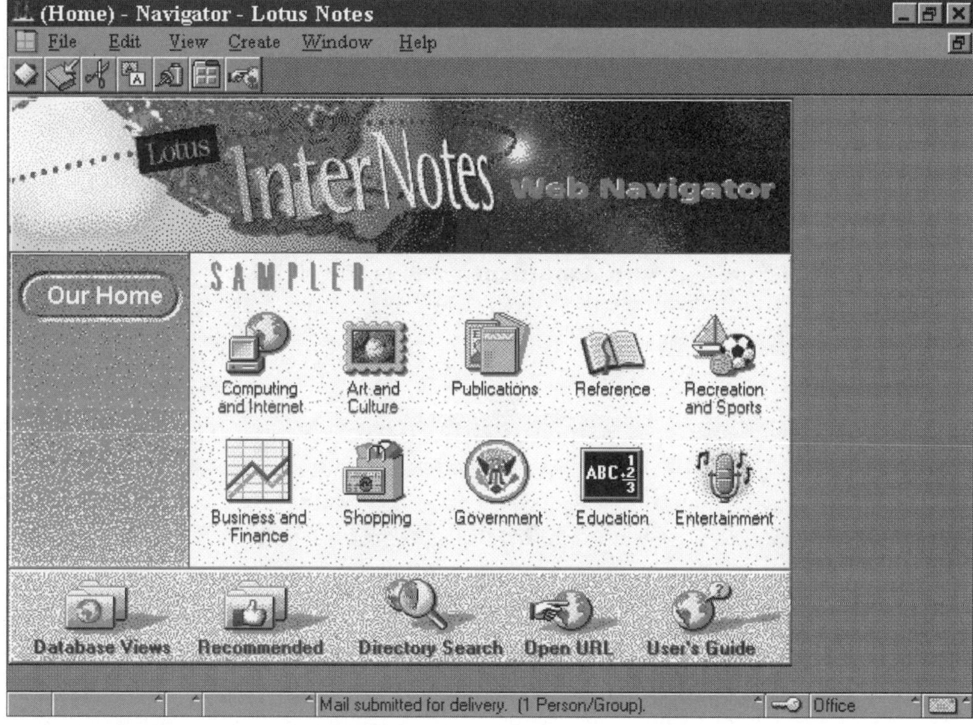

FIGURE 14.8   InterNotes Web Navigator user interface. The initial screen for the InterNotes Web Navigator database presents users with multiple options, including some predefined links. The user interface makes use of the Notes Release 4 Navigators for graphic presentation. As with all Notes Navigators, they are customizable, as are the links.

THE LOTUS INTERNOTES WEB NAVIGATOR

The InterNotes Web Publisher, at its most basic level, lets Web users access Notes data. Release 4 of Lotus Notes includes the InterNotes Web Navigator, which provides interactive access to the World Wide Web for Notes users and developers.

The InterNotes Web Navigator is not merely a Web client. Rather, it uses the power of the Notes server to deliver full HTML documents into a Notes database for access by Notes users (see Figure 14.7). These documents look and behave like HTML documents, including the launching of SGI scripts and "jumping" to

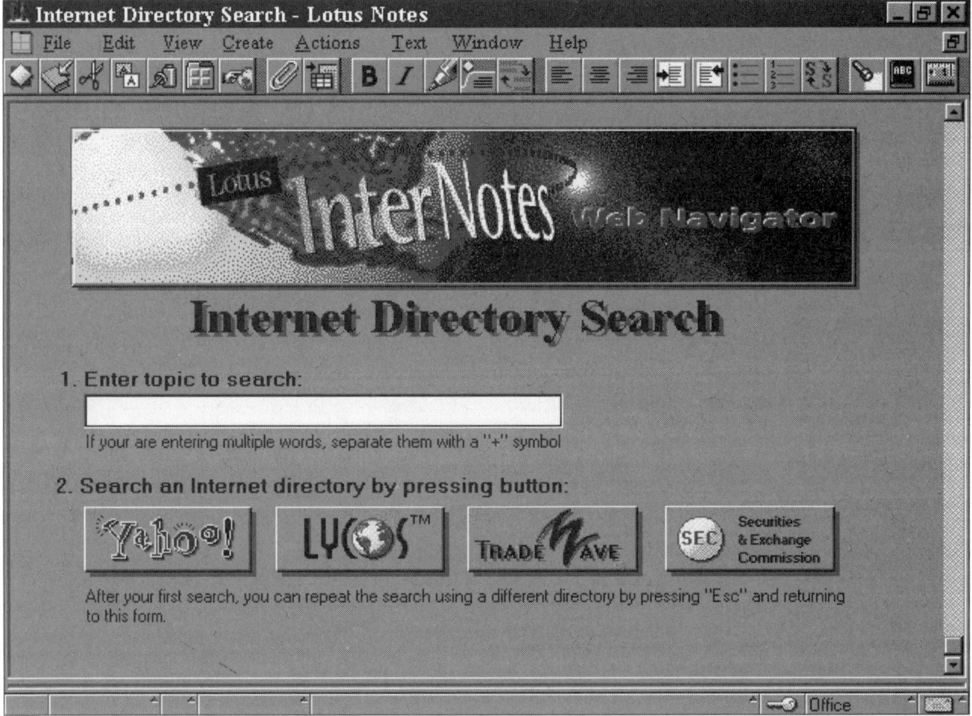

FIGURE 14.9   InterNotes Web Navigator search page. The Inter-Notes Web Navigator allows the user to enter one or more search terms and then select the search engine to use. The InterNotes Web Navigator comes with connections to search sites, such as Yahoo and Lycos. A Notes developer can easily change these or add more.

other URLs. From the users' point of view, other than the Notes user interface enhancements (see Figures 14.8 and 14.9), the experience will be identical to using a Web client (the user interface is very close to Netscape Navigator 1.x, and Netscape Forms and Tables are supported), including Next and Previous, Reload, and Bookmarks (see Figure 14.10).

The user of Notes also has all of the Notes functionality, including the ability to find documents via different Views (see Figures 14.11 and 14.12), using Notes full-text search, and running Agents against the document. In addition, the user can save or forward an HTML document, which, when opened anywhere in Notes, will behave as a Web document. In fact, any text in any database containing http: or ftp: can be clicked on and will automatically go to that site.

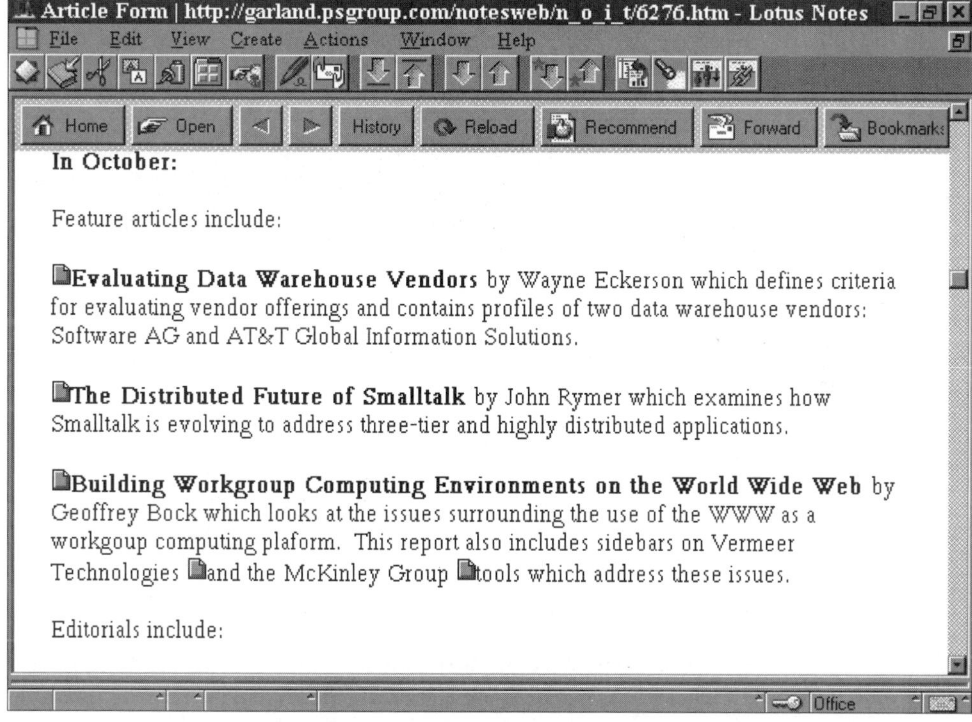

FIGURE 14.10 **A Web Document in Notes.** This is a Web document displayed in Notes. It looks and behaves like an HTML document (see Figure 14.6 for a comparison).

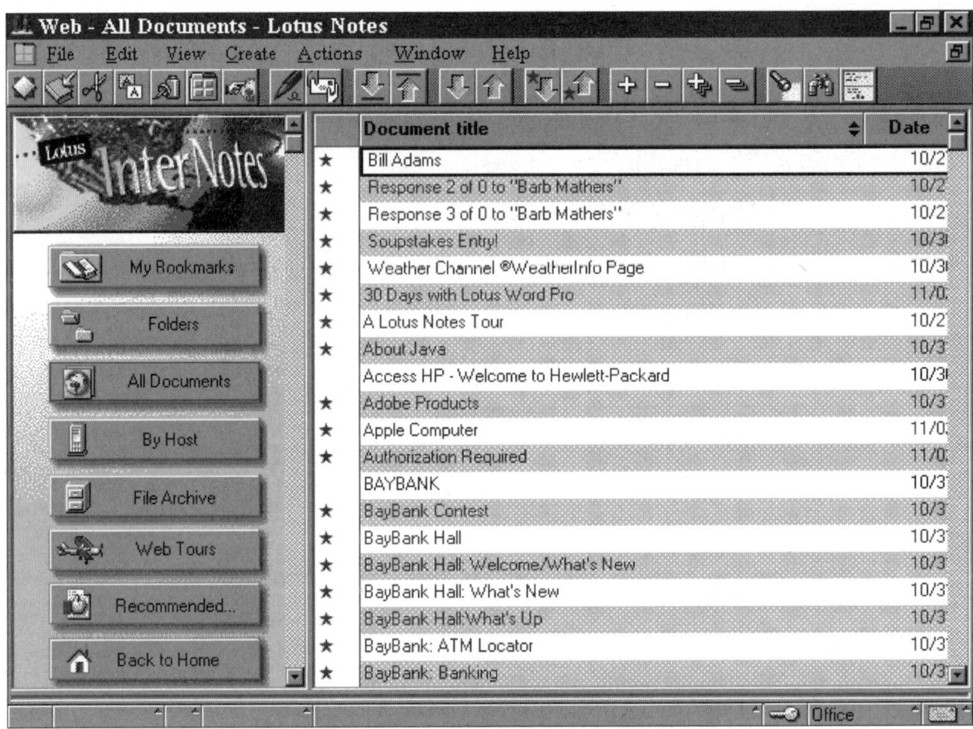

FIGURE 14.11 A Notes View of Web documents. In addition to
finding Web documents via links, URLs, and text searches, the InterNotes Web Publisher offers Notes Views for Navigation. This
View presents the user with all cached documents, sorted by document title.

The InterNotes server can be used to manage Web information
intelligently. For example, it can, on a scheduled basis, pull down
updated or new Web pages for users. Agents can also be run
against these new pages, and they can notify users when new information of interest to them has been posted on the Web.

Developers can include Web access as part of their applications via the new @OpenURL command. This enables:

- Loading a specific page/menu/file
- Refreshing cached pages
- Client navigation (forward/back/history)
- Search for a specific server (WAIS via CGI)
- Launch of a Web Worm or Crawler

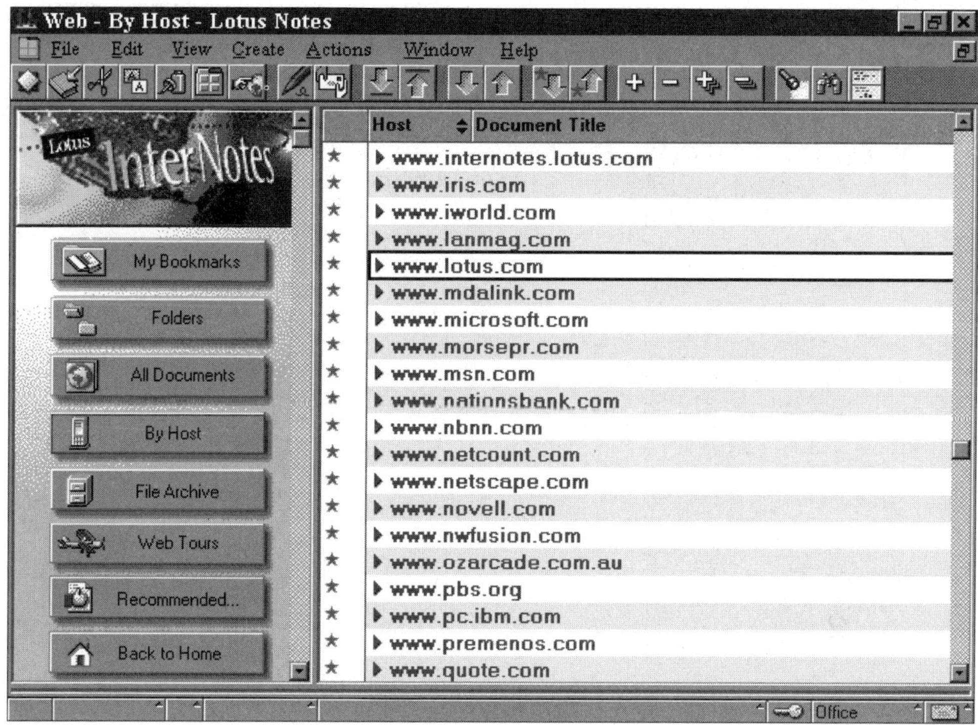

FIGURE 14.12 Another Notes View of Web documents. This View shows the users all documents sorted by server or Web site name. The user need only click on the server name to expand the View and see all of the cached documents.

InterNotes Web Navigator can be used to enhance the groupware experience of Web users. For example, Bookmarks can easily be shared, and a feature is provided for users to "rate" Web pages and sites (see Figure 14.13). And, since the HTML pages are stored as a Notes database, users can replicate all or part to their remote machines, and access the pages while offline.

For companies that use Notes, the advantages of deploying the InterNotes Web Navigator, rather than a separate Web client, will come in several areas, including:

- Consistent user interface and behavior for Notes users.
- Intelligent retrieval and caching of HTML pages by the Notes server. Using the Notes server may actually increase perceived performance for the user.

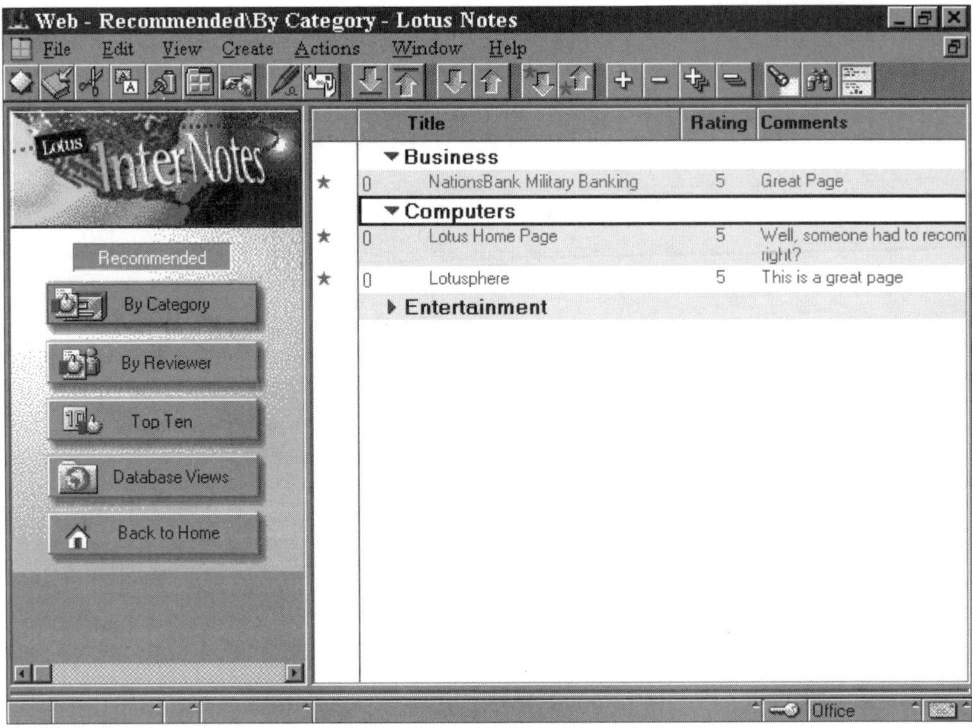

FIGURE 14.13 **Web page rating View.** Users can rate Web pages with a numerical rating and comments. Other users can view rated pages by topic, rating, or rater.

- Multiuser access to the same HTML document without multiple retrievals from the sources.
- Automatic, scheduled updating of HTML documents.
- Use of Notes agents to alert people to new, important information.
- Using Notes as a security firewall. This means that users do not require direct TCP/IP connection to the Internet.
- Support for mobile access and use of the Web.

15

The Future of Notes

Throughout its history, Notes has been viewed by many as a temporary player, a sort of placeholder until a more [fill in the blank with a term such as robust, open, advanced, less expensive] product appears. Every year, we see new products that claim to be a YANK—*Yet Another Notes Killer.* How many readers remember that in 1993 Microsoft's Windows for Workgroups was being hailed as the next-generation groupware product that would supersede Notes? The biggest mistake that companies have made to date is to wait for the next "Notes killer," while others—including their competitors—have transformed their businesses and created new opportunities using Notes.

Today there are two significant challengers to Notes: the long-delayed Microsoft Exchange (finally shipped in the first quarter of 1996), and the emergence of the internets and the World Wide Web. Each of these has been perceived to provide significant competition for two reasons: functionality and cost.

The functionality argument is as follows: "We can do most of what Notes does—messaging, conferencing, publishing—on Exchange or on the Web." This argument is then *always* followed by: "at a lower cost."

Today, neither argument holds. *You cannot do most of what Notes does on these other platforms.* Throughout this book we have seen that the value of Notes is not simple messaging, conferencing, and publishing. It is in supporting the business through customized applications, workflow, and interenterprise electronic commerce, and supporting distributed/mobile environments in these processes. Microsoft Exchange cannot compete with Notes in these areas (see "Microsoft Exchange versus Lotus Notes" below), and internets and the World Wide Web will require a lot more development before they can host these functions. As much as I support the Web as the future of computing, I cannot see how to build and deploy a sales force automation application to 400 mobile sales people in 8 weeks—something which is commonplace in the Notes world.

The insidious part of the argument is the promotion of the idea that Notes is more costly than Exchange or the Web. In the common perception, Notes has to be more expensive. After all, isn't Exchange free with Windows 95? Aren't Web browsers free? The answer, of course, is that neither is free. And each may be a more expensive platform on which to build applications that are already available in Notes.

Lotus has been faced with a severe challenge in answering these arguments, particularly vis à vis the World Wide Web. After some fits and starts, the company has embarked on a new Notes strategy that lowers the prices, emphasizes the value proposition, and proclaims tight integration with the Web.

LOTUS'S STRATEGY

At the end of 1995, Lotus took some bold moves to regain Notes momentum toward mass rollout. In December, Lotus CEO Mike Zisman and COO Jeff Papows presented a new strategy for Lotus, and a new vision of where Notes should fit in customers' future plans. We believe that this new strategy could be a key step in boosting the momentum behind Notes as a strategic application platform.

Lotus's new strategy can be summarized in three points:

1. Price will not be a barrier to customers buying Notes. For example, the Notes Mail client—which includes mail, discussions, document management/workflow, and Web browsing, is priced as Mail: $55. And Notes Desktop is priced at $69.

2. Notes will penetrate desktops as the most advanced client/server mail available. Lotus intends to go directly after the E-mail market as it moves from file-based to client/server

mail. Success in this area is key to Lotus's ability to get onto the tens of millions of desktops with Notes.

3. Notes versus the Web will no longer be an issue: Notes will become a key element of companies' Web strategy. This means giving Notes clients full interactive access to the World Wide Web, and providing full access to the Notes server from any Web browser—including full server support for HTTP, HTML, Java, and JavaScript.

PROSPECTS FOR NOTES: 1996 AND BEYOND

Today, I believe that there are two possible courses for Notes. This first will see the near- to mid-term future of Notes as a strategic infrastructure platform for supporting business processes. This means that most of the value will be in the Notes server and services, with the Notes client being one of a number of ways to access Notes data and services. The Notes client will most likely be used by those involved directly in Notes-managed processes, though, for the foreseeable future, it will remain the best client for mobile users of all applications.

The second scenario is based on Lotus being able to deliver on its new mail and Web strategy, and customers understanding the additional benefits that Notes can bring in these arenas. Under this scenario Notes could well become the user environment of choice for mail, Web browsing, and participation in business process applications. The Notes server could become the server of choice for developing/managing/hosting Notes/Web/Java-based applications on the Internet, intranets, or private nets.

Three major factors will determine the future of Notes and how it unfolds:

1. The impact of IBM

2. The impact of the direct groupware competition, most notably Microsoft Exchange

3. The impact of the World Wide Web

IBM AND NOTES

The most significant factor in the future of Notes is how IBM leverages it in its overall scheme. Since the acquisition of Lotus, IBM has tried to assure Notes customers and partners that Notes would remain open (multiplatform, support OLE, etc.) and would be strategic to IBM. Early in this process, IBM and Lotus outlined a series of product decisions, including the following.

- Lotus Notes is now IBM's workgroup client and its mail, messaging, and groupware server platform. cc:Mail will continue to support its current shared-file server and will also operate in client/server mode with Notes Release 4.
- Lotus SmartSuite has become IBM's desktop suite. Lotus's suite development team will evaluate technology from Star-Division GmbH, which IBM has licensed, for possible future inclusion in SmartSuite. (Since this public announcement, IBM and Lotus have started exploring a component-based desktop strategy.)
- Lotus is now IBM's brand name for PC application and workgroup software.

IBM'S IMPACT ON NOTES

According to Lotus CEO Mike Zisman, IBM brings major benefits to Notes. The first is a large increase in investment in the product—the majority of which is going into product development, with a significant amount into marketing Notes to a degree which Lotus had been unable to do.

The second benefit is to integrate the complementary strengths of Lotus's "front office" and IBM's "back office" capabilities into what is being termed an "extended transaction model." This will be done through integration of Notes and IBM products, such as MQSeries and CICS—work that had already begun before the acquisition. It will also manifest itself through enterprise- and inter-enterprise-level services that IBM will provide in the areas of consulting, application integration, service hosting, and outsourcing.

IBM and Lotus are also working on delivering integrated products, such as a Web/InterNotes server, code-named "Spike," and integrated imaging products. Another strong candidate for integration is a workflow system including Notes and IBM FlowMark.

The third key impact of IBM's ownership of Lotus is to allow Lotus to take a longer-range view. Previously, Lotus was forced to focus continually on the bottom line—generally in 3-month periods. Long-term investments, could be made, but not at the expense of current revenues. With a longer-term focus, Lotus can now take actions such as aggressive price reductions of Notes Mail and Notes Desktop.

MICROSOFT EXCHANGE VERSUS LOTUS NOTES

In the first quarter of 1996, Microsoft finally delivered a product designed specifically to compete with Notes. (No, Windows for Workgroups was not the "Notes killer" that some would have had us believe in 1993.) On the surface, Microsoft Exchange provides many of the capabilities that heretofore made Notes unique. Public folders, rules, custom forms, and views all sound as if they are aimed directly at "Notes applications." And, for those companies that have not yet tried Notes, Exchange will seem to be an appealing platform to build and deploy workgroup and business process applications.

ADVANTAGES OF NOTES

It is highly unlikely, however, that Exchange, when it first ships, will be able to compete with an environment as mature as Notes. Specifically, Exchange begins far behind in the following areas.

Support for mobile users. Notes is designed to provide, and Notes Release 4.0 greatly increases, support for mobile users. Exchange will have local replication—a feature that, though greatly welcome, we feel will be rudimentary compared to Lotus's mature technology (including R.4 enhancements such as location management, better selective replication, and Field-level replication).

Support for distributed applications. Exchange is optimized for connected environments. Occasionally connected environments, particularly where there are slow links, are at a disadvantage. Notes is built for occasionally connected environments that may have to communicate over slow links. And, as noted above, Notes Release 4 enhances this, particularly with Field-level replication, where only the Field in a document that changes has to be sent to other locations—rather than the whole document, as must be done today in Notes R.3 and in at least the first version of Exchange.

Integrated application development environment. The Exchange Forms Designer can produce nicer forms than Notes R.3 can. It does not compare with Notes R.4 functions, such as graphical Navigators, HotSpots, and Collapsible Sections. Exchange

Forms also lacks Notes-like functionality, such as real-time field updates and sophisticated input validation routines. If we add Visual Basic to the Exchange development environment, then it can compete in power, but it requires a much greater level of programming ability.

Workflow. Notes is essentially a workflow platform. Individuals work within business processes—Notes databases—and act on the information they need for their jobs. Notes supports this with rules-based routing, scheduled agents or rules, secure sections, and, with Release 4, a constantly available Action Bar and Notes/FX protocol. Exchange enables only simple mail-based workflow via rules running against incoming documents. The Exchange model is not workflow—that is, working within a business process—but rather individuals searching for ("exploring") information.

Interenterprise applications. As with Microsoft Mail, Exchange's interenterprise orientation is pretty much limited to delivering mail messages between companies. These capabilities are supported by interconnection and gateway services from providers such as AT&T, British Telecom, CompuServe GE Information Services, Sprint, and a number of others. Notes specifically enables different organizations to work with each other via public key/private key authentication and organization-level cross-certification. Setting up business relationships beyond sending and receiving E-mail is an easy and natural action via Notes, an act that seems to be forced, if possible at all, with Exchange. And the existence of public Notes carriers, such as CompuServe, WorldCom, and IBM, to host Notes applications relieves the burden of managing the infrastructure and setting up customers.

Third-party market. Initially at least, Exchange will not have the large third-party market of add-on and related products that has developed around Notes. Most large independent software vendors (ISVs)—including Powersoft, Oracle, Gupta, Novell, Great Plains, and Microsoft—have added Notes-specific features to their products. Hundreds of smaller ISVs are developing Notes-related products, and more than 10,000 companies are making businesses by building, integrating, and training Notes applications. There will be a great flurry around the release of Exchange, but it is likely to be several years before Microsoft can build a similar market.

ADVANTAGES OF EXCHANGE

Exchange has four specific advantages over Notes:

Exchange client on "every" desktop. Although there has been a lot of confusion about the Windows 95 default client, and this advantage is difficult to quantify, the existence of the default client may be too difficult to compete with no matter what the advantages of installing another product.

Calendar/scheduling. Lotus is now 4 years late on delivering a Notes-based calendar/scheduling system. The company does not have an answer to Schedule+ and its integration with Exchange. It will be at least mid-1996 until native Notes scheduling is delivered.

Visual Basic. As Visual Basic becomes the default corporate development environment, building Exchange applications will become more natural to corporate developers than building Notes applications.

Integration with Windows NT. Perhaps the greatest strength is the integration of Exchange with Windows NT and, in the future, with Cairo. From the administration, management, security, and purchasing points of view, the integration of Exchange with Windows NT and BackOffice makes things much easier for customers. At the same time, this is perhaps Exchange's greatest weakness. Customers who do not want to buy into a single server operating system or companies that want to build interenterprise applications where they cannot force their customers' platform choices are likely to reject Exchange outright as a strategic platform.

GOING FORWARD

Comparing Notes and Exchange is a difficult task. Over the past 2 years, Microsoft has continually redefined the functionality of Exchange, in general removing features that could have made it more directly competitive with Notes. At the same time, Microsoft has time and again changed the positioning of Exchange vis à vis Notes: At times, Exchange was the "Notes killer"; at times, Exchange was simply advanced messaging. As this book goes to press, Microsoft seems to be repositioning Exchange again, this time in combination with Microsoft Office as a workgroup, collaboration environment. And Microsoft has yet to connect Exchange to its emerging Web strategy.

Table 15.1   Notes vs. Exchange

	Microsoft Exchange	**Lotus Notes R.4**
Enterprise E-Mail	★★★? + Client/server + X.400/SMTP transport + MAPI/CMC + X.400 MTA + Some X.500 compliance + Integrated administration with OS ? Scalability − Single server platform	★★★? + Client/server + X.400/SMTP transport + MAPI/CMC ++ Multiplatform server ? Scalability
Groupware	★★★	★★★
Information Sharing	★★ + Public folders + Server-to-server replication − No replication for mobile users	★★★★ ++ Notes databases ++ Field-level replication +++ Support for mobile users
Conferencing	★★★	★★★★
Calendar/ Scheduling	★★★ +++ Integrated Schedule	★ + Notes as a transport for Lotus Organizer
Custom Applications	★★ + Forms Designer ++ Visual Basic − Everything looks like E-mail	★★★★ + Forms design + LotusScript + Navigators ++ Everything is an application
Workflow	★ + Event-based rules	★★★ ++ Schedule/event-based rules ++ Navigators, Action Bars, Notes/FX, etc. ++ Integration with third-party workflow products
Interenterprise		★★★★ ++ Notes security model ++ Notes replication model ++ Public Notes networks ++ Integration with WWW

It is clear, however, that in the key areas of support for mobile users, custom applications, workflow, and interenterprise applications, Exchange will not be able to catch up easily. And we certainly don't expect Lotus to stand still with Notes.

NOTES VERSUS THE WEB

As we discussed in Chapter 14, Notes and the Internet can currently be seen and best used as complementary technologies with overlapping functions, each with different strengths. And there are many opportunities to build hybrid applications that exploit the power of each.

That said, there is certainly a sense in which the World Wide Web can be considered a "Notes killer," or at least a major accomplice. As more and more companies provide Web access for their users, both to monitor their own company's presence and to participate with other companies and resources, the question of whether the Web will replace Notes looms large in some minds—and it is clear that a number of companies have delayed wide rollouts of Notes pending an answer to this question.

The key argument for the Web is that it is less expensive, more open, *and* can accomplish much of what Notes does. This is particularly true in the area of information publishing and, increasingly, for groupware functions such as information sharing, conferencing, and discussions.

Lotus's previous strategy was to enumerate the things that Notes does and the Web does not—authentication, replication, document management, and so on. This strategy was weak, as the speed of development on the Web runs at such a pace that the Notes differentiation seems to be decreasing constantly (it was less than a year ago that one could point to "Notes features" that were not available on the Web, such as full-text search, agents, threaded discussions, and document authoring).

Lotus is now changing its strategy to embrace the Web, and to bring into question the two major points of the argument: cost and openness. The cost issue is being addressed both by the decrease in client prices and by a number of scalability and manageability enhancements in Notes Release 4 that are designed to reduce significantly the cost of ownership of Notes.

The openness question may be more "religious" than technical. For many, Notes will always be a closed, proprietary system, even though it is inherently multiplatform and supports such standards as ODBC, OLE, TCP/IP, SNMP, X.400, and SMTP/MIME. For those willing to look past the religious questions, Lotus now has a pretty good story about being a good citizen on the Web, with the Inter-Notes Web Publisher giving access to Notes information to Web users and the InterNotes Web Publisher giving access to Web information to Notes users.

But Lotus is taking the argument one critical step further. The company is now getting ready to make and back up the claim that "Notes is itself a low-cost, standards-compliant, high-value Web product!"

THE FUTURE: NOTES IS THE WEB

In order even to conceive of making this claim, Lotus has had to undergo a key shift in thinking about the Web. This shift is from looking at the Web from a Notes-centric view (how do I publish my Notes apps on the Web, or how do I give my Notes users access to the Web) to a more Web-centric view. This Web-centric view portrays the value of Notes within a company's Web strategy, and asks the seemingly heretical question: Does anyone provide a better Web server or better Web client than Notes?

In order even to be able to ask this question, Lotus has to position Notes as a Web server. This positioning will become plausible and logical in the middle of 1996 when the Notes Web server ships. The Web server will provide direct support for HTTP protocol, HTML document storage within the Notes object store, and direct support for Java and JavaScript. In other words, Notes will be a full Web server supporting all standard Web browsers and all Web protocols.

Thus, when posed the question: "Why shouldn't I put my internal discussions and internal and external publishing on the Web?" Lotus's answer will be: "You Should! And Notes is the best Web server to deploy it on." The argument will be: At $495, the Notes server offers all of the standard functions of Web servers of its class, and it provides client/server mail, high security, full document management, replication, and much more.

On the client side, Lotus will put forth a parallel case: If all you need is a Web browser, then use anyone's browser to access the Web server. But if you also need client/server mail, or you need to manage users' access to the Web, or users need advanced capabilities such as Agents at no additional cost, then use Notes Mail as your browser. And, if the user needs to participate in the types of workflow applications for which Notes is best known, then Notes obviously is the best environment in which to combine the user's mail, browsing, and line-of-business activities.

These arguments are logical and will be extremely persuasive to current Lotus customers. We believe that if Lotus delivers this vision (and from our understanding of the technology, this is eminently doable), many customers will embrace this view and use Notes as a key element of their Web strategy. This will be particularly true of companies that see the Web as part of a whole Information Technology initiative, rather than an end in itself.

For Lotus the greatest challenge lies in convincing companies that are not looking at Notes (or that have no idea that Notes could help them in the Web space) to seriously consider Notes as core to their Web strategy. We predict that this will be most difficult with those most "into" the Web (the original "InterNauts" of a company), who will greet Lotus's claims in this field to be "unpure." We also predict that the new Lotus strategy will have great appeal to IT executives who are trying to manage their companies' role in this brave new world. Finally, we believe that in the coming years, people will look back at the announcement of this new strategy as a key turning point in the evolution of Lotus and of Notes.

THE VALUE OF NOTES TODAY

For most companies, the future of Notes should be a question more of theory than of practice. It is clear that today Notes provides the fastest, easiest way to build strategic communications, collaboration, and coordination applications that can affect the business directly. The biggest losers may no longer be those who sat and waited through the first half of the 1990s for something better than Notes to come along. Their loss may pale before that of those who wait out the second half of the decade for some combination of Microsoft products, Netscape products, Java, and others yet to be conceived to do the basic things that Notes does well today: allow control and transformation of your business!

Index